G000273054

DÖNITZ'S LAST GAMBLE

DÖNITZ'S LAST GAMBLE

The Inshore U-Boat Campaign
1944–45

Lawrence Paterson

Seaforth
PUBLISHING

Copyright © Lawrence Paterson 2008

First published in Great Britain in 2008 by
Seaforth Publishing,
Pen & Sword Books Ltd,
47 Church Street,
Barnsley S70 2AS

British Library Cataloguing in Publication Data
A catalogue record for this book is available from the British Library

ISBN 978 1 84415 714 3

Designed and Typeset by MATS Typesetters, Leigh-on-Sea, Essex
www.typesetter.biz

Printed and bound by Biddles Ltd in King's Lynn, Norfolk.

Opposite Title Page: The abortive U-boat attack on D-Day shipping in June 1944 showed just how
much Allied ASW weaponry and tactics had mastered Germany's conventional U-boat forces.

Contents

Dedicated to the memory of Cozy Powell

Acknowledgements

THERE ARE ALWAYS many people involved in the writing of a book such as this. I would like to begin by thanking Sarah, Megz and James of the Paterson clan (British Section), Ernie (American Section), Audrey 'Mumbles' Paterson and Don 'Mr Mumbles' and Ray and Philly Paterson of the New Zealand branch. Plus, special mention to Julia Hargraves who has been a constant source of encouragement throughout this and other books.

An inordinate amount of excellent and skilled research has been carried out by Axel Niestlé to whom this book owes a great debt of gratitude. His assessment of U-boat losses continues and he often makes his findings and general knowledge of the subject – which is unsurpassed in my opinion – freely available, which is extremely valuable and appreciated.

Special thanks for help and inspiration go to a long list of people, particularly: Jak Mallmann-Showell; Derek and Patricia Ancill; Mike, Sheila, Mitch and Claire French; Cozy Powell (RIP); Paul 'Beam' Robbie; Graham von Pentz; Carl Warner; Dave Andrews; Cath Friend; Tina Hawkins; Paul 'The Rög' Rogne; 'Blaze' Bayley Cook; Brian Johnson; Bonn Scott; Angus Young; Malcolm Young; Cliff Williams; Phil Rudd; Mark Evans; Chris Slade; and of course Nicko McBrain and Mikkey Dee.

Many men from the ranks of the Kriegsmarine, Bundesmarine and Royal Navy and their families have offered unparalleled glimpses into their experiences and much hospitality during visits. My thanks to all of them, but if I could single out some particular people I would like to mention the late Ludwig Stoll and his wonderful wife Inge; Jürgen and Esther Oesten; Gerhard and Traudl Buske; Georg and Frau Högel; Georg and Frau Seitz; Gesa and Hannlore Suhren; Karl and Annie Waldeck; Volkmaar König and Jürgen and Gisela Weber. Also, special thanks to all at the München U-Bootskameradschaft for many memorable evenings in Munich.

For the many people that have not been mentioned here, I have not forgotten your help and support and it is always appreciated. Cheers.

LAWRENCE PATERSON
NOVEMBER 2007

Faeroe Islands

Shetland Islands

North
Atlantic

Bergen

Oslo

Horten

Stavanger

Kristiansand

Orkney Islands
Pentland Firth

Skagerrak

Moray Firth

Outer Hebrides

North Minch

Aberdeen

North Sea

Kattegat

Dundee

Greenock

Firth Of Forth

Glasgow

Edinburgh

North Channel

Newcastle

Londonderry

Flensburg

Kiel

Belfast

Sligo

Isle of
Man

Lübeck

Irish Sea

Liverpool

Hamburg

Dublin

Bremen

Lowestoft

St George's Channel

Milford Haven

The Scheldt

Swansea

Cardiff

Antwerp

Portsmouth

Folkestone

Dover

Plymouth

English Channel

**Dönitz's Last Gamble
The Battleground
1944-1945**

Cherbourg

Le Havre

Western Approaches

Brest

Introduction

MUCH HAS BEEN made of the vaunted Type XXI U-boat developed by the Kriegsmarine during the final years of the war. Historians, both professional and amateur continue to debate the merits of this revolutionary new style of submarine, the so-called 'electro-boat' with its high submerged speed, automated torpedo reloading and advanced firing system. Indeed, the encounter on 4 May between K K Adalbert Schnee, captain of *U2511* and a British task force bound from Norway and centred on the cruiser HMS *Norfolk*, is often used as proof of the predatory prowess of the Type XXI in the hands of a true veteran submariner. Schnee approached submerged, plotted and fired on the cruiser, waited and then departed without the Royal Navy ships even being aware of his presence. The fact that only hours previously *Grossadmiral* Karl Dönitz had issued an order to cease fire from all U-boats, forestalled what could have been yet more tragic waste of lives in a war only days from ending in Europe.

In late 1944 and early 1945 western Allied naval commands harboured very real fears about a revitalised and revolutionised U-boat campaign to be launched by Germany. During 1943 the U-boats had been driven from the Atlantic after years of bitter struggle with the convoys that trailed worldwide towards what had been a beleaguered Britain. The ships in these convoys carried life-sustaining food, military material and troops to the sole remaining island bastion that defied Hitler's Germany. By the end of May 1943, due to a combination of numbers, improved convoy tactics, increased air cover and technological advantage – all held together by thousands of men of the merchant and military navies – Germany's young men of the U-boat service had been forced to concede defeat, leaving a trail of shattered U-boat hulks on sea beds that would ultimately stretch as far as Malaya. The casualty rates in the U-boat service had become horrendous, barely sustainable and yet, incredibly, they continued to sail.

June 1944 saw the Allies land on the French coast in the most famous of all D-Days. The immediate U-boat response was to sail a handful of veteran boats into the maelstrom of Allied warships and aircraft; this led to a slaughter on an almost unprecedented scale that once again demonstrated the Allies' comprehensive supremacy over conventional U-boats that the Germans had relied upon so heavily. As the first Allied troops stormed ashore in Normandy, others were already fighting on mainland Italy, as Churchill had pushed for his access to Europe

The revolutionary Walter boat, seen here trailing a marker for test purposes, promised large underwater speed and endurance though was never perfected.

through what he inaccurately described as the 'soft underbelly'. However, despite the arduous and costly fighting that inched up Italy's spine, the U-boats that had been assigned to the Mediterranean were also comprehensively beaten and eliminated by September 1944. With the invasion of France, the ports on the Atlantic coast from which Germany's U-boat aces had sailed during their mythical 'Happy Time' gradually either fell to Allied forces or were encircled and eliminated as viable staging posts from which U-boats could sail into combat. The German submariners retreated to their final bastion of Norway. The advance of the Red Army on land correspondingly destroyed the small U-boat presence in the Black Sea, the last of the six small U-boats stationed there being scuttled off the Turkish coast. In the Arctic, U-boats continued to sail against convoys to and from Russia but to less and less effect, since the almost complete victory over PQ17 in July 1942. The U-boat star had waned.

However, the Wehrmacht was not beaten yet. Allied forces were arguably guilty of underestimating the ability and resolve of their retreating enemy. The interception and destruction of the U-boats that had attacked D-Day traffic and the almost complete destruction of Germany's naval surface forces lulled the Allies into a sense of security that they were safe from the potential threat of underwater attack within their home waters. The first stirrings of disquiet were caused by intelligence reports of German development of a high-submerged-speed submarine, variously the 'electro-boat' or the experimental hydrogen peroxide-propelled U-boat, the so-called Walter boat. Mastery over the U-boats had been achieved against the conventional diesel submarines: slow underwater, easy to detect while surfaced and vulnerable to remorseless hunting once their location had been given away, usually when attempting to make an attack on a convoy. But in September 1944 began a fresh campaign using those same old U-boat tactics of attacking the enemy in shallow coastal waters – the inshore campaign. A handful of large Type IX boats made the journey to Canada and the northern portion of the United States to deliver the revived tactics in those waters, but this book deals with the unexpected commitment of 120 U-boats to the British coastal campaign.

The surprise attack by these boats, equipped with what now seem almost rudimentary snorkel systems to enable submerged charging of their inadequate battery banks, crewed in the main by new men without the benefit of harsh seagoing warfare experience, caused an almost unforeseen panic in the British Admiralty. The war-winning benefits of the convoy system, Enigma code breaking and radar were almost at a single stroke nullified by a change in German tactics and a dramatic Allied rethink was required to combat the fresh menace. The dire loss rate at the hands of radar-equipped aircraft aided by the ULTRA codebreaking of position signals had gradually forced U-boats to travel and operate primarily submerged, thus curtailing their ability to be detected by radar and send frequent radio messages, ironically proving a temporary saviour to the Germans. Just as American forces were thrown on the defensive by the land attack in the Ardennes during December 1944, so too did Allied naval and air forces grapple afresh with mastering Dönitz's final offensive.

Was Dönitz's intention to deliver a killing blow to the Allies with his inshore campaign? No. His purpose was to achieve a temporary stalemate at sea that would prolong the agony of Europe's war while his Type XXIs were perfected and readied for active service. Whether those boats could really have had the effect he envisioned once committed to battle will always remain a matter of conjecture. However, the renewed threat from conventional U-boats coupled with knowledge of the impending arrival of the 'electro-boats' altered Allied naval thinking and paved the way for the tactics that would define the postwar years of silent and undeclared battle with the new enemy of the west – Soviet Russia.

This book does not deal extensively with the Type XXI design other than in a contextual manner. Indeed the sole Type XXI to sail on an active war footing was in fact destined for the Caribbean and completely unsuited for coastal operations. Nor does it describe the death throes of the Kriegsmarine as a whole or their complex activities in occupied Norway. Those stories have either been told fully elsewhere or await their own treatment. It does, instead, look at the last battle of the conventional Type VII U-boats, reinforced by the smaller cousin of the 'electro-boat', the Type XXIII, as they sailed into the often crowded waters of Great Britain, a feat not achieved in strength since 1940. It was a forlorn hope, which, with the benefit of hindsight, can be seen as doomed to fail. But military history is not forged by hindsight but by high stakes gambles such as this of the Kriegsmarine in 1944.

CHAPTER ONE

The Crucible

Merchant shipping losses of the order of 70 rising to 90 ships
a month may possibly be expected . . . which could
in turn prejudice the maintenance of our forces in Europe.[1]

THESE WORDS FROM A forecast of possible U-boat depredation prepared by the
First Lord of the Admiralty painted a stark picture for Allied planners occupied
with the western front. Perhaps surprisingly they were also relating to possible
events during 1945, long past the heyday of the Kriegsmarine's U-boat service.

In May 1943 *Grossadmiral* Karl Dönitz had admitted defeat in the Atlantic and
had withdrawn his U-boats from the primary theatre of the commerce war to
which they had been applied. This, the battle of the Atlantic convoys was the
raison d'être for the prevalence of U-boats within the Kriegsmarine and their
mastery by Allied air and sea forces – assisted by the now famous breaking of the
naval Enigma codes – appeared almost complete. Dönitz had entered the war
using Type II, Type VII and Type IX conventional diesel submarines that had
changed little since the previous world war. Equipped with primary diesel propulsion units for surface travel they were at first indoctrinated in the virtues of
surface combat, attacking at night. Once submerged their electric motors could
attain only minor speed underwater, batteries eventually draining so that the U-
boat would be compelled to surface and recharge lest the propellers cease to turn
and the boat sink into oblivion. This was the Achilles' heel fully exploited by Allied
anti-submarine-warfare (ASW) forces.

Surprisingly, however, the addition of improved submarine ventilation
technology to existing U-boat designs coupled with fresh deployment to hitherto
largely untested coastal waters around the United Kingdom had brought a
startling reversal of fortunes to the Royal Navy during 1944. That, coupled with
the imminent commissioning of a pair of vastly improved U-boat designs, augured
ill for Cunningham's fleet, the merchant ships it was charged to protect and thus
the material support of the Allied front in western Europe. The consequences were
perceived as far reaching and potentially catastrophic. Ironically, the cause for these

Two U-boat commanders in Norway confer beside a Type VIIC, the near-obsolete design that formed the backbone of Dönitz's inshore British battles of 1944 and 1945.

concerns – Hitler's U-boat service – had already been mastered in the Atlantic and had been considered largely spent after years of harsh attrition in combat. Round-the-clock bombing of Germany had been supposed to nullify the nation's industrial capacity, yet under the dynamic control of Albert Speer military production had actually increased. Amongst the streams of tanks, weapons, rockets, and jet fighters were also the gravest naval threats: the Type XXI and XXIII and hydrogen peroxide-propelled Walter U-boats. Fast, silent and deadly, these U-boats could usher in a new age of submarine warfare for which the Allies were almost totally unprepared. Although true to say that Allied convoying and Enigma codebreaking would remain effective ASW tactics, the introduction of U-boats capable of high submerged speeds could render existing ASDIC technology obsolete, the speeds required by surface forces hunting the submerged U-boats probably deafening ASDIC reception. The Allies now had a vision of invisible predators able to operate more freely against convoy traffic than had been the case since the early years of the pre-radar war, when Type VII U-boats had attacked at night and surfaced. At the end of 1944 there was very real concern in Whitehall that defeat could yet be snatched from the jaws of victory in the battle at sea.

At right *Oberleutnant zur See* Wolfgang Seiler commanded *U37* during the tests
on the prototype Type XXI tower before being transferred to a staff post.

Included in the prototype tower were fearsome batteries of 20mm flak weapons
in enclosed cupolas, used also in the production models.

Development of the Type XXI involved use of the obsolete veteran Type IXA *U37*, shown here, equipped with a prototype Type XXI tower for tests during 1944.

In August 1944 Germany's western front against the Allied armies crumbled irretrievably. The U-boats' bases that ranged along the French Atlantic coast were placed under siege and either rendered untenable for all but static ground defence for the remainder of the war or, as was the case with Brest, taken in an urban battle that cost the lives of thousands of American and German troops. Whether stubbornly holding out against the Allied forces, or capitulating amid the wreckage of utter devastation, the bases were no longer capable of supporting the Kriegsmarine's U-boat service. Whatever boats remained were evacuated to Norway, packed with as many technicians and spare crewmen as they could carry. It was the final blow of defeat for the western U-boats, the Battle of the Atlantic having already been lost by the end of May 1943. Though U-boats continued to sail into the Atlantic for the remainder of the war, travelling once again to the coasts of the United States and Canada, they were no longer a war-winning threat. Their deployment was in reality a final desperate attempt by *Grossadmiral* Karl Dönitz to divert Allied ASW forces away from other areas and to keep as many such units as possible pinned to the Atlantic. Dönitz had begun to view the success or failure of the U-boat campaign as an issue of time – time needed to bring into service the Type XXI and Type XXIII electro-U-boats and the complete development of the Walter boats, which could revolutionise underwater combat. Until such time,

Schnorchel types varied as illustrated, though the function remained the same.

Professor Hellmuth Walter who not only pioneered the hydrogen peroxide propulsion unit, but also advocated the use of sectional U-boat construction.

the war would continue to be fought by the Type VII and Type IX designs, updated somewhat by additional equipment and armaments, but essentially the same U-boat models that had begun the war in 1939.

Indeed technological developments in all military arms had blossomed enormously during the Second World War. The pace of change was staggering, with radar, guided missiles, rockets and armoured-vehicle design leading the way. Medical advances had brought new life-saving abilities to the battlefields, while nuclear-fission research promised fresh methods of destruction. Germany's U-boats had long suffered from having development foisted upon them as a result of Allied advances, reacting to events rather than leading them. For example, radar detectors had gradually improved over the previous years due to Allied airborne centimetric radar developments. Arguably even the continuing development of new torpedo guidance systems and warheads were reactive to Allied weapons and tactics, forcing U-boats below the surface where they fought almost blind.

By August 1944 the fresh hope for U-boat crews fighting in near obsolete machines was firmly rooted in the *schnorchel*. This retractable tube – first properly developed by Lieutenant Commander J J Wichers of the Royal Netherlands Navy, and the two working examples mounted on *O19* and *O20* actually captured by German invaders in 1940 (though largely ignored until absolutely necessary), would allow U-boats to recharge batteries using diesel engines while remaining submerged. This necessity to recharge was the U-boats' greatest weakness; it kept them reliant on repeated surfacing, as underwater travel dwindled both battery power and breathable air aboard a submerged submarine. Ironically, Professor Hellmuth Walter, engaged in designing a closed-circuit gas turbine U-boat propulsion system at Kiel's Germaniawerft during the early 1930s, had first proposed development of a high speed U-boat in a communication with Naval Command on 5 October 1933. It incorporated the necessity of an extensible airshaft enabling air to be introduced into the boat for the engine operation while still running submerged or at least awash. In fact, Walter's proposal included many elements later used in the development of the Type XXI and XXIII electro-boats.

On 2 March 1943, with Atlantic defeat looming large, Dönitz conferred with Professor Walter once more about the future development of Walter's revolutionary high-speed gas-turbine-driven U-boats, as well as methods of regaining the initiative in the U-boat war. Walter once again raised the subject of his 1933 idea of the extensible air mast. Intrigued, Dönitz supported further development of the idea that became a reality during 1944.

In all possible haste Dönitz ordered his remaining conventional Type VII and Type IX combat U-boats fitted with the device to allow them to escape the terrible predation of Allied air power, which had helped to turn the tide of battle against him in the Atlantic. Indeed, on 1 June 1944, Dönitz ordered no U-boats to be sent

The revival of the *schnorchel* principle enabled Dönitz's boats to continue the battle, the small radar signature of such surfaced portions as shown here, a lifesaver.

to the Atlantic without a *schnorchel*. Despite this sound decision events five days later would force the commitment of many U-boats not yet fitted with the potentially life-saving equipment.

Of course the *schnorchel* was not without its problems. Perhaps the most serious was that if the head of the tube became submerged either through rough seas or bad depth keeping the valve would close while diesels continued to run. This would mean that the engines would suck air from the atmosphere within the boat itself, causing painful pressure on the crew's ears, often bringing men to their knees in pain, as well as venting exhaust gases into the hull. Potential carbon-monoxide poisoning from improper *schnorchel* usage thus also became a primary concern, the symptom of drowsiness sufficiently addling the brains of the crew that solving the problem was not as prompt as it would be otherwise. Plus, with extended periods beneath the waves there was no opportunity to rid the boat of rubbish and waste generated by the fifty men confined inside. Whereas these things were normally jettisoned by hand from the bridge they now had to be stored aboard until such time as the boat could surface for long enough to get rid of it. The resulting stench did nothing to enhance the already grim life aboard a combat U-boat. Perhaps most seriously, although the *schnorchel* enabled the boat dramatically to reduce its radar signature by running at speed submerged, this caused such oscillations in the search periscope that it became nigh on impossible to maintain a watch for enemy ships or aircraft. Indeed, the placement of a *schnorchel* on a Type VIIC U-boat was not ideal, situated as it was at the front of the conning tower on the port side. This meant that billowing exhaust frequently obscured whatever vision was afforded through the periscope that was only slightly abaft the *schnorchel* head. The hydrophones were deafened during speedy *schnorchel* voyages and sight was the sole remaining method by which to detect threats. Regular stops to use both the periscope and hydrophone were needed in order to operate with any kind of real security.

A large number of the Type VII U-boats that would feature in Dönitz's campaign within British waters were the improved Type VIIC/41 (see Appendix B). During 1941, with the opening of U-boat operations along the US Atlantic coast and in the Caribbean and Gulf of Mexico, considerable thought was given to how best to modify the basic proven Type VIIC design, in order to achieve enhanced performance and greater range while not upsetting current construction projects by making any real change to the boat structural design. The Type VIIC/41 was the result. The primary alterations were to the boat's weight, pressure-hull thickness and bow.

In February 1942 SKL/Ib had asked *Oberleutnant* (*Ing*) Friedrich Kiesewalter (Chief Engineer on the Type IXC *U157*) to compile a memorandum entitled 'Technical Development of the U-boat in the Light of War Operations'. Kiesewalter was mainly concerned with the fact that combat conditions would soon outpace current U-boat designs, an increased diving depth to escape depth charging a focus of his ideas: 'If we

U260 departs Saint Nazaire after having its *schnorchel* fitted.

cannot actually succeed in concealing U-boats from detection by ultrasonics, then only two possibilities remain: either one dives to 300 metres and waits until depth charging is over, or one must be equipped with an attacking weapon such as an acoustic torpedo with which to destroy the pursuer . . . At [300 metres] the effect of depth charges is greatly restricted and, furthermore, the time it takes for depth charges to descend to such a depth enables a boat to take avoiding action.'

Thus the VIIC design had various power and electrical systems replaced by smaller more compact designs saving a total of 11.5 tons of hull weight. This saved weight was then used to increase the thickness of the pressure hull from 18.5mm to 21mm, extending the test diving depth from 150 metres to 180 metres and the theoretical hull failure depth (frequently exceeded!) from 250 metres to 300. Coupled with this the forecastle was slightly widened and a 13cm extension to the bow – named the 'Atlantic stem' – fitted to improve seaworthiness and decrease water resistance. The first orders for the VIIC/41 were placed on 14 October 1941, applied to Type VIICs already under construction to utilise the new materials. However, the first VIIC/41, *U293*, was not launched until 30 July 1943.

On 6 June 1944, the Allied landings on the Normandy coastline had caught the Wehrmacht by surprise. A hurried U-boat response comprised largely of nine non-*schnorchel*-equipped Type VIIC and VIIC/41s, bolstered by eight with the new

U-boat crew outbound from Norway. By the tail end of 1944 these would be the last moments of sunlight glimpsed by many of the crew before sailing for British waters.

equipment, were rushed into the English Channel. Within days there were only five *schnorchel* boats left, the remainder either retreating damaged or destroyed. By the month's end twenty-one U-boats had been despatched to attack the invasion shipping, only two left on station and continuing to attempt offensive operations. However, the situation was not considered hopeless in BdU headquarters.

> Operational conditions appeared to correspond generally with our original expectations, the approach to the operational area proving very difficult, while the area itself offered considerable opportunity for successful attacks, with little enemy opposition because of poor conditions for ASDIC and radar location. However, these opportunities could not be fully exploited on account of torpedo failures and the U-boats' low speed and both boats [*U621* and *U764*] reported being frequently passed over by convoys without an opportunity to attack them.[2]

Indeed BdU had discovered some interesting advantages to the deployment of such forces, unseen in the English Channel since 1940:

> Appendix 2 to diary of 26 September 1944
> Experiences gained by boats operating in the Channel and inlets around England show that boats can operate successfully in shallow waters in spite of sea patrol.

Reasons:
  a) Density layering caused by coastal tides adds to the difficulty of picking up
     boats by hydrophone and asdic, and makes schnorchel sailing possible
     under hydrophone direction-finding to signal strength of 2, but special
     care must be taken to make all-round search about every 15 minutes.
  b) Ground echoes and density layering make location of boats lying on the
     bottom considerably more difficult.
  c) Lying on the bottom prolongs duration of submergence.

Exploitation of currents makes quick, noiseless alteration of position possible.

However, this somewhat optimistic appraisal of the chances of U-boat survival
against the D-Day traffic was soon overtaken by increasing Allied pressure on
attacking U-boats. The Royal Navy had already begun slowly to adapt from 'blue-
water' U-boat hunting to stalking the underwater enemy in difficult conditions as
it shepherded the huge and potentially vulnerable D-Day invasion armada and its
follow-up traffic. Myriad false contacts caused by the echoes obtained from wrecks
and bottom irregularities, each of which required scrutiny and investigation lest it
shelter a lurking U-boat, provided fresh challenges for the Royal Navy hunters.
Once thoroughly investigated the contact would be measured and classified using
new positioning technology, as existing wreck charts proved unreliable. The
warships of a single escort group or task force were regularly engaged on investigating several separate contacts at the same time making it impossible to maintain
a tight search formation. Shortly thereafter a new piece of equipment known as
QH3, a naval modification of the RAF 'Gee' radar was developed. This new set
used a triangular transmission system that was able reputedly to fix a ship's position
to within a cable length, allowing detailed charts to be pieced together of existing
bottom anomalies, in the hope of reducing false contacts. The QH3 later became
known as the QM set in the Royal Navy after 1945, two of its military designers
going on to form the DECCA Navigation Company after the end of hostilities.
  Meanwhile the introduction of the Kriegsmarine's Small Battle Unit technology
in manned torpedoes and other midget weapons had also yielded little, and led to
escort forces being intensified. Instead, conventional Type VII U-boats were
redirected in August to areas other than the Seine Bay, such as the Cornish coast
and Bristol Channel.
  While the French Atlantic U-boat bases hurried to equip evacuating U-boats
with *schnorchels* before they retreated to Norway, Dönitz summed up the situation
faced by his units in the English Channel and other coastal areas of the United
Kingdom on 28 August:

In spite of repeated requests to the remaining 7 boats in the Seine area to send
situation report at all costs, even if it meant leaving operational area, no report

was received. No clue was provided by radio intercept reports or ASV locations. The last reports received from boats spoke of intensification of Channel situation, the BBC announced losses of two boats by name, also an enemy report of destruction of one other boat which apparently attempted to break through the Channel at Calais in an easterly direction. These facts gave rise to considerable misgiving as regards the survival of the boats.

It was very probable that the enemy had not only strengthened his defence numerically but had also taken other defensive measures, for example the flanking of convoy routes by submarine barrages. Judging by a report from a boat in the Bay of Biscay it is also possible he is employing other defence measures ('anti-submarine kite'). Destroyers passed overhead while boat lay at depth of 180 metres on the bottom, towing explosive. One of the charges exploded on the boat's side and caused considerable damage. But this is the only case of such a thing happening according to reports from boats. (The old 'anti-submarine kite' is a very dangerous weapon in shallow water).

On summing-up therefore a fairly negative picture confronted operational staff: Complete ignorance with regard to the situation, no information concerning the boats and intensified defence.

For these reasons no further boats were sent to the Channel, and instead boats

Despite promises of the new 'wonder electro-boats' it was the Type VIIC
that carried the war into British waters in 1944.

sailing from Biscay were detailed to the west coast of England (Bristol and North Channel) in the expectation that these areas would be less heavily defended. The traffic situation according to the small amount of available data should be favourable.

Further, the remaining boats in the Channel were ordered to commence return passage as they still had the long journey to Norway in front of them, which would take at least four-and-a-half weeks reckoned by the present low day's run.

With this the submarine operation in the Channel was over, during which the old fighting spirit of the submarine arm had again proved itself with distinction. A retrospective survey showed that the operation was correct contrary to all previous fears and all continually renewed doubts, and brought satisfactory successes considering the extremely difficult circumstances and the heavy though bearable losses. They had a sharp though not decisive effect on enemy supply and thereby relieved the troops engaged in the land battle, and brought, apart from the numerous successes, important experiences and knowledge in the total field of submarine warfare, especially with regard to the new boats. Also it tied down considerable enemy patrol and escort forces which would otherwise have been free for other duties such as interruption of our own supply traffic along the Dutch coast and in the Norwegian area, as well as for heavier air attacks generally on supply communications to the western front.

The successes would have been considerably higher and the losses certainly lower, if the boats had been capable of greater submerged speed and longer operational radius submerged. As the new types were designed for these characteristics above all others, high hopes for the future are justified.

The effect of the *schnorchel* was certainly decisive, and operation in the Channel without it would have been quite out of the question. Only a few months ago it would have seemed impossible that a boat could operate for 42 days without breaking surface once. Only by means of the *schnorchel* was it possible to operate close to the English coast again and to bridge the intervening gap between the operation of the new and old types of boats.

The direct U-boat attacks on Allied shipping operating in support of the invasion of occupied France were at last curtailed in the face of impossible odds. Even the small battle units of the *Kleinkampfverbänd* – which included midget submarines, explosive motorboats and frogmen – thought to be difficult to detect and counter, had achieved little against the enemy. On 4 August American forces had pierced the Wehrmacht's defensive lines at Avranches and the Biscay U-boat bases were faced with certain encirclement. BdU placed primary importance on completing whatever equipping of *schnorchels* was being handled at Brest, Lorient and St Nazaire, while La Pallice and Bordeaux were made ready to house those boats for which there was no gear available. German land defences against the charging American forces in Brittany crumbled faster than anticipated, and the U-boats were forced to evacuate France at all possible speed for the German bastion of Norway.

With the fall of Norway to the Wehrmacht in June of 1940, the idea of stationing depot ships in the myriad fjords from which to resupply U-boats was immediately put into effect. Their strategic positioning was perfect for the Kriegsmarine to continue its offensive in both the North Sea and Atlantic, though the latter battleground was easier to reach within months of Norway's fall after naval bases on the French Atlantic coast were also taken. Eventually the fear of Allied air raids led to the Norwegian ports of Bergen and Trondheim being designated as U-boat ports, each planned to accommodate the edifice of a concrete U-boat pen in which the boats could be safely repaired and resupplied. Bergen's nine-berth shelter was completed and Trondheim's 'Dora I and II' shelters, totalling thirteen berths, were also completed. Narvik too would become established as a U-boat flotilla base after Hitler's declaration of war on Russia and the subsequent offensive against the Arctic convoy routes. However, there would be no dedicated U-boat shelter there, the boats being distributed through the outlying fjords and using exclusively depot ships.

In Trondheim work had begun on a shelter capable of accommodating seven U-boats simultaneously within five separate boxes. The first three were single berths, dry-docks where complex work could be undertaken on the boats, while the remaining two boxes were double berths and 'wet docks', six metres wider than the others. Designated 'Dora I' this complex was built by the Organisation Todt, utilising paid workers from Germany and Scandinavia as well as Russian prisoners of war. It was started in the beginning of 1941 and handed over to the Kriegsmarine on 20 June 1943. A second complex, named 'Dora II' was begun in early 1942. This was a similar project that shared the same harbour as its sister complex, and was planned to comprise two dry docks and two wet docks, allowing the total number of U-boats that could be accommodated in Trondheim at any one time to be increased to thirteen. Work was never completed on this bunker, however, the war ending with Dora II only 70 per cent completed.

In Bergen a U-boat bunker was constructed west of the town itself, comprising three wet and three dry docks, with a capacity of nine U-boats in total. Construction began in 1941 and although the 'Bruno' bunker hosted its first U-boats in 1944, work was never completed. Nonetheless it was primarily to Bergen that the evacuating French U-boats proceeded. There, the headquarters of the 11th U-Flotilla prepared for the addition of the evacuating Type VIICs to its complement of active U-boats.

The 11th U-Flotilla had been established in May 1942, under the command of *Korvettenkapitän* Hans Cohausz, primarily concerned with the interdiction of Allied convoys bound for northern Russian ports. Its most sweeping success as a unit had been the virtual destruction of convoy PQ17 during July 1942 in conjunction with the Luftwaffe, the U-boats of 11th U-Flotilla coordinated by

'Dora I' under construction in Trondheim harbour.

Reichsminister Dr. Fritz Todt masterminded the construction of Germany's colossal U-boat bunkers. Here he is seen handing over the edifice at Saint Nazaire to Dönitz for operational use in 1942. Todt was killed in an air crash.

Kapitänleutnant Jurgen Oesten in his role as U-boat liaison officer on the staff of *Admiral Nordmeer* before the post of FdU Nord had been established. Like most other combat flotillas, the unit's command did not exercise operational control over its boats. From Norway, BdU or eventually either FdU Nord or West directed them. However, the role of the flotilla command was not inconsiderable. Aside from the administrative duties and record keeping required by all military combat units, Cohausz's staff were charged with making provision to accommodate a new influx of crews and support personnel into the areas used by the flotilla, primarily Bergen but also Horten (near Oslo), Kristiansand and Trondheim. Indeed, after Allied aerial harassment became intolerable, U-boats began to be stationed in remote inlets within the labyrinthine Norwegian fjords. Various minesweeping and flak vessels, all coordinated with local patrol units by Cohausz's headquarters, also escorted U-boats entering or leaving port. Eventually, in December 1944, Cohausz departed and was replaced by another veteran combat officer *Korvettenkapitän* Heinrich Lehmann-Willenbrock who would lead the 11th U-Flotilla until the end of hostilities in 1945.

FdU West, *Kapitän zur See* Hans-Rudolf Rösing, arrived with a small group of

Korvettenkapitän Heinrich Lehmann-Willenbrock, commander of the 11th U-Flotilla from December 1944 until the war's end.

FdU West Hans Rudolf Rösing (left) with Adalbert 'Adi' Schnee who later commanded *U2511*, the sole Type XXI to sail on a war patrol in 1945.

officers in Bergen by train from Oslo during September 1944. The office of FdU West had existed briefly in 1939, though it bore little resemblance to the office that was created in July 1942 in Paris. During 1943 the FdU West moved to Angers, closer to the French Atlantic bases, until forced to evacuate late in 1944 to Norway after the Allied invasion of western France. FdU West was responsible for disciplinary and judicial matters within its region, as well as the U-boats themselves while they were within their French ports and in transit to and from the western edge off Biscay. While the boats were outside of these areas they remained directly under BdU command. On the other hand, FdU *Norwegen* had been formed in January 1943, *Kapitän zur See* Rudolf Peters stationed in Narvik. This latter command was answerable to *Marinegruppenkommando* Nord. Upon the arrival of FdU West in Bergen, FdU *Norwegen* was renamed FdU *Nord*, and unlike Rösing's command, exercised complete operational control over boats within its allocated area.

Rösing's remit included the complete maintenance of U-boats based in Norway, replenishment of their ammunition and supplies, as well as the supplies, housing and security of the personnel of the southern Norwegian flotilla and bases. It was a logistical task that was made progressively more difficult as transportation and communication links with Germany came under increasing pressure from Allied air and naval forces over the months that followed FdU West's relocation. Eventually Rösing would even begin to take on an increasing role as tactical coordinator for U-boat control. During the middle of January, BdU stopped compiling the daily *Kriegstagebuch* (KTB, German unit war diary), rather adding it as addendum to the diary held by *Seekriegsleitung* (SKL, the German Naval War Staff). This paralleled the gradual devolvement of control from the central source. With the relegation of radio traffic from U-boats in British waters to mere occasional passage reports and little else, a greater local control also became dictated by the inherent logic of immediate feedback from those boats that did return from action.

Among the first boats to sail for British waters was the 9th U-Flotilla Type VIID minelayer *U218*. *Kapitänleutnant* Ruprecht Stock's boat, a veteran of Atlantic and Caribbean operations, had already undertaken a minelaying mission off Land's End during July, during which the newly fitted *schnorchel* had developed a serious defect leading to the carbon-monoxide poisoning of several crewmen as exhaust fumes from the diesels were pumped into the pressure-hull interior. During August the boat laid its mines off Start Point, after which Stock headed for Norway and subsequent attachment to Bergen's 11th U-Flotilla.

Minelaying was an unpopular task among U-boat crews. Not only was it invariably undertaken dangerously close to Allied harbours and heavily patrolled waters, it also required precise recording of the location of the mines laid. Somewhat ironically, however, during the First World War and in the early stages of the Second, U-boat-laid mines had proved more effective than torpedoes, driving a desire within the Kriegsmarine for custom-designed U-boat minelayers to deliver the powerful moored SMA mines. Thus development of the dedicated minelaying Type VIID was approved. SMA (*Schachtmine* or shaft mine) mines were designed to be laid via specialised vertical tubes. An anchored mine, SMA mines were 2.15 metres in length with a diameter of 1.33 metres.

However, perfection of the TMB 'torpedo mines' deliverable by orthodox tube shots with minimal extra equipment required aboard a standard combat U-boat had negated the urgency for the dedicated minelayers, particularly after SMA mines were initially discovered to be defective; design faults were found to be a cause of premature explosions. Requiring several months of modification to correct, an embargo was placed on their use until March 1943. However, the desire remained at OKM for medium-sized submarines to be able to deliver the SMA in coastal waters where the other dedicated minelayer type, the Type XB – the largest U-boat constructed during the Second World War – would be too large and

Minelaying marked both the beginning and the end of Dönitz's inshore British campaign, carried out by the Type VIID *U218*, the last of its type still in existence by then. The mineshafts are clearly visible behind the engineering officer.

unwieldy. Given the proven reliability and versatility of the Type VIIC it was decided to develop this boat to serve the new purpose.

Conversion of the Type VIIC to minelayer was facilitated by the simple expedient of adding an entire 9.8-metre-long hull section aft of the control room, which incorporated five vertical mineshafts. Each shaft could hold three stored mines giving a total load of fifteen mines. The shafts were covered with slatted sheeting to provide ventilation, while the tube bottoms remained open to the sea; the stored mines were inaccessible from inside the pressure hull. Space within the extension that was not used by the shafts was given over to additional compensating tanks (which were flooded to compensate for the weight loss of a delivered mine), additional diving tanks and enlarged fuel bunkers giving the increased operational possibilities of extended range missions. However, because the VIID maintained the standard VIIC power plant and had the increased drag of the mineshafts, performance was slightly impaired in speed, manoeuvrability and diving time. Coupled with the mine capacity, the Type VIID carried the same conventional weapon load as a normal VIIC, allowing them to enter service as normal attack submarines (albeit with longer range) until the SMA mine was cleared for use. Six Type VIID minelayers (*U213* to *U218*) were ordered from Germaniawerft on 16 February 1940, *U213* launched that July. By August 1945 *U218* was the sole surviving Type VIID, the last to have been sunk being *U214*, depth charged while attempting minelaying off Start Point on 26 July 1944. As if to emphasise the particular hazards of minelaying, all the U-boats of this type that had been destroyed were lost in combat with all hands.

Meanwhile, within the French bases, eight U-boats newly fitted with *schnorchel* gear were approaching readiness as the evacuation gathered pace. With the decision to stop sending boats against the D-Day traffic in the Seine area, they instead were despatched to the Bristol and North Channels on Britain's west coast. *U667* had been operational within the Bristol Channel since the end of July and had reported sinking a destroyer and 15,000 tons of enemy shipping.[3] *Kapitänleutnant* Hardo Rodler von Roithberg's *U989* also scored surprise successes in late August when he damaged the American freighter SS *Louis Kossuth* and sank the British SS *Ashmun J Clough* southwest of the Isle of Wight, before being ordered to head for Norway as part of the general evacuation. Another 9th U-Flotilla boat *U480* that had left Brest in early August for the English Channel sank corvette HMCS *Alberni*, minesweeper HMS *Loyalty* and badly damaged SS *Fort Yale* northeast of Barfleur, before moving on to attack convoy FTM74 on the afternoon of 25 August. The convoy had overrun the submerged U-boat, the din of propellers easily audible throughout the German hull. The 5,712-ton straggler SS *Orminster* was torpedoed thirty-five miles northwest of Cap d'Antifer by *Oberleutnant zur See* Hans-Joachim Förster after which *U480* was hunted for seven hours but escaped, his ability to avoid detection enhanced by the *Alberich* covering – an early form of stealth technology – that had been applied during the previous May:

As always, the hard-pressed ships of the escort flotillas based in Norway came under increasing pressure from Allied attack as they shepherded U-boats to and from their harbours.

25 August 1944. 1508hrs. Am being pursued by four anti-submarine vessels, two of which are operating ASDICs; the third, which apparently acts as depth-charge dropper, approaches at intervals of from five to ten minutes and drops charges; the fourth can be heard to be running her engines at very low speed. Listening conditions are particularly good.

2140hrs. Beginning of dusk. Pursuit lasts until 2200 during which time we have covered five miles over the ground . . . I maintain my depth by shifting the crew. One of the A/S vessels frequently lies directly above us with her engines just ticking over, when the least sound aboard her is clearly audible and ASDIC impulses are extremely loud . . . The depth-charge dropper, which has lately been lying stopped, approaches and drops five or six depth charges at intervals. These cause such trivial damage that I am convinced that the enemy is unable to locate us with ASDIC . . . I attribute the enemy's failure to locate me mainly to the protection afforded by *Alberich* . . .

Alberich, named after the guardian of the *Rhinegold* treasure from Wagner's *Der Ring des Nibelungen*, consisted of 4mm-thick sheets of synthetic rubber, Oppanol, which possessed sound absorbing properties. The sheets were secured to the outer hull with adhesive, claiming a 15 per cent reduction in sonar echo reflection, as well as acting as sound insulation for the internal machinery of the U-boat. While *Alberich* itself was reliable, the adhesive used to secure its place on the hull was less so and experiments continued until the war's end to prevent sheets from being partially washed off and so flapping in the water stream creating both drag and noise.

The first U-boat to receive *Alberich* was the Type II *U11*, covered in the sheeting for initial trials with the 5th U-Flotilla during 1940. In 1941 a larger boat, the Type IX *U67* and then *UD4* were similarly tested, though the adhesive problem prevented its widespread use amongst combat boats. Not until the dawn of the '*schnorchel* war' was *Alberich* used on patrol, *U480* being the first U-boat to enter combat clad in the rubber sheeting. After Förster's enthusiastic appraisal of the material the decision was made to attempt to cover numerous Type XXIII U-boats with *Alberich*, though the first was not ready for service until February 1945 when *U4709* was commissioned. It was suggested that the huge unfinished 'Valentin' bunker in Bremen be given over to *Alberich* fitting, though the plan was shelved. In total there were more Type VIICs that ended the war with *Alberich* coatings, despite the fact that for every one of its type covered, two and a half Type XXIIIs could be so treated.[4]

More commonly used was *Tarnmatte*, a compound synthetic rubber and iron-oxide powder that coated the head of a U-boat's *schnorchel* to absorb enemy radar waves, and which was claimed to absorb 90 per cent of waves emitted by the ASV Mk III airborne radar.

Förster and *U480* would not make landfall until October, and his War Diary provides an interesting glimpse at the difficulties faced by U-boats compelled to remain submerged for long periods of time in transit to, from and within the combat zone:

Coupled with the *schnorchel*, *Alberich* also was applied to a few U-boats that operated in British waters, *U1105* pictured here.

12 September: 0511hrs. 300 miles west of Ireland. Surfaced for the first time in 40 days. The boat stinks. Everything is covered with phosphorescent particles. One's footmarks on the bridge show up fluorescently . . . *Schnorchel* fittings and flooding slots also glow brightly in the darkness. Because of a high stern sea the bridge is constantly awash and the men cannot stand up on the slippery wooden deck; it is therefore impossible either to change or to dismantle the AA guns. The shields of the twin AA guns cannot be opened; the hinges appear to have rusted up and cannot be attended to in the dark. The 3.7cm gun is out of action; so shall first transmit my situation report and then proceed on *schnorchel* until the state of the sea permits me either to change the AA guns or dismantle them for overhaul below.

2nd October: 1710hrs. Off the west coast of Norway. Surfaced. The whole flak armament is unserviceable. The gun shields have been torn away from their mountings and are fouling the guns. Everything, including the 3.7cm gun, is corroded and covered with growth.

The combination of seemingly weaker anti-submarine forces in this area and the ability perhaps to distract enemy attention from those boats heading to Norway prompted Dönitz to despatch the *schnorchel*-equipped *U963*, *U309*, *U953*, *U262* and *U714* from La Pallice, *U985* and *U758* from Saint Nazaire and *U247* from Brest

U985 passing out from training to combat status. In October 1944 after a patrol of the North Channel this boat was badly damaged by German mines near Norway and remained inoperative for the remainder of the war.

U247 commissioned into the Kriegsmarine, 23 October 1943.

for British waters. The North Channel would be patrolled by *U953*, *U963* and *U985*, while *U309*, *U262*, *U758* and *U714* would hunt the Bristol Channel. *U247*, destined also for the Bristol Channel, was, however, sunk in the western end of the English Channel on 1 September by HMCSs *Swansea* and *St John* of the Canadian 9th Support Group. Ironically the wreck of *U247* would later almost certainly have been the subject of an extended depth charge attack on 12 March 1945 by frigate HMS *Loch Ruthven* and sloop HMS *Wild Goose*, the pair claiming to have sunk their target which was initially – and incorrectly – assessed to be *U965*. The difficulties of locating combat ready U-boats amidst the reefs and wrecks that littered British waters would never totally diminish.

The newest sailings from Norway had also been redirected from their original planned forays to the Seine Bay to British inshore waters. *U482*, *U484*, *U248*, *U743*, *U680*, *U1004* and *U398* were all directed to the North Channel area, but

U248, U398 and *U484* all failed to reach their destination due to intensifying ASW patrols, the latter two boats being sunk near the Hebrides. The commander of *U398, Korvettenkapitän* Johann Reckhoff, was sharply reprimanded by BdU for a lack of aggression, and the U-boat was posted back to Baltic training under fresh command. Reckhoff, a former Watch Officer aboard the *Admiral Graf Spee* was posted to a reserve position, finally commanding a commandeered merchant ship in the last month of the war. For the captain of *U1004* there was a worse fate in store. The boat returned to Norway on 23 October with nothing but an unsuccessful attack against an enemy destroyer to show for its patrol. *Oberleutnant zur See* Hartmuth Schimmelpfennig was arrested and later court-martialled during January 1945. Reduced to the ranks he was posted to a naval infantry unit and killed in action against British forces on 27 April 1945. *U680* was detected, depth charged and forced to break off its patrol without success. The boat had suffered severe damage to the *schnorchel* (which was only partially operable), the main and sky-search periscopes, Q tank, 'Wanze G 2' radar and direction-finding gear, and had a leaking exhaust as well as myriad more minor faults. Nonetheless, Dönitz had made the first steps in opening a fresh U-boat assault on the British Isles – what has subsequently been labelled the 'Inshore Campaign' had begun:

> The west is no longer available as a base for operations. Its place has been taken by Norway and one or two ports in home waters, since those in the former were not sufficient. The operational possibilities are therefore limited . . . Operation of Type VIICs in the Channel will as a rule no longer be possible, as the outward and return passages alone last seven to nine weeks, and by that time as far as one can see the boats would no longer be in a condition to operate in such a difficult area. For these therefore, there only remain the coastal waters around England such as the Moray Firth, Minch, and North Channel, as well as waters off Reykjavik.
>
> With regard to enemy defence, it can be expected without the least doubt that it will be concentrated in Norway, the Atlantic passages, the North Sea and Baltic approaches. Theoretically it is possible for the enemy to set up such a thick patrol veil that the old boats which have to *schnorchel*-sail comparatively often would be bound to be picked up sooner or later and then have to bear concentrated attack.
>
> The loss of the West would have been of decisive importance had the submarine war to be carried on with the same types of boats as before. But a very great under-water range, high submerged speed and great diving-depth will enable the new type XXI boats to break through to the Atlantic in spite of concentrated defensive patrols, and to operate with success in the North Atlantic and other very distant areas.[5]

The first of the dedicated inshore U-boats to report satisfactory progress to BdU was *U482*, one of the initial Type VIIC boats to be equipped with a *schnorchel.* Having departed Bergen on 16 August, *Kapitänleutnant* Hartmut Graf von

The return of a combat U-boat to Norway, April 1945. As the flotilla commander strides ashore after welcoming the crew, the faces of the welcoming committee make Germany's military fortunes all too apparent.

Matuschka operated first between the Færoes and Shetlands before heading further west. During the mid-afternoon of 30 August he sighted convoy CU36 north of Malin Head. After manoeuvring his boat into a firing position, von Matuschka fired two torpedoes at a column of five of the convoy's ships that had split from the main body to proceed to Loch Ewe, hitting the last vessel, 10,448-ton turbine tanker SS *Jacksonville*, which was carrying 141,000 barrels of high octane gasoline. The first torpedo struck *Jacksonville*'s starboard side igniting the cargo, which immediately engulfed the entire ship, rendering the crew completely unable to attempt launching any lifeboats or rafts. The second torpedo struck thirty seconds later, breaking the ship in two, both halves remaining afloat in a nightmarish sea of flame that killed seventy-six of the seventy-eight crew, the surviving pair, one of the merchant's gun crew and a fireman, pulled from the sea by USS *Poole* after 90 minutes in the water.

Nor was this the end of von Matuschka's run of success. Two days after the destruction of the *Jacksonville* a single T5 *Zaunkönig* torpedo hit and sank escort corvette HMS *Hurst Castle* from B1 Escort Group, which was shepherding CU36 towards its destination. On 3 September convoy ONF251 lost the 4,115-ton

Norwegian merchant SS *Fiordheim* to *U482*. The ship had left Belfast bound for Halifax the previous day, carrying 4,000 tons of anthracite coal. Proceeding at seven and a half knots in heavy swell under a clear sky none of the three bridge lookouts saw any sign that they were under attack until the torpedo exploded against the starboard side between number 4 and 5 holds. The Norwegian vessel had been a target of opportunity, travelling as the fifth ship in the sixteenth column of a seventeen-column convoy. After the first sharp blast she began to sink immediately. There was no fire, though crewmen remembered an odour similar to mustard coming from the impact area before they took to the boats a minute after impact. HMCS *Montreal* and SS *Empire Mallory* rescued thirty-five survivors aboard four lifeboats and three life rafts as the ship rapidly sank, exploding six minutes later when water reached the boilers.

U482 then moved to the west in order to avoid roving ASW patrols, sighting convoy HXF305 inbound from New York to Liverpool. In the early morning of 8 September von Matuschka fired a spread of torpedoes followed by a single T5 *Zaunkönig*. The unmistakable sound of detonation and sinking noises heralded the destruction of British steam tanker ST *Empire Heritage* carrying 16,000 tons of fuel oil and 1,942 tons of deck cargo, which included Sherman tanks, trucks and half-tracks. The ship, hit in the stern, capsized and sank after the fuel cargo had been ignited by the blast. Fifty crewmen, eight gunners, an army storekeeper and fifty-three passengers lost their lives. The 1,346-ton rescue ship *Pinto* neared the floating survivors and was spotted by von Matuschka while lying stationary during rescue attempts. A single T5 arced toward the *Pinto*, hitting and sinking her and killing the ship's Master, six crewmen, eight gunners, a signalman and two of *Empire Heritage*'s rescued survivors. The remaining survivors from both ships were later rescued by HMS *Northern Wave* and put down in Londonderry.

It was considered a spectacular success for a U-boat on its maiden patrol at that late stage of the war, and von Matuschka was awarded the German Cross in Gold by radio on 12 September the day after BdU had noted the following situation appraisal provided by the young captain:

> In ten days sighted three large convoys with destroyer and air escort. Convoy route over AM 5282 – 5387 – 5397. Noise buoys concealed convoys. During night while at depth of 40 metres two convoys were picked for first time as they passed overhead. Diving attack. Strong defence by sea and air. Over 300 depth charges dropped, none dangerous, no destroyer came near. Hydrophone and location conditions very bad. Mobile noise buoys. Depth-charge attacks by night undisturbed.[6]

U482 now headed to Norway, sighted twice during this voyage between the Færoes-Iceland gap by British aircraft, but crash diving to safety. Von Matuschka triumphantly entered Bergen on 26 September.

On 2 October BdU radioed fresh information on Allied convoy routes within the North Channel to the four U-boats supposed to be within that operational area – *U1001*, *U309*, *U953* and *U743*. They also reported that, as far as German intelligence could show, there was little or no merchant traffic outside the routes given, only strong anti-submarine forces aimed at driving off approaching boats. However, it was too late to make any real difference to the success rate of Dönitz's first wave of inshore boats. Indeed messages radioed to both *U484* and *U743* fell on deaf ears, as both boats – on their maiden patrols – had been sunk with all hands on 9 September. *U484* was destroyed south of the Hebrides by HMCSs *Dunver* and *Hespeler*, supported by a Sunderland from 423 Squadron, RCAF; *U743* northwest of Malin Head by HMSs *Helmsdale* and *Porchester Castle*. This latter U-boat was not listed in the BdU War Diary as presumed lost until 6 October:

This boat left Trondheim on 28 August and went into the North Atlantic via the Iceland Passage. She did not make any passage report on entering the North Atlantic and was given an operations area off the North Channel. According to

Approaching the U-boats' pens. These were built using the same construction techniques that were used for the bases in occupied France although priority was not given to Norwegian harbours so shelters were fewer.

her supplies she should by now be on return passage, but has not reported despite several orders. She may have been lost in the Iceland Passage on her way out or otherwise by anti-submarine hunt in the North Channel.

Similarly *U484* was not officially listed as *Vermisst ein Stern* until the last day of October, its supply state unable to keep the boat at sea for eleven weeks and demands for situation reports remaining unanswered. The Allies too were unsure about the destruction of *U484*. The Sunderland had spotted the U-boat's *schnorchel* and delivered an immediate depth-charge attack while homing three Canadian warships to the spot. HMCSs *Dunver* and *Nene* attacked what they believed to be schools of fish, or possibly whales, while the corvette *Hespeler* obtained ASDIC contact on what was considered a positive U-boat. Two attacks using the ahead-throwing three-barreled mortar known as the 'Squid' followed, after which large air bubbles broke the surface astern of the passing attacker. The Canadian commander reckoned that the U-boat had at least been damaged, but subsequent study of the ASDIC recorder trace by the U-boat assessment committee decided that the target was not only on the bottom, but also suspiciously near the site of a known wreck, and so concluded that there was 'insufficient evidence of the presence of a U-boat'.

Thus despite the success of *U482*, for Dönitz this brief victory was ultimately hollow:

> In spite of *U482*'s good start, the last nine boats to operate in the North Channel have not had any successes. Six boats have entered port meanwhile, one is presumed lost on her way out [*U743*], two others are plotted on their return passage, but have not reported so far. With the exception of *U482*, none of the boats that have entered port observed any traffic and only experienced slight anti-submarine activity.
>
> Short reports show that the boats did not press far enough forward, ie, never reached the areas of densest traffic, which would certainly have been possible with the weak defences reported. Experiences gained have been radioed to the new boats approaching, *U246*, *U1006*, *U978* and *U1200*. It remains to be seen whether these boats can penetrate far enough into the North Channel to pick up the convoys there.[7]

The 'Squid' was an improvement on the depth charge as a U-boat killer. The use of depth charges meant that as the surface ship was above the suspected position of the target U-boat, the ahead-looking ASDIC lost contact for valuable minutes. This, coupled with the roughly fifteen minutes before the disturbed water settled enough for ASDIC to become effective again could be exploited by an experienced, and lucky, U-boat commander. With the 'Squid' this problem was avoided and the target could be kept locked in an ASDIC trace during the crucial last seconds as the weapon was launched.

The first such Allied weapon to have been developed was the 'Hedgehog', a 24-

The Hedgehog (shown here) and Squid ASW projectors were more effective than standard depth charge attacks in shallow British waters.

firing-contact fused bomb 'spigot-mortar'. A spigot mortar operated on the principle that the propellant charge located at the top of the tubular tail of each projectile was fired, the explosive force working against a spigot on which it was mounted. This allowed the weight of the base plate and firing unit to be kept to a minimum. The twenty-four bombs were fired in a staggered series of six-bombs, each in an arc that was designed to land all twenty-four projectiles simultaneously in an elliptical area approximately thirty metres in diameter at a fixed range of 230 metres before the ship's bow.

The advantages of the 'Hedgehog' were immediately apparent. First, the target U-boat could be held by ASDIC throughout the attack. Secondly the depth of the target was irrelevant, as the weapons were fused to explode on contact. Thirdly the explosion of a single direct hit by a Hedgehog bomb – particularly once the tried and tested Torpex explosive was used instead of less effective TNT – could rupture a U-boat's hull, as opposed to the large number of depth charges usually deployed.

The three-charge Squid mortar in action off the bow of a Canadian destroyer.

Lastly, the weapon provided no warning of when it was being deployed. Hydrophone following of a ship deploying depth charges gave U-boat commanders a logical idea of when the actual attack was taking place, whereas the 'Hedgehog' could literally come out of nowhere.

However, the weapon was not without limitations, the primary one being that results could only be achieved using a contact fuse by a direct hit rather than damage from near misses possible with timed explosives, and in the same year that it had been issued, the improved 'Squid' mortar was rushed into service. The first production unit was installed on HMS *Hadleigh Castle*, after which it went on to be installed on seventy frigates and corvettes during the Second World War. The first successful use was by HMS *Loch Killin* on 31 July 1944 against *U333*. This weapon was a three-barrelled, 12in mortar, the barrels mounted in a laterally staggered series to result in a spread of projectiles. This entire frame mount could in turn be rotated through ninety degrees to enable loading. Most 'Squids' were mounted in pairs aboard ship, all six bombs fired in salvo. The 'Squid' was automatically fired from the ASDIC range recorder at the exact moment calculated to achieve success, fulfilling the true potential of sonar as a U-boat killer. The ASDIC 'programmed' a clockwork fuse to detonate the explosive at the correct depth. The pattern of explosives from a single installation would form a destructive triangle at a range of 250 metres before the ship. Two weapons firing the opposing triangular spreads set to detonate above and below the target would create a pressure wave capable of crushing a U-boat's hull.

Concurrent with this improved weaponry was the development and construction of the *Loch*-class frigate, which would feature extensively in the new hunt for inshore U-boats. This frigate's ASW striking power was centred around the 'Squid', with only fifteen depth charges being carried within a single rack and a pair of stern throwers. Additionally, new sensors were incorporated in the form of the Type 277 radar that utilised the cavity magnetron, transmitting on centimetric wavelengths for target location. It was found that this new radar could detect a periscope or *schnorchel* amidst the usual surface clutter, although the danger of chasing assorted other surface debris was correspondingly magnified. Alongside the American air-launched Mark 24 'Fido' homing torpedo and sonobouys, the technological war gathered pace in Allied quarters as well as within the Kriegsmarine.

CHAPTER TWO

Courage and Dash

THE MONTH OF October had not produced the onslaught against British shipping envisaged by Dönitz after von Matuschka's promising beginning. On 6 October he radioed all of his boats at sea:

> During the last few days four boats [including the lost *U743*] in the North or Bristol Channels have reported no traffic. It is known for certain, however, that several convoys passed through the areas while these boats were operating. Failure to find the traffic can only be explained by the fact that boats were not on the convoy routes or in positions where shipping is concentrated, but remained further out to sea.
>
> The sole aim of every Commanding Officer must be to attack. This means: going at it with courage and dash, holding out with determination, but with intelligence, in areas which promise success even if there is strong anti-submarine activity.

His commanders were exhorted to take their boats as close as possible to the narrowest parts of harbour entrances and channels through which merchant traffic would be compelled to pass. While British ASW forces were operating at a radius of up to 150 miles from shore, the closer the U-boat sailed to shore the greater its chances of both survival and victory in the shallow waters of the British Isles, amidst jumbles of natural reefs, currents and the detritus of centuries of maritime war and wreckage.

During September *U281*, *U1199* and *U1226* had all sailed for the British Isles; the Moray Firth, North Minch and English Channel respectively, the last destination now customarily reached by a circuitous route around the north of the British Isles, west of Ireland and entering from the Atlantic end of the Channel. In October nine more would also be sent to British waters, while *U300* was tasked with patrolling near Reykjavik, Iceland. Here *Oberleutnant zur See* Fritz Hein, *U300*'s commander, attacked convoy UR142, which had been scattered by heavy weather, south-southwest of the port on 10 November, and successfully sank two ships: the 6,017-ton British tanker SS *Shirvan* and the 1,542-ton Icelandic SS *Godafoss* – Iceland's largest passenger ship – which had stopped against orders to rescue survivors. A third vessel, British steam tug *Empire World* departed Reykjavik to assist the stricken *Shirvan*, which was abandoned but still afloat for some time

U1058 and *U1109* in British captivity. Both boats display their different *schnorchel* arrangements.

following the attack. The small tug disappeared, and though often credited to Hein, its fate remains unconfirmed. It was the second patrol of Icelandic waters for this young commander, his first having been terminated by depth-charge damage from a Canadian Canso aircraft of RCAF 162 Squadron in August that year.[1] Only good fortune had saved the U-boat on that occasion, after Hein rashly attempted to dive to safety with damaged periscopes and a cracked ballast tank. Forced to the surface by the explosions, his gunners managed to drive their attacker away and, aided by drifting fog, Hein limped ignominiously home to Norway.[2]

Once more the new boats' dispositions were spread between three main operational areas: *U483* and *U1003* to the North Channel; *U1061* and *U1202* to the Bristol Channel and *U246*, *U978*, *U1006*, *U991* and *U1200* to the English Channel. Again, enforced radio silence due to prolonged *schnorchel* passages denied BdU its customary instant feedback on progress or problems, the operational command in Berlin transmitting blind instructions to all U-boats in the hope that they would be received at some point. While this hampered the German command view, it also denied British ULTRA intelligence, a great asset against the U-boats, and limited the effectiveness of the highly developed radiolocation system that had so often swung the tide of battle against the U-boats. They could intercept instructions telling where the enemy were supposed to be – but not where they were in

Eberhard Godt, head of BdU Ops during the
inshore campaign of 1944/45.

reality, as the German commanders had also been given considerable latitude in how to conduct their operations.

Meanwhile, on 14 October Hinrich Mangels' *U1200* aborted its patrol with mechanical difficulties, entering Bergen on 17 October and putting out again two days later.

The BdU War Diary reflects this incomplete knowledge of the situation within the combat area. On 19 October *U246*, *U978* and *U1006* were all ordered to make a standard report (Channel Operations Order Serial No.36), which briefly notified BdU of the state of boats and crews, while presumed to be west of Ireland and preparing for the passage into the Western Approaches and ultimately their Channel operations area. Three days later the same trio of boats were reminded to make this report in order for BdU to determine the feasibility of their planned deployment in the Seine Bay.

The destroyers of the 6th Escort Group, covering the Western Approaches, further reduced the numbers of this Channel group when *U246* was found and depth charged southwest of Ireland on 23 October. *Kapitänleutnant* Ernst Raabe had taken his boat around the British Isles running surfaced as much as possible in darkness and proceeding by *schnorchel* for the remainder of his transit. They had observed little enemy traffic throughout the journey and Raabe had just ordered the boat's *schnorchel* lowered with batteries full when his hydrophone operator detected warship engines. It was too late; the noise of ASDIC location followed, and depth charges exploded above and below the slow moving U-boat. Both periscopes were damaged as well as diving tanks three and five. With blowing vents partially unserviceable, Raabe decided to head back to Norway, creeping away from the destroyers above who continued to probe with ASDIC, the 'sawlike' noise of their 'Foxer' torpedo decoys plainly audible. More depth charges were dropped further away from *U246*, which successfully evaded pursuit and returned to port for repair. It was assumed that the Escort Group had been lying stationary as the U-boat approached while using its *schnorchel*, rendering hydrophones inoperative and periscope use difficult due to the normal speed travelled. This was the most dangerous period for U-boats using the new apparatus; fresh directives were issued to maintain regular listening and periscope-observation pauses during travel.

Konteradmiral Eberhardt Godt, BdU Chief of Operations, recorded the situation within the BdU Diary on 26 October, the day after *U978* finally reported as ordered that the boat and crew were fit for their Channel operation. Their recorded average distance covered during a single day from Bergen was approximately fifty-five miles and they were ordered to make for Seine Bay as originally planned. With now only two boats believed to be headed for the Channel, Godt ordered *U991* to replace *U246* and make for the grid square AM79 covering the Western Approaches. The sole remaining unknown boat, *U1006*, was again reminded to report their condition before entering her operations area. With still no reply they were given instructions to make for the Seine Bay or for AM9817

– the northwest entrance to the Bristol Channel – at the commander's discretion. On the penultimate day of October Godt noted:

> If *U1006* does not intend to operate in the Seine area, she will have an operations area between the latitudes and longitudes of AM9898 and AM9487, concentrating off Milford Haven and Pembroke . . . It is intended to send *U991*, on her way out, to the same area. It is possible that the main shipping route lies through the centre of the St George's Channel, as *U262* and *U714* have seen no traffic in the coastal area off Cape Land's End to Trevose Head, and *U758* has seen nothing off the south coast of Ireland. An operation off Milford is therefore considered very promising, especially as there has not been a single U-boat in this area for three years. Details of traffic situation have been radioed.

However, *Oberleutnant zur See* Horst Voigt's *U1006* had already been destroyed by the time of this entry, depth charged to the surface and sunk in a surface torpedo and gun duel against HMCS *Annan* south of the Færoes on 16 October.

> HMCS *Annan* exchanged ferocious machine-gun fire with *U1006*, which had been forced to surface by depth-charges.
> To the bridge came the heart-stopping report: 'Torpedo. Red Four-Oh, sir.' Seconds later, the deadly fish passed by the frigate's port side by only yards.

It had been a desperate attempt at torpedoing their pursuer – a T5 *Zaunkönig* fired from the stern tube – as gunners fired their flak weapons at the Canadian. Another member of Canadian Support Group 6, HMCS *Loch Achanalt* moved in to assist after fixing the U-boat on radar.

> 'Their guns were shooting something that looked like .5 stuff,' Lieutenant John Corbett said. 'It was pretty stuff, all colours, blue and pink and red. But it was coming too close just to stand and watch it.'

HMCS *Annan*; victor over *U1006*.

Riddled with 4in and Oerlikon rounds and blasted by a depth charge that landed directly on her, the U-boat went down for the last time. Forty-six German survivors were plucked from the sea.

Lieutenant Commander C P Balfry gave the order to splice the main brace (a double tot of rum for his crew). 'I've been commanding ships for three years,' he said, 'and this was my first actual brush with a U-boat. I knew my luck would change one of these days.'[3]

In fact it had been more bad luck for the U-boat that the attack had happened at all, the contact having been dubbed dubious at best by the accompanying ships of Support Group 6.

Uncertainties resulted from problems with detection equipment, which made it difficult to locate the enemy, then just as difficult to confirm a kill. U-boat hunters thus had to rely on a large helping of luck if they were to be successful (and credited with success), which may account for the continuing heavy reliance on depth charges – they were most suitable for quick attacks. Such was the case with HMCS *Annan* in October; patrolling with Escort Group 6, it had been obtaining good contacts from whales, which were no doubt identified by their breeching. At just before 1800, however, a target appeared at twelve hundred yards, which the operator classified as 'doubtful'. Taking no chances, the ship carried out a depth-charge attack, though two of the ten devices jammed at the rails. A search revealed further echoes, but after much 'to-ing and fro-ing'. It was thought that a tight circle of fish, or a number of whales had been attacked and dispersed.

Annan thus rejoined its group, which had not bothered pursuing the doubtful target, but an hour later the ship's radar gained a surface contact. What followed was a chaos of star shell, gunfire, and the staccato of machine guns, with shallow depth charges bringing the battle to an explosive close. Prisoners-of-war revealed that the first attack, which *Annan* had concluded did no more than disperse some fish, had caused so much damage that the boat was forced to surface.[4]

The survivor of BdU's Channel Group, *U978*, continued on its path towards the Seine Bay and in so doing *Kapitänleutnant* Günter Pulst and his crew carried out the longest *schnorchel* war patrol, lasting seventy-three days in total, starting near the Norwegian island of Hellisoe. Originally assigned for Arctic operations during September, Pulst's boat had been diverted to Atlantic operations on 2 October, their first operational cruise.

After 24 days Pulst entered the English Channel and headed for the Allied landing zone in the Seine Bay, patrolling the approaches to Cherbourg at a distance of between two and five miles off the coast. Between 19 and 23 November Pulst recorded three convoys attacked, each with one freighter sunk. The first

U-boats of the 11th U-Flotilla moored in Bergen.

unidentified troop ship Pulst estimated at 7,000 tons, sinking six minutes after being hit by torpedoes. The second claimed was British Landing Ship Infantry (LSI) SS *Empire Cutlass*, which had taken part in the original D-Day landings on 6 June. The last was the American Liberty ship SS *William D Burnham*. It was only this latter attack that has since been confirmed by Allied sources.

The *William D Burnham* was carrying 3,917 tons of food and 166 vehicles to Barfleur when, during mid-afternoon on 23 November, a single torpedo – a T5 *Zaunkönig* – hit the stern. The Liberty ship had been supposed to meet convoy TMC44, but had failed to make the rendezvous and was sailing independently with a sole escort, armed drifter HMS *Fidget*. The blast physically lifted the ship from the water, blowing off the rudder and breaking the propeller shaft. Flooding soon caused the ship to settle by the stern, and Pulst opted to finish her off. However, with strong tide conditions it took nearly an hour to achieve a fresh firing position, whence Pulst launched a single LUT torpedo, which struck the ship's port side forward of the bridge and opened a forty-foot hole in the hull. The American's Master, Emil Rosol, had already ordered lifeboats made ready and this second blast destroyed one of the prepared boats, killing eighteen men in and around it. With all chances of saving his ship lost, Rosol ordered her abandoned and the fifty survivors lowered the three remaining lifeboats. The Liberty ship failed to sink; she was later taken in tow and beached off Cherbourg where she was declared a total loss.

For Pulst, believing that he had destroyed three laden merchants it was a highly successful voyage, and *U978* then returned via the Atlantic to Bergen, where Pulst was awarded the *Ritterkreuz*.

Meanwhile *Oberleutnant zur See* Hinrich Mangels' *U1200* had radioed its required short report on boat and crew state on 2 November, reporting both to be ready for Channel operations. BdU directed *U1200* to the same area as *U978* (the sea area between longitude BF2610 and BF3610), with the addendum that if the target shipping situation warranted a change of location the commander had the freedom to move eastwards. However, on Armistice Day 1944, four Royal Navy corvettes of Support Group 30, which was escorting convoy HX317, located the boat with radar as it sailed surfaced south of Ireland heading east. The corvettes deployed in line abreast as the U-boat dived, locating the twisting target on ASDIC and destroying it with depth charges and Squid attacks. A can stamped with a Hamburg address was retrieved from a small debris field, all that marked the end of Mangels and his fifty-one crewmen. *U1200* was not listed as missing from unknown causes until December.

The sole other success of that wave of U-boats was recorded by *Kapitänleutnant* Hans-Joachim von Morstein aboard *U483* who, on 1 November, torpedoed British frigate HMS *Whitaker*. This was the second attack of von Morstein's patrol. A week earlier he had fired three torpedoes at an *Erebus*-class monitor ship, (HMS *Erebus* was being used for shore bombardment as part of 'Operation Infatuate', the Allied assault on Walcheren in the Netherlands); they all missed, however, exploding between eight and ten minutes after firing and were thought to have hit the ground at the end of their runs in water only forty-four metres deep. Success came when von Morstein fired two LUT torpedoes at a convoy sailing off Malin Head. Two explosions and subsequent sinking noises led von Morstein to claim a definite ship sunk, estimated at 5,000 tons and a second probable, though in fact he had blown the bow off *Whitaker*, killing ninety-two crewmen. The crew eventually halted the flooding and extinguished fires aboard the ship, after which it was towed to Londonderry and on to Belfast where it was declared a total loss.

Three days later von Morstein was forced to abort his patrol after his forward hydroplane developed a fault. It was not the first mechanical malfunction suffered by the U-boat crew. In the voyage's early stages a fault had developed in the *schnorchel* leading to several cases of carbon-monoxide poisoning. *Funkmaat* Gustav Hoffmann died on 12 October from pneumonia contracted following poisoning by the exhaust fumes.

On 20 November as *U483* headed home, Luftwaffe aircraft sighted what at first they reported as a 'large target' probably a cruiser southwest of the Shetlands. BdU gave *U483*, at that time off Stavanger, the opportunity to follow and attack the target, until fresh sightings downgraded the vessel to a motor torpedo boat.

The following day von Morstein entered Bergen harbour, and extracts from his short report featured in the BdU War Diary. In general the notations regarding von Morstein's report were favourable for future inshore operations, listing the fact that, despite the frequent detection of day and night air patrols, there were no attacks made on the boat. Conditions inshore were considered excellent with shallow water, rocky bottoms and thick salinity layering giving good protection from hydrophone and radar detection, as well as affording favourable conditions for *schnorchel* use.

Likewise Dönitz cited the report made by returned skipper *Kapitänleutnant* Rolf Nollmann heavily during a conference with Hitler on 3 December 1944 in favour of *schnorchel* use. Nollmann had claimed an (unconfirmed) 8,000-ton freighter sunk during his patrol off Peterhead and Aberdeen, which included fifty days of schnorchelling, thirty-one of them spent within the operational area. However, Nollmann found submerged listening conditions very bad and periscope visibility also hampered by thick fog, by which he accounted for a lack of further success. He scorned the enemy ASW patrols as 'ill-trained' as, despite their almost constant presence, the U-boat was not detected once. For BdU it confirmed once more that the old model Type VIIC U-boat was feasible as an attack craft in British inshore waters while the Kriegsmarine awaited completion of their new electro-U-boats. Dönitz further proposed during this Führer conference that seven U-boats equipped with *schnorchels* be stationed outside Scapa Flow in order to attack carrier task forces. Although Dönitz planned for Arctic U-boats to operate within this area, at least two of his Atlantic U-boats were also destined to patrol the approaches to the Orkney anchorage.

Meanwhile, *Kapitänleutnant* Diethelm Balke's *U991* – presumed by BdU to be in the Bristol Channel – had in fact already moved into the English Channel. On 27 November he mounted an unsuccessful attack against a large steamer south-southwest of the Isle of Wight, although the two end-of-run detonations led to claims of hits and damage to the target. The boat's fortunes did not improve, a claimed Liberty ship torpedoed and sunk on 15 December during the return to Norway remaining unconfirmed. It was to be the boat's only war patrol; having left Norway once more for refit in Germany it was prevented by the end of the war from sailing again operationally.

Kapitänleutnant Rolf Thomsen also made quite significant unwarranted claims for kills on his boat's maiden war patrol. *U1202* had departed Kristiansand on 20 October for the sea area off Milford Haven in the Bristol Channel. *Maschinenmaat* Anton Worbel, responsible for the electric motors, recalled the voyage:

> We departed Kristiansand by foggy night. Once in open sea we began our submerged journey . . . We were destined for the St George's Channel in the Irish Sea. But stretching from Ireland to Land's End was a thick minefield . . . but, Ireland itself was neutral and the coast free from mines. So at night, in stormy seas, we dived and headed at high submerged speed close inshore and behind the English mines. We entered the Irish Sea, but found absolutely nothing. During our return voyage in the dark night within the St George's Channel the float valve on the *schnorchel* jammed and for three to four minutes air was sucked into the engines from the boat's interior.[5]

Men aboard *U1202* prepare victory pennants after their first war patrol.

On 10 December Thomsen attacked a convoy northwest of St David's Head, Pembrokeshire, and recorded sinking four ships. The sole confirmed success was the American Liberty ship SS *Dan Beard*, travelling in ballast outbound from Barry alone and unescorted. Ironically, the ship's Master, William Robert Wilson, had been ordered by the Admiralty to sail alone as the Irish Sea was reported clear of U-boats. The first torpedo struck the port side at number three hold, a second hitting the stern, blowing off the rudder and breaking the propeller shaft. The ship already had a plate welded over a previously discovered crack in the hull almost exactly where the first torpedo had hit; this weak spot soon broke in two whereupon the ship's stern sank rapidly. It was Thomsen's sole success, though after successfully reaching Bergen on 1 January 1945 he was awarded the Knight's Cross, presented by FdU West Hans Rudolf Rösing.

The question is often asked as to why such incredible over-claiming took place within the U-boat service. The awarding of Knight's Crosses to U-boat commanders that had in actuality achieved little appears to postwar eyes to have

The crew of *U1202* head toward their Norwegian barracks
at the end of their maiden voyage into British waters.

devalued the decoration. The stringent requirements of confirmed tonnage sunk in order to be recognised were gradually relaxed as the war progressed until, by 1945, men were awarded the coveted decoration with what, by comparison to the heady days of 1940, were relatively paltry combat records.

The answer is largely twofold. First of all events within the Wehrmacht were on a considerable downward trend by the last year of the war, and the award of Germany's highest decoration could have been seen as a morale-boosting exercise. The second reason is perhaps more prosaic. By the mid- to late war, torpedo attacks were increasingly made from underwater. While early war doctrine had preached the value of attacking while surfaced and using the U-boat's high surfaced speed and small visual silhouette, these advantages had been removed at a single stroke by Allied radar advances. Forced beneath the surface in attack, commanders were hamstrung by their lack of submerged speed and mobility. Thus they fired whenever possible, often at extreme ranges. Once the attack had been made the U-boat tended to begin a withdrawal to forestall the inevitable Allied ASDIC hunt that could spell doom for slow submerged conventional U-boats. Technological advances in pattern-running torpedoes allowed a virtual 'fire-and-forget' approach as the weapon raced on its path and began a pre-programmed search pattern. Designed to be used against massed enemy convoy traffic the theory was that if fired correctly it was bound to hit something sooner or later, while the U-boat retreated to safety. A final torpedo development – the T5 *Zaunkönig* homing torpedo that targeted propeller noise – demanded that the firing U-boat dive immediately after the weapon was discharged lest it circle and home on the U-boat itself. Thus, once the attack was launched, the U-boat submerged and was rendered blind. Amidst the surprising cacophony of underwater sounds that assailed both the crew and boat's sensory capabilities, such things as premature explosions, defensive depth charges or 'end-of-run' detonations that could be caused by either the torpedo sinking to crush depths and exploding once its propellant was exhausted or, in shallow waters, impacting the seafloor, rocks or even wrecks, were often taken as conclusive proof that a hit had been made. The wish became the father of fact, and U-boat claims far exceeded the reality of their achievements.

North of Scotland, patrolling between Pentland Firth and Cape Wrath, *Oberleutnant zur See* Erich Taschenmacher's *U775* torpedoed and sank the frigate HMS *Bullen* on 6 December. The single T5 *Zaunkönig* broke the ship in two as the frigate sailed as part of 19th Escort Group. Stoker Petty Officer Frank Hughes later described the attack:

It had just turned 10 o'clock and I was down below keeping the forenoon watch. I felt the explosion that lifted me right off my feet. I managed to pick myself up and felt to see if I was all right . . . I looked around to see what was happening. All the lights had gone out . . . I turned on the emergency lights and reached for my torch so that I could check the bilges. I noticed that there was a slight list on the ship, but for the moment we were dry and there seemed to be no water coming in.

Then I saw the Engineering Officer pass, so I put my head through the hatchway and called out 'Sir, what's happening?' He said, 'You had better come up – they are abandoning ship.' I got all the stokers up and out before shutting all the hatches down. I looked outside on the upper deck and could see she was in a very bad condition. She was sinking and as I looked over the port side to the forecastle, I saw that she was awash.

There were only a few left on the forecastle by that time and as I had no lifebelt at this moment, when I saw Mr Crook, I asked him if there was a spare one. He said that he had one that might do. Stoker Dale said that his didn't fit him but, as it would fit me, he would have the other . . . I then went over the port side and started to swim for it.

As I swam . . . I thought I would have a rest and looked back. The mast was going over. Then I saw the net and life raft and started to swim over to them. I again looked around for the ship. She was now in two. The bows were going up to meet the stern.[6]

Coupled with what have now become the familiar edifices of huge Organisation Todt constructed bunkers, U-boats based in Norway were often sheltered in more secluded and dispersed mooring places such as this pier.

As the frigate went down, HMS *Goodall* obtained ASDIC contact with *U775* and the U-boat was hunted for fourteen hours by HMSs *Loch Insh* and *Goodall*. Eventually, however, Taschenmacher escaped and managed to return to Bergen on 21 December, forced to curtail his patrol due to engine trouble. For their part, the hunting Royal Navy ships later claimed the destruction of a U-boat, postwar reckoning listing it as *U297*, though in actuality they had failed.

Like *U775*, *U739* – one of the U-boats intended for attacks against carriers off Scapa Flow – was forced to return to Trondheim because her port diesel had broken down. *U296* had been allocated the North Minches as its hunting ground alongside *U775*, though achieved nothing and returned to Norway on Christmas Day.

A more troubling issue had come to the attention of BdU as the loss of *U1006* became the subject of a brief attempt at disinformation by the Allies. Espionage had silently raged in all the combatants' countries since – and often prior to – the outbreak of war in 1939. German attempts at planting spies in Great Britain had met with mixed success not helped by MI5's superb ability at finding and turning agents, some of whom maintained their role as double agents until the end of hostilities. MI5 established a covert detention centre at Ham Common where suspected agents could be isolated and interrogated. Their first major breakthrough came with the 'recruitment' of Welshman Arthur Owens who had been arrested in September 1939. Owens owned a battery company and had frequently visited the Kiel shipyards, reporting his observations of German rearmament to the Secret Intelligence Service (SIS). Unfortunately for him, he was careless and a routine mail intercept revealed to his SIS masters that he was also in touch with the Abwehr. Following arrest Owens offered to make radio contact with the Abwehr while acting under control of MI5, helping Bletchley Park decipher the Abwehr's Enigma circuits once they had encoded his transmissions and passed them on. He also betrayed incoming German agents, the trail of which eventually led to Danish-born Wulf Schmidt.

Schmidt had been born in 1911 at Abenra, South Jutland, serving briefly in the Danish army before accompanying a consignment of cattle to Argentina. He made a second trip and then settled in the Cameroons to grow bananas. The South Jutland region had belonged to Prussia until 1919 and Schmidt obviously felt kinship with the Reich to which he returned after the outbreak of war. He was recruited by the Abwehr as an agent, operating first in Copenhagen until the successful conquest of Scandinavia by the Wehrmacht, before volunteering to parachute into England during 1940, confident that German forces would shortly invade. On the night of 19 September 1940 *Hauptmann* Karl Gartenfeld took his black painted Heinkel 111 bomber from Brussels with Schmidt aboard, the Dane leaping into British territory equipped with a new identity as Harry Williamson. He drifted down close to RAF Oakington's flak defence battery near the Cambridge-shire village of Willingham. Schmidt's wristwatch had been smashed during his exit from the aircraft and the following morning he walked into Willingham and bought a new pocket watch, stopping to wash a slightly swollen ankle in the village pump and buying a copy of *The Times*. After breakfast in a small local cafe he began to retrace his steps to the field where he had hidden his wireless and suitcase.

His evident confusion concerning ration cards and the English monetary system had aroused suspicion, however, and, as he crossed the village green, he was challenged by a private of the Willingham Home Guard and escorted to their headquarters in the Three Tuns public house. Here, Colonel Langton, the commander of the Home Guard detachment began to interrogate him. His explanation that he was a refugee was considered insufficient and police arrived to take him away, eventually handing him over to MI5. Schmidt resisted interrogation for thirteen days before he cracked and turned to the Allied side in exchange for escaping the death penalty. MI5 codenamed him 'Tate' due to a supposed resemblance to the music hall comedian Harry Tate; his first transmission was made on 16 October 1940, continuing until 1945. 'Tate' proved highly successful in the early years, even becoming a naturalised German citizen and being awarded the Iron Cross First and Second class all by radio. MI5 had become skilled in including just enough accurate information in each report for the Abwehr to be confident of its veracity. In September 1944 'Tate' began transmitting reports of false minefields back to his controllers in Hamburg as the Admiralty struggled to contain the menace of the *schnorchel* U-boats.[7] Godt recorded the fresh intelligence sent by 'Tate' in the BdU War Diary:

According to agent's report *U1006* was lost by striking a mine ... On 15 November an agent's report was received stating that according to one of the

TOP OF TUBE FITTED WITH A NON-RETURN VALVE TO PREVENT ENTRY OF SEA-WATER.

ENGINE EXHAUST.

SURFACE.

CRUISING PERISCOPE.

ATTACK PERISCOPE (LOWERED).

STREAMLINED MAST CONTAINING AIR AND ENGINE EXHAUST PIPES.

ONE DIESEL ENGINE KEEPING BOAT UNDER WAY; THE OTHER ENGINE CHARGING BATTERIES.

FIXING CLIP.

FORWARD JUMPING WIRE.

RAISING AND LOWERING GEAR.

WATER-TIGHT JOINT AND HINGE.

TROUGH IN DECK FOR STOWING DIESEL MAST.

EXHAUST PIPE FROM DIESEL ENGINE.

FRESH-AIR PIPE FOR BOTTLES AND THE BOAT GENERALLY.

GALLEY.

DIESEL ENGINE ROOM.

BATTERIES.

CONTROL ROOM.

ENGINE-ROOM ARTIFICERS' QUARTERS.

ATTACK PERISCOPE CASING.

OFFICER AT CRUISING PERISCOPE.

BALLAST TANKS.

PORT FORWARD HYDROPLANE.

The development of the *schnorchel* was not a well-kept secret.
This feature from the *Illustrated London News* was from 23 December 1943.

crew of an English minelayer, the boat was sunk in the minefield south of Ireland during the last week in October. The boat sank after surfacing again for a short time. Forty-four survivors were taken prisoner. The same agent's report stated that new minefields have been laid north and south of Ireland to combat submarines operating in coastal waters.[8]

The loss of *U1006* in the newly laid mine barrage south of Ireland made it necessary to inform *U991*, who is already in the Bristol Channel, and *U1202*, who is en route there, that the boundaries of the declared mined area must be respected, for the latest information shows that it must be assumed that barrages have been laid. Radioed shipping routes are taken as swept channels.[9]

The agent that reported the loss of *U1006*, has now reported from England that new minefields, aimed at new types of submarine that do not need to surface, are being scattered in small groups close to the sea bed. As the mines are deep laid they are outside the declared mined zones and in mine-free channels to counteract submarines that are stalking convoys. Minelayers *Plover* and *Apollo* laid over 2,000 mines north of Ireland during September. Information was obtained from a member of the crew of an English minelayer.

A further report showed that the abovementioned minelayers are to lay similar minefields south of Ireland.

Report is considered here as doubtful, as there is no proof that the agent is still reliable. He has already spent three years in England. He is suspected of working for the enemy too.[10]

Although BdU had correctly judged the information as dubious, the very fact that the British would attempt such a deception partially showed their understanding of the German plans for a renewal of inshore U-boat combat. In reality the Royal Navy had been involved in minelaying within the region since 1941; however, the revelation via ULTRA intelligence at the end of October 1944 of the probable renewal of U-boat operations between Land's End and the Bristol Channel prompted fresh Admiralty minelaying plans. Starting that same month British minelayers laid deep fields across St George's Channel, within the entrance to the North Channel, northwest of the Hebrides, and within the centre of the English Channel.

BdU did indeed reverse its previous conclusion and in November reconfirmed the presence of mines within the ascribed area. The same report mapped the supposedly known mine-free British coastal convoy route through which expected traffic was thought likely to comprise various independently sailing vessels and three daily convoys between Bristol and the Channel ports.

U680, which had resailed on 18 November after its previously aborted patrol, had been the first U-boat directed to the convoy route mapped out within the situation report, although the boat was redirected to the Channel after *U978*'s successful situation report was received by BdU. Instead *U400* – which had sailed at the same time – was redirected to the north Cornish coast as a replacement for *U680*. *U680* meanwhile, though detecting and reporting enemy shipping movements in the Channel, failed to make a successful attack and returned empty handed to Bergen in January 1945.

The invaluable ULTRA intelligence gleaned from successfully decrypted BdU transmissions informed the British Admiralty of the U-boats' movements and planned deployment areas. Thus a policy signal was issued to C-in-C Western Approaches on 15 November stating that:

... further consideration has been given to the relative importance of anti-U-boat minefields in the NW and SW Approaches. Routing of ocean convoys south of Ireland not only renders this the more attractive area but U-boats' course of action can to some extent be anticipated. In the NW Approaches, mine-laying operations must follow rather than anticipate U-boat activities. ...

Consider therefore as a matter of policy that mine-laying operations should be concentrated in the SW Approaches.

To fulfil this policy the minelayer HMS *Apollo* was ordered on 25 November to lay three lines of deep mines off Trevose Head, in an operation codenamed 'HW'. This ship was to be assisted by minelayer HMS *Plover* in December in order to continue laying fields along the swept channel between Trevose Head and Hartland Point in operation 'HY'. Thus, between 29 November 1944 and 3 January 1945, the two minelayers laid eleven deep minefields using over 1,200 Mk XVII moored mines across the Cornish coastal convoy route that BdU had confirmed as mine-free. The moored mines were used for the fields, as ground mines sensitive enough to catch slow-moving U-boats could also have posed a threat to Allied surface ships.

Recent research by German historian Axel Niestlé, combined with the wreck-hunting expertise of Innes McCartney, has helped to prove the effectiveness of the British minelaying. *Oberleutnant zur See* Horst Creuz's *U400* was on its maiden patrol from Norway when it was redirected to the approach to the Bristol Channel northeast of Land's End. (Creuz's departure from Germany to Norway had not been without incident; the boat had become caught in a net barrage in the Kattegat and had had to be towed to Aarhus by the large tug *Otto* (Net Tender 26) of the Baltic *Netzsperrflottille* to have her screw, hydroplane and rudder examined.) *U400* was carrying one of the first U-boat service test pieces of the the improved 37mm Flak LM43U, equipped with a new gas-operated breech that improved firing rates while also reducing the weapon's overall weight.

Like other U-boats despatched to British waters *U400* made no radio contact with BdU after departing Norway and was plotted in Berlin on assumptions of the boat's speed and destination. On 17 December, thirty miles south of Cork, a U-boat

The fast minelayer HMS *Apollo*.

attempted an attack against a convoy that included the 16,385-ton New Zealand passenger steamer SS *Rimutaka*, which was carrying Prince Henry the Duke of Gloucester and his wife the Duchess to Sydney, where he was due to begin his Governor Generalship. Designated 'Operation Aintree' the transport ship was shepherded by the cruiser HMS *Euryalus*, two destroyers and five frigates of the 18th Escort Group.

Escorting frigate HMS *Nyasaland* detected the submerged U-boat fine on the *Rimutaka*'s port bow, which would have placed the U-boat in a perfect firing position as the convoy was about to begin a turn to port as part of routine zigzagging. The frigate signalled alarm to the remainder of the convoy which turned in the opposite direction. This left *Nyasaland* to attack with depth charges and a Hedgehog salvo, which was followed by a violent underwater explosion that physically lifted the frigate and brought diesel oil to the surface, confirming the U-boat as sunk. The U-boat Assessment Committee labelled the destroyed U-boat as *U400*, though Niestlé's painstaking research has revealed the more likely target U-boat to have been *U772*, which had sailed on 19 November destined for operations in the English Channel. On 4 December BdU recorded the boat's progress:

> *U322* and *U772* are moving into the Channel with focal point off Cherbourg. In case operations are impossible there because of condition of the boat or crew, operations will be authorised off Milford or in the area of *U400*.[11]

Less than two weeks after this entry was written *U772* was gone. In all likelihood *U400* perished at about the same time, its wreck now found to be lying amidst the minefield HYA1 north of Trevose Head and identified by the equipment carried, including the LM43U gun mount. *U772* is now reckoned to also have been the U-boat attacked by a Norwegian Sunderland of 330 Squadron and frigate HMS *Ascension* west of the Shetlands on 24 and 25 November respectively. The U-boat was listed as sunk and assumed to have been *U322*, however the most recent analysis places it as likely to have been *U772* in transit, escaping the scene. *Oberleutnant zur See* Gerhard Wysk's *U322*, it appears, did actually operate within the English Channel. On 18 December BdU recorded his presumed disposition:

> At present *U680*, *U322* and *U772* are off Cherbourg, three more boats (*U485*, *U1209* and *U486*) are on their way there. No special attack areas will be allocated. Cherbourg is the focal point for all boats, as the greatest chance of picking up and attacking shipping is in this area. Submarines are to utilise the experience gained by the boats who were stationed here earlier when they operate against shipping concentrations that they themselves observe.

Oberleutnant zur See Gerhard Meyer began a brief rash of Channel sinkings on 15 December when he torpedoed British steamer SS *Silverlaurel* of convoy BTC10

By 1945 the face of the U-boat war was vastly different to the glory days of 1940, time spent above the waves increasingly rare in those days of the submerged struggle for survival.

south of the Eddystone Lighthouse. The ship, bound for Hull and carrying 2,949 tons of cocoa beans, 2,423 tons of palm oil, 758 tons of timber, 303 tons of lumber, 317 tons of rutile (titanium dioxide), 66 tons of coffee, 30 tons of ramie (fibre) and 195 tons of rubber, sank with no loss of life. Meyer's next target of opportunity was not to be so fortunate.

The day following the sinking of SS *Silverlaurel*, German forces opened their Ardennes offensive; the main thrust codenamed *Wacht am Rhein*. The planned – and hugely unrealistic – goal was to split the British and American Allied line in half, going on to capture Antwerp, after which four Allied armies could be encircled and destroyed forcing the Western Allies to agree a negotiated peace with Germany.

Though the plans formulated at OKW far outstripped the capabilities of German ground and air forces the initial attack caused great alarm within the Allied command, as the region was considered dormant and was largely held by troops already wearied by months of combat and pursuit of the retreating German Army. In the picturesque wooded hills of the Belgian Ardennes, thousands of American soldiers used the time to regenerate both themselves and their equipment, comfortable in the knowledge that their commanders considered the narrow roads of this region impassable to German troops. They were as safe as if behind the elaborate fortifications of the Siegfried Line. The fact that French commanders had made the same error in judgement during 1940, and the Germans had done the impossible and attacked with tanks through this improbable terrain seemed not to have registered. Warfare is always harsh on those who fail to learn the lessons of history.

In the early morning mists of 16 December, German storm troops infiltrated the weakly held American lines, paving the way for armoured units of the *Heer* and Waffen SS. A full-scale assault spearheaded by fighting units that included battle-hardened veterans of four years of war, ripped the American lines to tatters, sending bewildered Allied troops into an unexpected retreat. Hitler made his final lunge for Western victory. As Eisenhower and his generals raced to restore order to the chaotic brawl taking place in dense woodland and crowded ancient villages, the call went out to England for more reinforcements. While a huge salient had been forced into the Allied line, confidence was increasing that it could be contained and then countered. But more men were needed, both in the battle and in immediate reserve.

Near the town of Dorchester, England – in one of the many staging areas for units of the American Army – the 66th Infantry Division was biding time before the expected orders in the New Year. Christmas was only a day away, and there was no sign of immediate movement. The troops, who all sported the snarling Black Panther of the unit's insignia on the right shoulder of their jackets, prepared for Christmas in the relative comfort of their compound. Developments in the Ardennes soon changed everything. The men were placed on alert and ordered to prepare for immediate movement to Southampton. From there, unit commanders were informed, they were to embark troopships bound for Normandy and transit to the front line. News of the battle raging in the Ardennes was sketchy at best, and many knew nothing about the struggle underway. There was little good humour to be found among the troops moving from warm comfortable billets into

SS *Leopoldville*, the 11,500-ton Belgian steamer sunk by *U486* on Christmas Eve 1944 inflicting one of the worst losses of American troops at sea of the Second World War.

a winter night so close to Christmas. There was even less when they arrived in Southampton.

The division was to embark on two transport ships. The first of these was the British ship HMT *Cheshire* the second a Belgian veteran, SS *Leopoldville*, the 11,500-ton steamer whose primary pre-war role had been plying the route between the Belgian Congo and Antwerp. By 1939 she had already begun to show her age, worn and a little shabby, her crew approaching maintenance in little more than a workmanlike fashion.

In drizzling rain 2,235 men of the 66th Infantry Division trudged wearily up gangplanks rising from Southampton's Pier 38 and disappeared into the cavernous holds of the Belgian steamer, captained by Belgian Master Charles Limbor. The customary confusion of military movement had been compounded by a clerical error. Hours before the Black Panthers began embarkation, *Leopoldville*'s holds had been packed with American paratroopers bound for France. In what was to turn out to be a stroke of good fortune for those young men, the error in their deployment was discovered and they were disembarked, replaced by the grumbling 66th infantrymen. An unfortunate result of this confusion was that loading manifests became worthless, units were told to find whatever area they could and stay put. Units became disorganised and wandered leaderless through the ship. Further to this, responsibility for supervising loading and unloading usually fell onto the thirty-four English troops aboard responsible for the ship's defensive guns – most of whom had been caught out by the unexpected departure and were still on Christmas leave. The remaining men of the division were embarked on HMT *Cheshire*, while heavy weapons and transport were loaded aboard LSTs for the crossing.

By 0800hrs on Christmas Eve the ships were ready for departure and eased from their mooring berths. Convoy WEP3 began to steam towards the open sea, escorted by three British destroyers – HMSs *Brilliant*, *Anthony* and *Hotham* – and the French frigate *Croix de Lorraine*, which would rendezvous with the troop carriers outside of the Isle of Wight. Nine hours was the scheduled duration of the crossing and it promised to be uncomfortable for the thousands of American soldiers sandwiched below decks. The fetid atmosphere of a poorly ventilated troopship, coupled with a deep rolling swell, conspired to spread misery among the Americans. There were feeble attempts to instruct on lifeboat awareness, but few listened. There was no drill and men were merely told where to proceed in the event of emergency. *Leopoldville* carried fourteen lifeboats, four large rafts, 156 Carley Floats and 3,250 life preservers, more than enough for those aboard. But they were neither distributed nor their locations pointed out, so they lay largely ignored by troops wrestling with seasickness, fatigue and boredom.

At 1400hrs convoy leader HMS *Brilliant* ordered the train of ships to begin zigzagging. Shortly after she hoisted the black flag of a submarine contact and charged away to drop depth charges on the vague contact, the other warships following. Further warnings were given and charges dropped, but no firm sighting made. Aboard *Leopoldville* the commotion was regarded as probably due to false alarms, much to the good fortune of *U486*.

Three days after sinking *Silverlaurel* Meyer had unsuccessfully attacked an Allied destroyer in the Western Approaches, making a hasty retreat from the scene as its intended victim combed the area with ASDIC. Reasoning that the waters off Cherbourg would be the most likely area for targets *U486* approached the waters north of the Cotentin Peninsula. By Christmas Eve *U486* was only five miles from Cherbourg when Meyer's searching produced perfect results. At 1745hrs, beneath a darkened winter sky, he sighted convoy WEP3. Two large ships were clearly visible, heavily laden and accompanied by smaller, equally heavily laden vessels that he took to be LSTs rolling ponderously through the greasy swells.

Meyer prepared to launch his attack against the obvious troopship and fired two torpedoes. His first torpedo passed astern, while the second ran true. With a deafening roar it impacted the starboard hull of *Leopoldville* at number four hold. Packed inside this area of the ship were 355 American soldiers, most of whom were attempting to sleep the voyage away and almost certainly never knew what happened.

With escort pursuit inevitable Meyer dived away from the scene as pandemonium engulfed the *Leopoldville*, so the U-boat commander never actually saw the ship go down.[12] Just one hour after the torpedo impact, the *Leopoldville* began to sink. The order to abandon ship was issued although, as it was announced in Flemish, many of the American troops did not understand. Scores of men calmly waited on deck for further instruction that would never come. Meanwhile the Congolese crewmen aboard attempted with some degree of success to lower a small number of lifeboats, duly boarding them and rowing away from the stricken vessel. The American soldiers were neither equipped nor trained in lowering lifeboats and the resultant fiasco caused numerous extra injuries to the inexperienced infantrymen. The order to abandon ship had still not been received in English by the Americans, standing on the tilting deck in heavy greatcoats designed to keep winter's chill at bay. During this whole period Captain Limbor stood as if in a trance – the event had overwhelmed him and he played no further part in the evacuation of his ship.

While this calamity was growing from bad to worse the British destroyers were still seeking targets for their depth charges and HMS *Cheshire*, although not far away, was sheltered from the terrible situation on board the *Leopoldville*, the chaos hidden by winter's darkness and the noise of the wind. Eventually the Royal Navy destroyer HMS *Brilliant* realised what had happened and signalled for urgent assistance, the first signal to be received on the French shore only five miles distant. The signal then had to be passed onto rescuers who, in the middle of various yuletide activities, took longer than normal to prepare themselves. The commander of *Brilliant* deftly brought his ship alongside *Leopoldville* to embark

Men of the US 66th Infantry Division shown on the outskirts of Saint Nazaire after their decimation during the sinking of SS *Leopoldville*.

bewildered survivors. If help had been summoned earlier by the *Leopoldville* herself then there was a good chance that the huge ship could have been towed and beached on French soil, averting the catastrophe to follow.

High seas began to buffet the two ships and the awful certainty of the liner sinking became apparent to the men aboard *Leopoldville*. Chaos ensued as they struggled to board *Brilliant* and the first rescue tugs arrived from Cherbourg, where knowledge of the events unfolding off shore had finally registered. Then, at 2030hrs – one and a half hours after being hit – the *Leopoldville*'s bow lifted from the water while her boilers began to explode within the huge hull, and she slid stern first to the bottom. There were now hundreds of frightened men struggling in the cold water, many sucked under with the ship, others weighed down with greatcoats, boots, webbing and rifles, unable to stay at the surface and sinking to their deaths.

After dawn on Christmas Day, once the shocked survivors were huddled in tents near Cherbourg, it was found that the 66th Infantry Division had lost 802 men in the disaster, 500 dying in the freezing water. Captain Limbor was the only officer from *Leopoldville* to lose his life, as well as the ship's carpenter and three Congolese crewmen. The 'Black Panthers' were decimated, their combat worthiness as a cohesive unit so shaken that they were posted to stand opposite the dormant front line surrounding Lorient and Saint Nazaire's fortress cities until the war's end in May 1945.

Approaching the Norwegian coast. Despite heavy artillery units stretched along the crenelated coastline and the presence of flotillas of patrol and flak ships U-boats became increasingly vulnerable to Allied attack in such friendly waters as the war neared its climax.

U486 would again make her presence felt near Cherbourg two days later, with the sinking of British frigate HMS *Capel* of 1st Escort Group on 26 December. Fifteen minutes after the British frigate began to go under Meyer audaciously launched another torpedo at another frigate HMS *Affleck*, seriously damaging her and ultimately consigning her to the scrapyard. Despite limping to Cherbourg she was later towed to Portsmouth where she was judged unworthy of repair. A third member of the Escort Group, HMS *Gore*, successfully 'combed the tracks' of a final salvo fired by *U486*.

The first operational voyage of *U486* had been remarkably successful. She put in to Bergen on 15 January with four victory pennants fluttering from her periscope – accounting for 17,921 tons of Allied shipping.

Elsewhere *U325* had been despatched from Norway to the English Channel on 9 December, returning empty handed but intact on 14 February. Likewise the veteran of the battle against the D-Day landing fleets, *U764*, as well as *U905*, *U979* and *U1009* all returned to Norway with no confirmed success to their credit. *Oberleutnant zur See* Hanskurt von Bremen's *U764* had suffered a malfunction of its *schnorchel* after the exhaust conduit had become compressed following a deep dive, leaking exhaust gases into the U-boat interior when both diesels were running. Von Bremen was only able to operate his *schnorchel* thereafter in calm seas and with a single diesel running alongside an electric motor. Nonetheless the noise still prevented use of the hydrophone to detect the enemy, as evidenced on 14 January when the U-boat was virtually overrun by a three-funnelled liner, SS *Isle de France* carrying nearly 1,000 troops. It was detected too late by the hydrophone operator for a firing position to be reached. Von Bremen recorded in his KTB:

> The approach directly under the English coast further proved our superiority when equipped with a *schnorchel*. Material defects forced the boat to return. The negligence of a hydrophone operator deprived it of a big success.

However, *U764*'s flotilla-mate *U322* had been more effective. On 23 December it is believed that *Oberleutnant zur See* Gerhard Wysk could have torpedoed two ships previously attributed to the deceased *U772*: SS *Slemish* from convoy WEG14 and SS *Dumfries* from convoy MKS71. The former was hit behind the forecastle, the hull splitting in two and sinking with six dead crewmen and a gunner aboard, survivors rescued by escort vessel USS *PC553*. SS *Dumfries* was travelling from Algeria to the Tyne with 8,258 tons of iron ore when the ship was hit and sunk a little before lunchtime southwest of the Isle of Wight.

On 28 December the Landing Ship Infantry (LSI) SS *Empire Javelin*, which had taken part in the landings on Omaha Beach, was sunk northeast of Cherbourg while on passage from Portsmouth to Le Havre, again probably by *U322*. It is also probable that *U322* attacked and damaged SS *Black Hawk* and SS *Arthur Sewell* the following day. The pair of steamships was travelling in ballast in the two-column convoy TBC21 outbound from Southampton when *U322* attacked seven miles southeast of Portland Bill Lighthouse. Both ships were hit and although later towed ashore they were both judged damaged beyond repair. One of the escort ships, however, *Flower*-class corvette HMCS *Calgary*, fixed the U-boats on ASDIC and mounted a depth-charge attack that destroyed *U322* only one mile from where TBC21 had been attacked. Previously this attack has been credited with destroying *U772*, the wreck now visited by divers. However, recent revision of the fate of the lost Channel boats confirms it as *U322*.

The last of the Channel U-boats – *U1209* and *U485* – achieved no success. *Kapitänleutnant* Friedrich Lutz's *U485*, coated in the experimental anti-sonar rubberised *Alberich* material, entered the Channel on or about 18 December – the last boat to do so in 1944 – making a single unsuccessful attack against an enemy destroyer. Problems with the boat's *schnorchel* caused several cases of carbon-monoxide poisoning among the crew, before Lutz returned to Bergen at the end of January empty-handed.

Oberleutnant zur See Ewald Hülsenback's *U1209* was less fortunate. Sailing submerged near the Scilly Isles on 17 December the boat was detected by HMCSs *Ribble* and *Montreal*. Earl B Sullivan, an engine room Artificer 4th class aboard the former, remembered:

On December 17, 1944, we made a contact off Wolf Rock on the southwest coast of England. We attacked with Hedgehog and were sure we had made a hit. However, nothing showed. We continued to make intermittent contact over (the next day), when we were finally ordered out of the area by the Admiralty. We were only a few miles off when an aircraft flying over signalled us that bodies

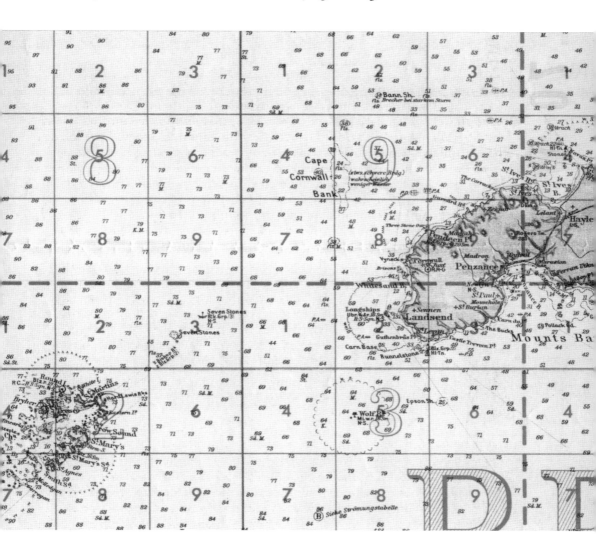

Close up subsection of Kriegsmarine chart 3270. To the southwest of Land's End can be found Wolf Rock where *U1209* fatally grounded.

were popping up in the water astern. We turned back. We picked up 18 survivors and the HMCS *Montreal* 19. One of the Germans we picked up died on board and a plain white sheet was used in place of a German Flag and the prisoners were permitted to carry out their own service. Prisoners stated that our first attack had knocked out their lights and they'd been largely in the dark since.

Hülsenback's boat may have been damaged by the Canadian attack, but it was the natural elements that proved fatal to *U1209*. A German survivor later recounted that they had been in search of a reported British aircraft carrier:

> The boat had been lying on the bottom in shallow water for nearly four days. The commander decided to go to periscope depth but found the sea so rough and so went down again. That's when it happened. We landed on a rock and water was coming in all over the place. Still the commander decided to go up again, only to periscope depth. However, the leading engineer was of a different opinion – the boat had to be blown up or else we would all drown. My job was to destroy the secret documents and then abandon ship. When I climbed up to the tower a half of the boat was already under water . . . I wondered what to do now. Then a big wave came along and that was me in the water.

The U-boat had run aground on Wolf Rock where Lighthouse Keeper Jack Cherrett, outside his charge and about to 'spend a penny' witnessed *U1209* hitting the rocks: 'High and dry she came,' he said – 'before a huge wave carried submarine *U1209* back into the water, where she threshed her way clear. But she was holed and sank within an hour.'

Cherrett swiftly relayed news over an open radio channel to Trinity House and from there to the Admiralty, who despatched the two Canadians to investigate. Sure enough as they approached the U-boat could be plainly seen wedged between the lighthouse rock and another rock running parallel to it. Gradually the boat, holed badly aft, slid sternward into the sea, nine of the crew killed during *U1209*'s disastrous grounding. The boat's young commander, Hülsenback, was rescued alive, but died shortly afterward of heart failure aboard HMCS *Montreal*. BdU recorded:

> According to an enemy radio broadcast report early on 18.12., *U1209* ran onto rocks off Wolf Rock Lighthouse. Boat then surfaced and the crew took to rubber dinghies. The boat must be assumed lost, as according to dead reckoning she was in this area. Although the crew apparently had sufficient time to destroy confidential books, the key-word will be altered at 1200 on 21 December.[13]

Dönitz's planned deployment of U-boats to attack carrier and cruiser forces off Scapa Flow also failed to fulfil its promise. Though officially deemed an operation for Arctic boats stationed in Narvik, both *U297* and *U1020* were involved:

26 December

U1020, U297 and *U312* who are off Scapa Flow . . . have had their operational orders changed. Attack on any target is now sanctioned, instead of only on cruisers and above, provided that the submarines have not been detected.

The order was given as *U1020* and *U297* had already spent twenty days in the operational area and had apparently not been detected. Hence it must be assumed that the submarines have not yet been able to attack any large targets.

30 December

According to Radio Intercept Intelligence, brisk anti-submarine measures are being taken in the sea area round Scotland (probably off Scapa Flow) . . . As two submarines from Northern Waters have arrived off Scapa Flow (*U278, U312*) and two more are on the way (*U313, U315*), the two Atlantic boats (*U297, U1020*) at present there are being withdrawn.

U297 has been told to make for AM 3850 (Loch Ewe).

U1020 is proceeding to the south and has a free hand in the Firth of Moray (AN1756). If this area is not favourable, boat is to operate off Aberdeen and Peterhead.

The following day *U1020* torpedoed and damaged the destroyer HMS *Zephyr* west of the Orkney Islands. It was the last recorded action of *Oberleutnant zur See* Otto Eberlein's boat, which was posted missing during January, lost to unknown causes. Likewise *Oberleutnant zur See* Rudolf Zorn's veteran *U650* that had sailed from Bergen bound for the Channel area disappeared, lost to unknown causes sometime in December or January.

And, as in so many other cases, messages and information regarding *U297* painstakingly recorded in the BdU War Diary were ultimately transmitted to empty seas. *Oberleutnant zur See* Wolfgang Aldergarmann's boat had been located west of Strathy Point in the Orkneys and sunk by depth-charge attack with all fifty hands aboard. Ironically it had been *U775*'s success against HMS *Bullen* (see pages 55–56, this chapter) that led the British to *U297*. A Sunderland of 201 Squadron, 15 Group Coastal Command, piloted by Flight Lieutenant Denis Hatton, had been alerted to assist in the hunt for a possible U-boat after *Bullen*'s sinking. The Sunderland searched the area, observed the sinking frigate and prolonged his hunt for *U775* until, after widening his search area and in fading light after sunset, white smoke was sighted at a distance of approximately five miles. Investigating the sighting, the Sunderland crew soon spotted a definite wake, most probably from the *schnorchel* as *U297* headed west. Hatton then attacked:

Our aircraft crossed the wake's track ahead of the smoke, turned to port and made an attacking run at a height of fifty feet along the path of the wake from astern. Unfortunately the depth charges failed to release, but as no faults were found a similar attack was made. We closed in on the same course and height; this time the depth charges functioned and a straddle of six fell in a straight line up the wake . . . Three depth charges entered the actual wake, with the other three reaching ahead at spacing of 60ft. The wake and smoke immediately disappeared. Our aircraft circled the area and five minutes later a pear-shaped oil patch and ochre coloured scum was noted.[14]

Subsequent discovery and examination by divers of the wreck of *U297* show that the *schnorchel* itself had been broken off, probably by the depth charges, which would have rapidly flooded the U-boat.

Despite these losses and the large number of Allied surface warships and Coastal Command aircraft operating within the English Channel, U-boats had operated successfully within the restricted space of that busy waterway. From Coastal Command's point of view:

It had become clear that while we had succeeded in keeping the enemy under, and had thus greatly limited his power of attack, he, by his skill with the snorkel and with aid of radar warning devices, had succeeded in eluding us. The situation is indicated by the reduction . . . in the totals of sightings and attacks during the autumn months, when between 50 and 70 U-boats are known to have been at sea.

September: twenty-one sightings, ten attacks.
October: ten sightings, three attacks.
November: twelve sightings, ten attacks.

It was a situation, moreover, that called for new counter measures, for although the enemy was doing little damage to us . . . we were getting no better success against him and a stalemate was in view.[15]

The First Sea Lord, Admiral of the Fleet Sir Andrew Cunningham even stated at the turn of 1944 that 'We are having a difficult time with the U-boats . . . the air are about 90 per cent out of business. The ASDIC is failing us.'

Chapter Three

Commander's Instinct

New Year's day 1945 found Germany's land forces struggling against Allied forces in their great push towards Antwerp. By Christmas Eve 1944 the main German advance had effectively stalled short of the Meuse River with British troops reinforcing the American defence. Wehrmacht and Waffen SS forces had stretched their supply lines to breaking point. Ammunition had run dangerously low and crucial, though vaguely planned captures of American fuel never materialised. In an attempt to reignite the offensive Hitler launched Operation Nordwind on the first day of January, with Army Group G beginning what would become the final major German offensive on the Western Front. Despite early promise this fresh

Life ashore for the ever-younger U-boat crews remained largely the same in 1944 as it had in 1939; military drill still required.

push was over by 25 January. In reality the Battle of the Bulge had already ended by that stage, Hitler having agreed to extract forces from the main Ardennes offensive to the south, the cutting edge of that operation. His SS Panzer divisions were withdrawn for use in ultimately futile operations to the east, where Stalin had launched the Vistula-Oder offensive in Poland and East Prussia. An all-or-nothing gamble by the Luftwaffe, Operation Bodenplatte, which involved the attack of Allied airfields in the Low Countries, had also been launched at the beginning of January. Despite destroying and damaging hundreds of aircraft it was a forlorn hope. Allied losses could be made good in mere days, whereas the 277 German aircraft also lost in the process shattered the already fragile Luftwaffe.

At sea there was little that Dönitz's U-boats could do to influence the outcome of the fighting on continental Europe. Fresh weapons – the midget submarines and explosive motorboats of the *Kleinkampfverbände* – were readied for operations in the Scheldt estuary amid the vital waterways leading to the Allied supply head at Antwerp. In British waters his conventional U-boats would continue their attack on Allied merchant shipping in the hope of prolonging the battle until the new electro-boats could enter service. Indeed, with the situation on the Russian front deteriorating rapidly, Dönitz even offered Hitler all of the men from Danzig's U-Boat Training Division (about 900 non-commissioned officers and 600 men) for transfer to the infantry in order to help defend the port city. Hitler, fortunately and correctly, declined, on the grounds that these men were valuable specialists, and that every U-boat in action against the enemy would be more valuable than any action at the front by their diverted crews. Dönitz issued a forceful proclamation for his U-boat men on New Year's Day, in which he exhorted them to continue their struggle into 1945 until, 'The striking power of our Service will be strengthened in the coming year by new boats. It's up to us to give them full effect.'

U2332 shortly after launch in October 1944. Behind the new boat can be seen another slim silhouette of a Type XXIII in the left hand floating dock and two Type VIIs in the right hand dock.

Within the Baltic several Type XXI and Type XXIII boats were beginning 'working up' trials, in an attempt to iron out problems and defects caused by the groundbreaking modular construction of the U-boats as well as the dislocation of Germany's industrial capacity and transport system due to Allied bombing. These factors, combined with inevitable design flaws and underdeveloped innovations, kept the boats pinned to training within seaways increasingly hindered by Allied aerial mining. Bomber Command had begun mining the Skagerrak and Kattegat and the southern coast of Norway, forcing U-boats transiting from German ports to the frontline stations in Norway to proceed surfaced. Since there were now far fewer opportunities to destroy U-boats in the Atlantic, Coastal Command began intensive attacks on those surfaced boats heading north, Liberators attacking by night and Mosquitoes and Beaufighters hounding them by day.

Unfortunately for the Admiralty though, it was hard to convince Allied planners of the strategic bombing campaign of the seriousness of the threat posed by a renewal of U-boat warfare using improved models. While the Ardennes Offensive raged, concentration was firmly placed on oil and industrial targets more directly related to the war on land. U-boat ports and related industry, both in Germany and occupied territories, had in the past been targeted as a matter of course – indeed, the first raid targeted specifically against the U-boats had taken place on Hamburg's Blohm & Voss yards on 18 May 1940 – but not as a matter of urgent priority. However, in 1944, fresh Admiralty fears begged a specific targeting of Dönitz's new U-boats. Somewhat ironically, Bomber Command and the US Eighth Air Force had in fact already begun their attack on the infrastructure of U-boat building, albeit almost unwittingly, when they focused on Germany's beleaguered transport system. The large prefabricated segments of the Type XXI U-boats could only be transported to their final assembly yards by canal; the canals were heavily attacked from November onward. On the night of 2 December 504 Bomber Command aircraft once more almost unwittingly began a more direct attack against U-boat construction when they bombed the town of Hagen, destroying a most important factory responsible for making U-boat accumulator batteries, vital for the new 'electro-boats'. It had previously been raided on 1 October 1943, though the damage was made good by the workers of Organisation Todt within six months.

By the end of 1944 thick, roofed, concrete shelters had been constructed at several of the major U-boat building yards. In Hamburg's Finkenwerder yard the ten-berth 'Fink II' had been finished in October 1942, a four-berth shelter also constructed at the Howaldtswerke at the same time, named 'Elbe II'. In Kiel's Howaldtswerke the eight-berth 'Kilian' bunker had also been completed. All were used as priority for the construction of Type XXIs.

The first of the refreshed dedicated attacks on U-boat production was made on 31 December, when 526 B17s of the Eighth Air Force targeted oil and industrial targets in Hamburg. For the loss of 27 B17s and damage to 289 others, 740 tons of

The wreckage of Type XXIII segments within this German shipyard illustrates the need for shelter from Allied bombs. Disruption of Germany's construction and transport systems greatly hampered electro-boat production.

bombs were dropped on the Blohm & Voss U-boat yards, destroying three Type XXI U-boats and damaging three others, as well as delaying construction of the first Walter Type XXVI experimental U-boat *U4501*. Hamburg would again come under daylight American attack on 17 January when seventy-three B17 aircraft hit the Blohm & Voss yard, destroying three commissioned Type XXIs and severely damaging nine others. Two salvage ships engaged on lifting *U2532*, which had been sunk in the previous raid, were also destroyed. The air attack on Dönitz's last source of hope would only intensify into 1945 until, by the war's end, there had been 138 specific raids on U-boat construction yards – including precision attacks by Mosquito bombers, code-named 'Boomerang' by the German High Command – augmented by four saturation bombing raids against related industrial targets.

However, despite this added pressure and delays in bringing the new U-boat models online, the conventional U-boat inshore campaign continued. On the evening of 3 January Dönitz reported to Hitler in private discussion about the state of his U-boat war:

Latest reports turned in by U-boats with *schnorchel* equipment and information submitted by radio intelligence prove that these boats too, can achieve success even in waters where German U-boats were forced to cease operations more than three years ago, ie the Cherbourg area, the Irish Sea, Scapa Flow and Peterhead. However, this success will serve to forewarn the enemy that a new German U-boat offensive has begun. Therefore we will have to be prepared for strong countermeasures in the immediate future, even before the new submarine models are ready for operations. Since it is difficult to combat these submarines at sea because of their ability to remain submerged, these countermeasures will of necessity be directed against submarine bases and yards and against the routes used by the submarines entering and leaving harbours.[1]

As we have just seen, Dönitz was correct when he predicted the intensification of Allied air attack against the shipyards and bases, though he overstated the effectiveness of the *schnorchel* boats. Because of the lack of radio signals from the U-boats operating in British waters, dead reckoning and presumed positions were used for prolonged periods of time when recording developments in the battle. Indeed, by the end of 1 January 1945, from twenty-three U-boats deployed in the inshore campaign, including those in transit to and from their operational areas, fifteen achieved no confirmed success against the enemy and seven (*U297, U322, U400, U482, U650, U772* and *U1200*) had been lost already. The 'ghost' positions of these lost boats continued to be plotted until their missing-in-action status was confirmed either via intelligence services or the fact that the U-boats' supply situation simply could not support their continued survival at sea.

Kapitänleutnant Hartmut Graf von Matuschka's *U482*, the most successful of the first wave of U-boats directed into British inshore waters (see chapter 1) had, it appears, been among those to have met an inglorious end. Recent research appears to show that the boat was lost to mines off Malin Head, its operational zone allocated by BdU. Since von Matuschka's last visit – and largely as a result of his unqualified success – the area had been mined with two deep anti-submarine fields designated CGA1 and CGA2. These had been laid on 8 and 11 November respectively, and each comprised two lines to a depth of 150 feet with a total of 156 mines in each field. It is presumed that *U482* hit one of these mines on or about 1 December. Previously it had been believed that *U482* had reached and patrolled the North Channel and been destroyed by depth charges there on 16 January. But it now seems that the depth charges dropped that day were directed against one of the myriad non-submarine targets that U-boats used so well to their advantage when attempting to avoid ASDIC detection.

BdU continued to record a summary analysis of the situation both known and presumed at sea, which clearly indicated the direction that the operational Type VIIC *schnorchel* U-boats would continue to follow:

Even narrow areas such as North Minch, the North Channel and the Bristol Channel, through which traffic putting in and out is sure to pass, are 'wide' from the point of view of stationary submarines. This fact is stressed by events in the Channel. Boats in this area, as far as we know, contacted and operated against traffic while it was off Cherbourg. During recent months this has been the most fruitful area, with very heavy traffic strongly defended. As, however, in all coastal areas, these strong defences were not nearly as powerful as they seemed when it came to the point, as submarines are particularly difficult to contact by hydrophone gear and underwater location, owing to currents and density layers. Only rarely did depth-charge hunts 'on the old scale' take place in coastal areas, during which three or more destroyers would hunt a submarine for hours at a stretch. Mines are only considered to be dangerous on the outward routes and are not taken much into consideration in the attacking areas or in the areas through which enemy traffic proceeds on a large scale.

1) It is impossible to occupy only areas that offer the greatest opportunities for attack, eg, the Channel . . . as the enemy would discover this very quickly and would concentrate his defences on them. He is now forced to defend himself from attacks on all sides, to divide up his forces to cover different areas and thus weaken them . . . Another advantage in occupying several operational areas at the same time, is the information obtained of new measures and methods of enemy defence, and a better idea of the development of enemy dispositions.

2) We expected to lose greater numbers of submarines as more *schnorchel* boats were sent to the more difficult operational areas. That this did not occur, on the contrary, there was a decrease compared to the losses incurred in 1941 and 1942, illustrates the immense value of the *schnorchel.*

3) In comparison, the numbers of boats lost in relation to those at sea, are taken during the months of November–December 1944 and April–May 1944 (when the *schnorchel* was being introduced and afterwards):

April/May 1944: Lost 23, average number at sea 42.

Nov/Dec 1944: Lost 7, average number at sea, 49.

4) This sudden change at the end of 1944 not only gave the captains and crews in action at the time new faith in this weapon, but it also showed that the basic idea of this new type of boat, namely the 'underwater boat' with its higher submerged speed and greater staying power, was justified, and opened up great possibilities for success. This change also made it clear to the enemy that the danger from submarines was by no means over . . . In January 1945 the first two boats of type XXIII will be ready, and we can take it for granted that these new boats will fight outstandingly well in calm waters.

At the beginning of January BdU had the following actual deployment of U-boats within their operational areas in British waters: *U1020* in the Moray Firth, though the boat was soon declared missing; *U485, U486* and *U650* in the English Channel,

Oberleutnant zur See Herbert Zoller and his crew of *U315* are welcomed home in Trondheim.

though the latter disappeared so its presence in its planned patrol area remains unconfirmed.

In transit from Norway to operational areas were: *U1051* and *U825* to the Irish Sea; *U285*, *U1055* and *U1172* to the Irish Sea and St George's Channel; *U325*, *U764*, *U1017* and *U1199* to the English Channel.

U680 was returning to Norway from the Channel, as were *U905* and *U1009*, the last never having reached its patrol area due to *schnorchel* problems. *U979* was also returning from a dual-purpose voyage, first as a weather-reporting boat and then on patrol within St George's Channel. *U773* lingered off Southern Ireland for a period of time, although the boat was actually returning from running ammunition to St Nazaire, and so was not truly a part of the inshore wave of boats just yet.

Additionally, Arctic U-boats had begun operating frequently between the Orkney Islands and the Scottish coast. *U278* of Narvik's 13th U-Flotilla was also approaching the waters of the Pentland and Moray Firths hunting for British carrier groups, ultimately unsuccessfully.[2] *U312* attempted to enter Scapa Flow itself, but was forced onto rocks in Hoxa Sound by the strong current, which damaged her rudder and forced a retreat to Trondheim. *U313* took her place but to no effect. This pair of boats was later allowed freedom to manoeuvre along the Scottish east coast as far south as the Firth of Forth, though again with no success.

Victorious return of a Type VIIC to Norway.

This virtually marked the end of Dönitz's plan to station U-boats off Scapa Flow. On 3 January BdU noted the return of *U315* to Trondheim with engine damage. The boat had been intended to form part of the Scapa Flow task force but had not even reached its patrol area where it should have been on hand to make attacks on carriers. Various U-boats had been off Scapa for that purpose since 7 December with no success, and when the three U-boats that were already in the area exhausted their supplies it would mark the end of deployments there.

The North Channel was also reported as becoming increasingly dangerous due to Allied minelaying. On 11 January BdU recorded:

Until further notice, no boat is to pass through the North Channel to the Irish Sea. The four boats in the North Channel en route for that area are to proceed south instead. *U1009* has insufficient provisions to make the detour through the St George's Channel, and is therefore permitted to continue through the North Channel and operate there.

In St George's Channel *U1055* was the first U-boat to announce its presence with a rash of sinkings that began on Tuesday 9 January. *Oberleutnant zur See* Rudolf Meyer had departed Norway on 11 December bound for the Irish Sea. Convoy ON277 sailing from Southend to New York was two days into its recorded voyage and still gathering when American Liberty ship SS *Jonas Lie*, travelling in ballast, was hit by a torpedo in the Bristol Channel. A single torpedo struck the starboard side and shattered the bulkhead separating the engine room and number four hold, killing two men on watch below. With a gaping hole in the waterline and both steam and electric connections severed, the ship lost way and began listing to port. While the majority of the crew abandoned ship, the Master Carl Lionel Von Schoen, his chief officer, bo'sun and a single seaman remained on board for three more hours before finally leaving the ship to drift in the tide. The following day these four, with six other men would reboard the ship – which by then had drifted into Allied minefields – and attempt to facilitate towing by steam tug. The tow parted in heavy seas, and eventually SS *Jonas Lie* foundered. She was the last of eighty-one ships lost to U-boat attack from the 307 'ON' convoys that had seen 14,864 ships sail to North America and the Caribbean.

Meyer now headed north and two days later attacked three ships off Holyhead that had just dispersed from a coastal convoy. Within thirty minutes Meyer missed his first target, Yugoslav SS *Senga*, the torpedo exploding in its wake, but hit and sank two others, the 2,606-ton American SS *Roanoke* travelling in ballast and the 1,428-ton British SS *Normandy Coast* carrying 266 tons of steel plating towards London. Within two minutes this last was gone, though the American's bow stubbornly refused to sink for a further hour.

Now firmly alerted to his presence, a Coastal Command Liberator sighted *U1055*'s *schnorchel* the following day and launched an attack, but Meyer escaped. Fresh radio directions from BdU soon followed for *U1055* which would shortly begin its return voyage:

> According to a spy report, new minefields were laid against submarines off the North Channel. Traffic is alleged to proceed between 'Inishtrahull' and/or 'Rathlin' and 'Festland', just off the coast. Although this seems unlikely, as there are very swift currents here and channels which are very hard to navigate, *U1009* was instructed not to proceed into the Irish Sea via the North Channel, but to proceed SW from her present position to off 'Inishtrahull'. The submarine is to proceed over these longitudes and not to the east.
> The three submarines in the Irish Sea (*U1172*, *U1055* and *U285*) were ordered to return to base instead of proceeding to the southernmost point of Ireland as had originally been ordered, on the basis of the same spy report.[3]

As a parting shot *U1055* torpedoed and sank the British tanker MV *Maja* on 15 January, an unescorted ship carrying 10,680 tons of gasoline. Hit west of

With air attack in Norwegian waters an increasing hazard; bridge watches began wearing the unwieldy Wehrmacht helmets.

Drogheda, seventeen crewmen and eight gunners were lost, the survivors being rescued by a Belgian trawler *Hendrik Conscience*. Meyer successfully docked in Stavanger on 1 February 1945 after his voyage of a little under two months. Somewhat ironically, given that he had been directed to his hunting area in response to Knight's Cross winner Rolf Thomsen's unjustified reported success, the far more successful Meyer was awarded the German Cross in Gold for his performance.

Oberleutnant zur See Jürgen Kuhlmann's *U1172*, engaged on its maiden patrol within the North Channel and Irish Sea during January, also experienced some brief success. En route to his final destination Kuhlmann passed through the North Channel where he made two attacks. At 1328hrs the escort carrier HMS *Thane*, sailing to Greenock to offload aircraft after suffering storm damage while escorting convoy CU53, was hit on its starboard aft quarter by a single T5 torpedo as it approached the Clyde Lightship. The blast blew the starboard aft 5in gun and its sponson completely off the side of the ship, displacing the stern aircraft lift and causing it to become wedged within its well. The main steering failed and she lost way as the propeller shaft had been severed. The carrier was not the only craft present; the trawlers *Cypress* and *Cirisinio*; Norwegian oiler MV *Spinanger* and troopship HMT *Isle de France* were all nearby, while the carrier's screen destroyers, HMSs *Caprice* and *Oribi*, were four miles astern. The two destroyers closed to investigate as *Isle de France* accelerated from the area lest the event be confirmed as a torpedo attack.

Within half an hour of hitting *Thane* Kuhlmann torpedoed the 1,599-ton Norwegian MV *Spinanger*, again hitting the ship with a single T5 torpedo. The ship had arrived in Londonderry from New York as part of convoy HX329 on 13 January, then departed without escort for Greenock two days later. That same day a single torpedo hit the starboard side aft while *Spinanger* was about one nautical mile off the Clyde Light Vessel. Three engine-room personnel were killed and another four severely injured, one dying later as a result of his burns. A doctor from a nearby destroyer was brought aboard to treat the injured until an RAF rescue launch ferried them to port. *Spinanger* was later taken in tow to Rothesay, where she was eventually repaired. The German B-Dienst established that *Spinanger* had been hit before Kuhlmann had reported his success, the Norwegian's initial distress call intercepted and passed to BdU.

Meanwhile damage control measures had stabilised HMS *Thane*, which also was eventually taken in tow and berthed at Greenock where the grisly task of removing ten bodies from the impact area began. The ship was later declared a constructive loss.

U1172 remained undetected and escaped the scene, sailing south toward Anglesey. There, Kuhlmann claimed his final victim when he sank the 1,599-ton Norwegian freighter SS *Vigsnes* carrying 1,936 tons of coal from Cardiff to the Mersey on 23 January. The freighter had recently left convoy MH1 (Milford Haven to Holyhead) when a single torpedo hit the starboard foreship. Steam and smoke engulfed the engine room making it impossible to stop the engine; *Visgnes* listed heavily and the crew abandoned ship. Within fifteen minutes the steamer was gone.

This hit was, however, to be *U1172*'s swansong. Four days after the sinking of SS *Vigsnes*, frigates HMSs *Bligh*, *Keats* and *Tyler* of 5th Escort Group detected Kuhlmann's submerged boat during a routine ASW sweep and depth charged her. The U-boat went down with all fifty-two men on board. This was the second kill in which ships of 5th Escort Group had participated in as many days.

On 21 January *Oberleutnant zur See* Heinrich von Holleben's *U1051* had just reached its station in St George's Channel when he torpedoed and sank the 1,152-ton Norwegian freighter *Galatea* which was travelling alone from Liverpool to Barry in ballast. The ship sank rapidly, its sole survivor, stoker Harald Hvidtsten, being picked up from a raft by frigate HMS *Tyler*. Four days later Holleben struck once more when he hit frigate HMS *Manners* with a single torpedo twenty miles

Despite the combat situation having dramatically changed for Dönitz's U-boats by the fifth year of war, Type VIIC U-boats continued to be built despite their near obsolescence.

from Skerries on the Isle of Man. The frigate, which had locked its attacker's position with ASDIC immediately before being hit, broke in two shortly afterward, the stern sinking with the loss of four officers and thirty-nine ratings and fifteen injured. The shattered foresection of the vessel was later towed into Barrow in Furness and was declared a total loss. Ships of the 4th Escort Group east of Cork responded immediately to distress signals from *Manners*, which had managed to maintain ASDIC contact with *U1051*. Immediately the Escort Group raced to the scene, alongside HMS *Aylmer*, leader of 5th Escort Group. Upon arrival the reinforcements found *Manners'* foresection still afloat, and *Manners'* captain passed over information on the whereabouts of the U-boat before the remains of his ship were towed away. *U1051* had gone to ground in the shallow water, hoping to evade the combing ASDIC traces amidst the numerous wrecks on the seabed. Eventually HMS *Calder* detected the submerged boat with ASDIC, while HMS *Bentinck* made a number of runs with her echo sounder to confirm the silhouette of a U-boat rather than scattered wreckage.

HMS *Calder* made a Hedgehog attack and scored a direct hit, which forced *U1051* to the surface, whereupon HMS *Aylmer* rushed forward and rammed the U-boat. Holleben's boat immediately sank, taking all forty-seven men to the bottom, while HMS *Aylmer* limped into Liverpool docks to have her bows rebuilt.

That same day *Kapitänleutnant* Rolf Nollmann's *U1199* was also destroyed after a successful attack. Nollmann encountered coastal convoy TBC43 and torpedoed the Liberty ship SS *George Hawley* near Wolf Rock at the western end of the

English Channel. *George Hawley* had joined the two-column convoy during the previous day near the Isle of Wight, bound for Cherbourg in ballast apart from seventy-seven bags of Royal Fleet mail. At 1538hrs the next day the Liberty ship reeled under a single torpedo impact on the starboard side amidships. The explosion destroyed the engines and completely flooded the engine room; an officer and one crewman on watch below were killed almost immediately as a small fire started in the galley. *George Hawley* began to list to port as the British coastal tug *TID74* and fellow convoy member merchant steamer SS *Wiley A Wakeman* stood by. The remaining seven officers, thirty-two men and twenty-seven armed guards abandoned ship in all four lifeboats twenty minutes after the hit. Several hours later, the master, chief mate, bosun and another crewman reboarded the vessel in order to attach tow lines to the floating hulk, which was eventually towed to Falmouth the following day. It was declared a total loss shortly thereafter.

Nollmann had obviously betrayed his position with this attack, and was located on ASDIC by one of the convoy's escorts, the corvette HMS *Mignonette*. The corvette and destroyer HMS *Icarus* both began a series of depth-charge attacks that brought wreckage to the surface. Nollmann and his forty-six crewmen were dead.

In the English Channel, new boat *U1017* captained by *Oberleutnant zur See* Werner Riecken had been given freedom to manoeuvre, according to his already standing operational orders and situation reports. Riecken was reminded by BdU radio transmissions that his main target remained Cherbourg merchant traffic, but if defences there were found to be too strong he was free to close the English coast and make opportunistic attacks on any convoys he encountered.

On 6 February southeast of Durlston Head *U1017* torpedoed the 5,222-ton British steamer SS *Everleigh*, which was a member of convoy TBC60. Though Riecken claimed two 6,000-ton freighters hit, *Everleigh* was the sole success of the attack. The ship went down, but fifty of the fifty-six men on board were rescued by British landing craft HMS *LCI33*.

Five days later *U1017* struck again. Riecken hit and sank the 5,382-ton Belgian SS *Persier*, the commodore's ship in convoy BTC65. Hit four miles from the Eddystone Lighthouse, the ship was taken in tow but sank during the night in Bigbury Bay. Once more, despite the huge presence of Allied warships in the English Channel and Western Approaches, *U1017* evaded detection and returned to Norway on 2 March 1945. Riecken was awarded the German Cross in Gold.

On 27 January *Oberleutnant zur See* Gerhard Stoelker's *U825*, only recently having been cleared for its first combat patrol, attacked convoy HX332 in Cardigan Bay, damaging the Norwegian tanker MV *Solör* and the American Liberty ship SS *Ruben Dario*; the latter later broke in two and was declared a total loss after being beached. Swift counter-attack by convoy escorts damaged *U825*, though Stoelker escaped. *U825* returned to Norway in February without any further successes.

BdU opened a new area of inshore operations during January 1945. *Korvettenkapitän* Friedrich Schumann-Hindenberg, a former artillery officer aboard the *Tirpitz* and specially selected for the task, was ordered to take *U245* to the eastern end of the English Channel and attempt to attack convoy traffic plying the Thames-Scheldt route. Previously this shipping had come under attack by units of the *Kleinkampfverbände*, but their lack of success prompted Dönitz to allocate a conventional U-boat to the task. His briefing for what became known as 'Operation Brutus' was full and detailed, much of it appended to the BdU War Diary on 13 January 1945:

1) Attack supply traffic proceeding from the Thames to Antwerp. Supplies on this route are of the greatest importance to the battle on the Western Front. Every ship sunk has an effect on this battle. The lives of many German soldiers will be saved by the destruction of such important war material. The captain should think of this while operating, and should carry out his task ruthlessly.

2) The submarine is to follow Operational Orders 'Brutus', the verbal instructions from BdU, and otherwise to act according to the situation. The success of the operation depends on the captain's ingenuity . . . and his daring. When opportunities for attack are unfavourable because of sand banks and minefields in the area, the captain himself is left to decide whether the chances of success, by advancing to the west or the east on to the convoy route, through the mined area, justify the risks incurred . . .

Execution

To put out from Kiel when ready for action. All preparations and tactical repairs should be made very carefully, as, if the submarine were forced to return to base owing to damage, the intended operation might be discovered. The crew are not to be informed before putting out, but only when the boat has reached the open North Sea, and it is obvious that she will not be forced to return to base because of technical damage.

All secret documents which are, in the commander's estimation, absolutely necessary, to be thrown overboard. Measures to be taken for destruction of secret cipher material (especially operational orders with appendices) in case of need.

The boat is to put out on receipt of verbal instructions from Senior Officer Flotilla, after orders issued by Naval Chief of Command North. Give out the following to camouflage the real reason for the intended departure through the Kaiser-Wilhelm Canal: The installation of important apparatus in Bremen. Ice-protection will be required, instructions concerning use and distribution will be issued by the Flotilla Senior Officer . . .

Navigation

Absolutely accurate navigation is necessary to the success of the operation, especially before entering the operational area, as the attacking area is very small . . .

9) Behaviour in the Operational Area

No binding rules. The commander's 'instinct' is essential to the conduct of the operation. The submarine will only be successful on the convoy route itself, therefore calculate the exact position of the convoy route and remain close up to it. Buoys are the best means of navigation.

    a) All information gathered from radio intercepts, and observations made by Fortress Commander Dunkirk, will be transmitted to the submarines using the list of cover names enclosed in Appendix (a).

    b) As the submarine is fitted with *schnorchel*, she is naturally to try and attack by day. If this is impossible, and the convoy has gone by in the dark, the captain must see whether an attack by night without visual sighting (if the moonlight is not bright enough) is likely to succeed, taking into consideration the enemy's speed and course, or whether it would be better to surface before firing. As the boat can get into position right on the convoy route and thus face the convoy, it is not necessary for her to haul ahead. Also LUT torpedoes make it possible to fire at the convoy from ahead or astern, with reasonable prospects of hitting.[4]

Antwerp lay 129 kilometres from the open sea along the Scheldt River; the estuarine approaches to this waterway contained drainage from numerous large rivers and smaller waterways from the Netherlands, France and Belgium. Antwerp was in operational Allied use from mid-November, shortening supply lines to front-line units that had previously been relying on Normandy beachheads and Cherbourg. Meanwhile the small units of the *Kleinkampfverbände* had been operational within the Scheldt estuary, though with only meagre success. *U245* was the first of Dönitz's conventional boats to be specifically targeted against the convoy traffic bound for Antwerp.

Schumann-Hindenberg took his boat from Flensburg on 3 January, stopping at Heligoland for a week, berthed inside the Nordsee III bunker on the small island, the first U-boat shelter built by the Kriegsmarine in home waters, before departing for his search area west of the Dogger Bank on 14 January. There *U245* began its hunt for the Antwerp-bound convoy traffic. Despite an apparent abundance of merchant targets it was not until 5 February that *U245* made its first successful attack.

Convoy TAM71 had departed Margate Roads that day bound for Antwerp when Schumann-Hindenberg sighted the merchant train. That evening he launched his attack against the convoy's starboard flank, hitting the last ship in that column. Lookouts aboard the American Liberty ship SS *Henry B Plant* sighted their attacker at a distance of only 300 yards, though it was too late to avoid the torpedo that hit the ship abreast of number 4 hold. The explosion ruptured the main deck, severed steam lines, blasted hatches and beams overboard and probably set off the after magazines. The American ship was carrying 9,300 tons of engineering materials, including iron landing strips, sewer pipes, acids and oils,

Oberleutnant zur See Hans-Heinrich Hass hosts *Grossadmiral* Dönitz (left) and *Generaladmiral* Hans Georg von Friedeburg aboard *U2324*, the first Type XXIII to sail on active duty. Dönitz's pennant is streamed from the commander's flagstaff.

and within five minutes had sunk stern first in forty-two metres of water with sixteen dead: one officer, eight crew members and seven armed guards.

Henry B Plant appears to have been *U245*'s sole confirmed success of the patrol. (The Dutch tanker SS *Liseta* was torpedoed on 15 February, its attacker thought to have been a *Seehund* (Type XXVII midget submarine) *U5332*, though *U245* claimed the attack as well.) It was the end of Operation Brutus. *U245* returned to port, docking at Heligoland, a port that had not been used by U-boats for two and a half years prior to *U245*'s visits. Here Schumann-Hindenberg began preparation for a second mission in the 'Brutus' vein.

While *U245* had added its meagre weight to the inshore campaign against the British Isles, elsewhere a new chapter opened for the Kriegsmarine. On 31 January 1945 a small U-boat, *U2324*, slipped out from Norway to begin its tour of operations in the Firth of Forth. *Oberleutnant zur See* Heinrich Hass had learnt his trade as watch officer aboard *U96* and *U543* between 1941 and 1944 before being transferred to his first command in July 1944. Then, as part of the 4th U-Flotilla in Stettin, he began the working-up trials of *U2324* within the Baltic. *U2324* was the first Type XXIII to leave Germany, sailing from Kiel to Kalundborg on the Danish island of Zealand on 18 January in order to rendezvous with military escorts, and then onto Horten where she berthed at 1700hrs on 23 January as part of the 11th U-Flotilla. Finally, Hass and his crew took their U-boat from harbour bound for the Firth of Forth – the first Type XXIII U-boat to sail for combat.

CHAPTER FOUR

New Designs

THE TYPE VIIC and IXC U-boats, which had altered little from pre-war designs or, for that matter, from the most successful U-boat types of the First World War had carried the brunt of the Battle of the Atlantic until their defeat at the end of May 1943. Forced to remain surfaced for great periods of time in order to recharge the batteries that enabled underwater operations, they were on the losing side of a technological battle successfully waged by the Allies. Radar, particularly that mounted on long-range bomber aircraft, had been a key ingredient of the Allied triumph. While in the war's early years U-boats had attacked convoy traffic surfaced at night, using the top speed attainable by the boats' diesels and the small silhouette of the conning tower to its full advantage, surface radar had, at a stroke, nullified these advantages. The battle became a three-phase Allied operation: detection at range by air or surface convoy escorts; attack to drive the U-boat underwater where it was reduced to a virtually blinded slow-moving vessel, then hunt to exhaustion using ASDIC. The U-boat would eventually be forced to surface as its battery power drained and the air inside became unbreathable. Once surfaced, radar would once again locate the target, which now did not have the luxury of diving to comparative – and dubious – safety.

Professor Hellmuth Walter – who was responsible for perfecting the *schnorchel* following his discussions with Dönitz on 2 March 1943 as Atlantic defeat loomed – had since 1933 been developing his truly 'underwater' boat. Within his initial proposal had been several ingredients that addressed key technological problems faced by the U-boat arm:

> The outer casing is shaped like a fish, with a completely smooth exterior presenting no sharp projections. A small amount of positive buoyancy is present when the boat is travelling on the surface, and the boat does not break surface in the usual sense of the term, ie, it does not travel 'on the water'. In effect it 'sticks its essential organs up through the water surface' – those organs that are necessary for the suction of air, for combustion, and for navigation.[1]

Long before the defeat of the U-boats in the Atlantic, the forward-looking Dönitz had been immediately impressed with Walter's ideas, whose first small experimental U-boat, *V80*, was demonstrated for the then-head of the

One of the prototype 'Walter boats' is launched in Germany.

Kriegsmarine *Grossadmiral* Erich Raeder on 14 November 1941. Built at Germaniawerft in Kiel, the crew of four drove *V80* to a speed of twenty-eight knots submerged. Such high submerged speeds would enable a truly offensive U-boat to enter action and Dönitz enthusiastically backed the project, as long as the boat's radius of action could reach the north of the British Isles with a payload of at least four torpedoes.

The answer to Dönitz's requirements seemed to come with the four Type XVIIA experimental U-boats *U792*, *U793* (both Wa201 types built by Blohm & Voss),

(*Opposite*) The scale and improved design features of the finished Type XXI, as seen here with *U2502*, are evident.

U794 and *U795* (Wk202 types built by Germaniawerft). The first was launched on 28 September 1943 and commissioned that November. By April 1944 the last of them had been commissioned and all four were involved in trials to attempt to solve problems with the hydrogen-peroxide drive system. Their top submerged speed of twenty-five knots promised to revolutionise U-boat warfare. The Walter propulsion system required no air intake at all, as it was a close-cycle engine, and thus was obviously the correct concept to produce high underwater speed. But technical difficulties dogged the project and it was clear from an early stage that it would be some time before a workable, combat U-boat could be produced using this engine. Indeed, it was at a meeting organised by Dönitz at his Paris head-quarters in November 1942, primarily to discuss progress with the Walter boat, that a new answer to U-boat design began to take shape.

The main problem with Walter's propulsion system was the fuel it required. A highly flammable concentrated form of hydrogen peroxide, known as Perhydrol, was not only extremely corrosive, but inherently explosive. It operates at peak efficiency as a propellant in high concentrations. The heat of the decomposing hydrogen peroxide becomes strong enough to vaporise liquid stored at a standard temperature and transforms it into a heated gas. This combined gas and steam was used to generate thrust via a turbine, promising potential speeds of more than twenty-five knots underwater. The Walter U-boats also required a high fuel consumption rate, which would thus require an enormous fuel tank. Walter therefore proposed a fresh design that incorporated a figure eight when viewed in section. The upper part of the hull would hold crew, engines and torpedoes, while the lower part acted as fuel bunker. This proposal was later named the Type XVIII and it was here that electro-boat design received its first real stimulus.

Two of the Kriegsmarine's shipbuilding engineers, Dr Friedrich Schürer and Councillor Broecking recommended using the new Walter hull design for the Type XVIII but instead of using the lower half of the figure eight to hold fuel, suggested installing additional batteries there. This would effectively triple the battery capacity of the boat and provide the high underwater speed required from a new boat. Though not likely to attain the same velocity as the Walter boat itself, it was nonetheless calculated to be higher than average Allied convoy speeds, so sufficient for the task in hand. Walter himself recommended combining this modification with a *schnorchel*, allowing what Dönitz recorded in his memoirs as the first '100 per cent underwater vessel'. By the end of January 1943 designers had completed their first theoretical calculations and in June of that year Dönitz received initial blueprints for what would become the Type XXI electro-boat. Alongside these were preliminary projections for smaller, coastal U-boats, recommended for use in the shallow waters of the North Sea, English coast and Mediterranean, and designated the Type XXIII. While they failed to fully capture Dönitz's imagination in the same way that the large ocean-going Type XXI did, BdU authorised further development of the idea, adding that the boat must be

The special crane and trailer equipment used for road transport of Type XXI sections, this being Section 8 captured by the Allies in Kiel's Deutsche Werk.

capable of being transported by rail to combat areas within the Black Sea and Mediterranean.

The primary characteristics of the Type XXI were a planned displacement of 1,620 tons; a streamlined hull with six forward torpedo tubes that incorporated a semi-hydraulic reloading system; a top underwater speed of eighteen knots that could be maintained for one and a half hours; retractable *schnorchel* and improved onboard electronics. The Type XXIII on the other hand would displace only 234 tons, have a similarly streamlined hull with no external weaponry but carry only two bow torpedo tubes and no reloads. Likewise it would be equipped with a *schnorchel* and improved systems, capable of twelve knots maximum submerged speed.

In July 1943 Dönitz presented the electro-boat designs to Hitler and final approval to begin construction was granted, though not at the expense of further conventional U-boat construction. Dönitz, however, was initially disappointed by the construction estimates produced by Reichs Armament Minister Albert Speer. He reckoned that full construction would take at least eighteen months to

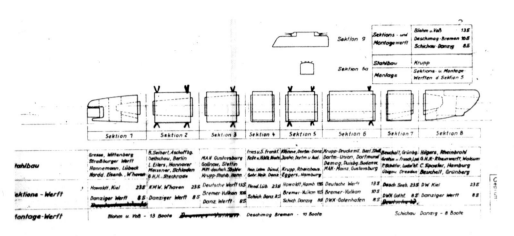

German blueprint breakdown of the sectional construction of a Type XXI.

complete using traditional shipyard methods, meaning that the first prototypes would not be ready until November 1944, a timeline totally unacceptable to BdU. Speer consulted with his newly appointed Director of the Main Committee for Ship Construction, Otto Merker, who possessed considerable experience in the mass manufacture of automobiles. Merker firmly believed that current production methods were unduly time consuming due to the convention of building on a single slip from keel to finished boat. He recommended adopting the methods of mass production enabled by sectional construction. By this means, different sections of the U-boat could be built in parallel in various industrial centres throughout Germany, the completed sections then transported to a single location – Type XXI sections by canal, Type XXIII sections by rail – and assembled in the manner of modern production lines. There would be no prototypes produced in order to save time, trials after launching deemed sufficient to resolve teething problems. By this method it was estimated that an entire Type XXI U-boat could be built – from acquisition of raw materials to finishing work after launch – in 171 days, or six months, of which only the eighty days of final completion required the dedicated use of a shipyard slipway.

The Type XXI would be built in nine sections:
    Stern with stern compartment (65 tons, 12.7 metres);
    Electric motor room (130 tons, 10 metres);
    Diesel engine room (140 tons, 8.4 metres);
    Aft living quarters (70 tons, 5.3 metres);
    Control room and galley (140 tons, 7.6 metres);

Forward living quarters (165 tons, 12 metres);
Torpedo stowage room (92 tons, 6.8 metres);
Bow compartment with torpedo tubes (110 tons, 14 metres);
Conning tower superstructure with double flak mounts (14.1 tons)
The smaller Type XXIII would require only four sections:
Stern, steering installation, silent speed motor, gearing (11.5 tons, 9.2 metres);
Main engines and motors (14 tons, 6 metres);
Control room, forward living quarters (18 tons, 7.5 metres)
Bow compartment with torpedo tubes, the rest of forward living quarters (16.25 tons, 10 metres).

The initial order for the construction of Type XXIII U-boats was issued on 20 September 1943 to Hamburg's Deutsche Werft (series number beginning at *U2321*). A second order was later given to Kiel's Germaniawerft on 7 July 1944 (*U2332*, *U2333* and *U4701* upwards). At first it had been planned to assemble the Type XXIII from its prefabricated parts at Toulon, Genoa and Monfalcone for use in Mediterranean areas and Nikolayev on the Black Sea. Thus the completed boats would be in place for local operations. Hamburg was reckoned to be convenient for those boats required in the North Sea, but by July 1944 foreign yards had failed to fulfil their potential and faced possible capture or at least isolation by enemy troops, so Kiel took the role as second yard. On 6 November 1943 a final order for the construction of Type XXI boats was submitted to the three shipyards: Blohm & Voss, Hamburg for 130 U-boats (*U2501* onwards); Deschimag AG Weser, Bremen, for eighty-seven U-boats (*U3001* onwards); Schichau, Danzig, for seventy U-boats (*U3501* onwards).

The initial segments were ready from February 1944 and the Type XXIII *U2321* was the first boat to be laid down on 10 March 1944. It was launched on 17 April after only thirty-eight days in the yard and commissioned into the Kriegsmarine on 12 June 1944. The first Type XXI boat to be laid down was *U2501* on 3 April 1944, launched on 12 May 1944 and commissioned on 27 June 1944. By the end of 1944 the Kriegsmarine had commissioned thirty-one Type XXIIIs and sixty-four Type XXIs into service. Allied fears appeared to be justified.

The ambitious new style of U-boat production encountered problems, however, particularly with the more complex Type XXI. While the principle of segmented construction was sound, several of the companies involved had never been constrained by such fine tolerances as were mandatory for U-boat construction. By the time that the finished sections came to the shipyard for assembly, faults that normally would not significantly hinder the construction of a surface ship rendered the U-boat virtually inoperative at worst, and vulnerable to pressure and depth charge damage at best by creating weak spots in the welded hull. This issue was exacerbated by the timesaving expediency of not creating a prototype with which to attempt to rectify any problems. These workmanship issues began to be resolved in the latter part of 1944, but by that stage bombing had begun to be

Reichsminister Albert Speer and *Grossadmiral* Karl Dönitz aboard a Kriegsmarine surface ship. Speer's genius for the logistics of armament production was severely tested by the intensifying Allied bombing campaign.

concentrated against the now improved U-boat assembly yards. Transporting the sections by Germany's beleaguered waterways also proved more problematic than at first envisioned, and once at the shipyard those boats not sheltered from air attack by purpose-built bunkers remained vulnerable to the increasing air attacks. The time required to complete each Type XXI U-boat was thus lengthened from Speer's optimistic projection. Fierce competition for Germany's increasingly scarce industrial resources also contributed to the delays, as evidenced by minutes of a meeting with Hitler attended by Dönitz and *Reichsmarschall* Hermann Göring on 13 April 1944:

> As a result of the priority granted the Luftwaffe, Types XXI and XXIII have been delayed causing other armament to suffer. An example of this occurred in the Augsburg Division of the Maschinenfabrik Augsburg-Nürnberg [MAN]. The engines were not completed because too few construction workers were employed to repair bomb damage. And the ready submarine sections could not be welded together because the engines were not ready. The Führer admits this

is a great disadvantage. However, from a broader point of view, the *Jägerstab* [Fighter Command] will have to have this priority. Otherwise industry might be destroyed still more, and thus submarine construction completely halted. The *Reichsmarschall* agrees wholeheartedly.[2]

The first Type XXI to reach the water was *U3501* on 19 April 1944 – one day before Hitler's birthday. However, it was a launching for prestige not trials or combat, as the boat was not even watertight and was immediately towed to a floating dock aided by external buoyancy. There it remained until July. The first completed Type XXI was *U2501*, which entered service on 28 June 1944. Almost immediately faults in this boat were discovered during its trials. With unsatisfactory construction of section 2, seawater was able to enter the electric motors' lubrication system and the boat was immediately placed back in dry dock for ten days. Other boats experienced similar catastrophic problems that arose from the lack of a trials prototype. One of the most serious issues was revealed when reversing electric motors underwater were found to drive the diesel system in the same way, leading to seawater being sucked through open exhaust vents and into the diesel-engine cylinder heads.

The extending *schnorchel* also proved troublesome. As the Type XXI was modelled on Walter's original design, which had not incorporated a *schnorchel*, the extensible model – as opposed to the externally raised mast added to existing Type VII and Type IX boats – was considered the only way of incorporating it into the Type XXI without hull-design modification. However, they were found to be not sufficiently watertight in trials, due to high vibrations against the mast itself when moving at speed. Other systems such as bilge piping and pumps, hydraulic controls for periscopes, flak weapons and torpedo hatches, and the general layout and accessibility of the boat's compressor were all found wanting once the Type XXI finally began trials.

Once a Type XXI was complete, training for the fifty-seven crewmen would also take longer than traditional U-boat training. Where it took an average of about three months to train a new conventional U-boat crew, the preparation involved for the crews of Type XXIs could take up to seven months. With improved underwater capabilities and weaponry came fresh tactics that training units developed as they progressed. Feedback was taken from all boats involved in training, and ultimately given to the veteran commander *Konteradmiral* Erich Topp who compiled the commander's manual for the Type XXI. Delays in training were also exacerbated by British aerial mining of the Bay of Danzig, which ultimately led to its complete abandonment for training purposes; the boats moved to Lübeck Bay where they came within range of Coastal Command's strike aircraft. Erich Topp later recalled his posting to oversee testing of the new U-boats in his autobiography:

The enclosed bridge of the late Type XXI *U3037*, designed to increase the protection afforded against enemy aircraft.

In August 1944 I became Director of Testing and Training of Type XXI and Type XXIII 'Electro' U-boats. Carl Emmermann, a Crew comrade [ie, somebody from Topp's naval graduating class of 1934] of mine, assisted me in the assignment. Our primary task was to test the new superboats with their huge batteries under tactical conditions and to write up the manual for operations against the enemy.

We received the first boat of the larger Type XXI series. Her commanding officer was yet another Crew comrade of ours, Adi Schnee. Gerd Suhren served as Chief Engineer and Conny Lüdders as executive officer. We went through all traditional tests and individual exercises and then practised attacks against convoys along with other boats of the 27th Tactical U-boat Flotilla. The results were impressive. The new boat displayed superb characteristics when operating alone. It also enjoyed far greater survival chances when hunted thanks to superior manoeuvrability both laterally and vertically. But the boats did by no means live up to the boasts that Dönitz had made to Hitler and us U-boat officers ...

Compared to the older Type VIIC boats, the Type XXI version undoubtedly represented progress and innovation. But it could never by itself have turned the tide in the war at sea, let alone in the overall conflict.[3]

The same problems existed for the Type XXIII, though by virtue of the smaller scale of the vessel, so too were its difficulties. With fewer sections to construct, which could be transported by rail as well as water, the Type XXIII progressed at a great pace. Crewed by fourteen men the boats began training for coastal operations using the same interactive method as Type XXI, crews learning by trial and error, the manual primarily compiled instead by the veteran commander *Korvettenkapitän* Carl Emmermann.

Erich Topp, pictured here as the highly successful captain of *U552*, later responsible for authoring the commander's handbook for the Type XXI U-boat.

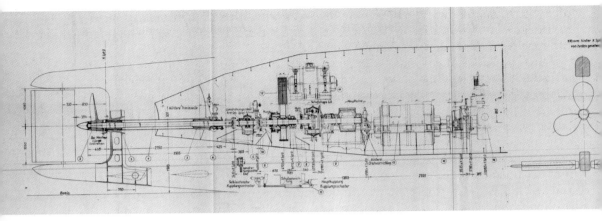

Extract from the 'Engineer's Sketch Book' for the Type XXIII, showing the propulsion unit.

The first Type XXIII to begin assembly was *U2321* in Hamburg's Deutsche Werft on 10 March 1944, the boat launched on 17 April. Once more the boat was launched almost to maintain the illusion of adhering to Speer's schedule, and required extensive work in the dockyard before finally being commissioned on 12 June 1944. Once launched the Type XXIIIs suffered far fewer technical difficulties than the larger Type XXI. In fact the Type XXIII attained performance that closely matched the projections of its designers.

Being designed principally for submerged performance meant that surface speed was effectively reduced to a maximum of ten knots, a reduction due to water resistance against the high bridge, itself a requirement for detection of the enemy – the boat was so low in the water that an exaggeratedly high conning tower was essential for viewing the distant horizon. Submerged, however, the boat was able to make more than twelve knots, and could make full use of its diesels when running with the raised *schnorchel*, the first U-boat type so to do. When running at 'creeping speed' of two-and-a-half knots in twenty metres of water the propeller noise was almost undetectable. The Type XXIII possessed no negative buoyancy tanks but instead simply blew ballast if stationary (submerging fully in twenty-one seconds), and combined this with forward hydroplanes if moving (submerging fully in fourteen seconds). The steep angle of descent required swift adjustment of the forward dive planes in order not to exceed the boat's operating depth, reckoned to be a designed depth of 100 metres, test depth of 150 and destruction depth of 250 metres. The first deep-diving test was undertaken on 24 January 1945 under the close supervision of Naval Construction Advisor Professor Otto Grim off the Norwegian coast, and attained 150 metres without problem. In fact the speed with which the Type XXIII could submerge was the cause of the loss of the first of these boats on 10 October 1944 when *U2331* sank while travelling surfaced during trials off Hela. It appears that the boat was moving astern with after hydroplanes set at four degrees upwards, causing the boat to dive accidentally and so suddenly that the crew were trapped by inrushing water and killed.[4]

The Type XXIII was found to be easy to control once submerged. It was possible to make its small turning circle – as little as 150 metres at full rudder – regardless of the speed at which the boat was travelling. Even surfaced the U-boat could make a 250-metre circle at full rudder and full speed, the rudder itself able to be taken completely across its lateral position – from full port to full starboard – in only fourteen seconds. The first *true* German U-boat had become operational.

By January 1945 three Type XXIIIs had been lost. In addition to the afore-mentioned training accident, *U2323* was sunk on 26 July 1944 after striking a mine laid by the RAF as part of their 'Forget-me-not' field in the Kieler förde off Möltenort on 26 July, just eight days after commissioning. Two men were killed in the explosion, *Leutnant zur See* Walter Angermann and eleven of his men managing to escape. The boat was later raised and decommissioned in Kiel.

On 24 December *U2342* was proceeding amid frequent snow storms in convoy with nine other Type XXIII and XXI U-boats from Neustadt to Swinemünde

Korvettenkapitän Carl Emmermann, a veteran of U-boat combat, was largely responsible for authoring the commander's handbook for the smaller Type XXIII electro-U-boat.

Type XXIII *U4706* after commissioning on 7 February 1945. The boat was never deployed, the war ending before working up was complete and the boat scuttled at Kiel.

under escort from minesweeper M502 of the 2 *Sicherungsflottille*. At 2200hrs an aerial laid ground mine (part of the British 'Geranium' field) exploded on the U-boat's starboard side, and the U-boat sank with the loss of all but five of her crew.

At 1800hrs on the last day of January 1945, *Oberleutnant zur See* Hans Hass took *U2324* from Kristiansand to its operational area off the Scottish coast in the Firth of Forth. Within seven days he had arrived in his patrol area, sighting a distant steamer but was unable to close the target enough to mount an attack. Finally his chance came on 18 February when he sighted and engaged a small coastal convoy in bad visibility fifteen miles east of Coquet Light on its small island off Amble. Hass fired his two torpedoes at a freighter, but missed due to a gyro-angling failure. Dejected, Hass headed back to Norway, berthing in Kristiansand on 25 February where the boat was put into the Bredalsholmen shipyard to prepare for its next patrol. Hass would not be commanding the small boat on its second sortie. Instead he was replaced by *Kapitänleutnant* Konstantin von Rappard who had begun his naval career as a watch officer aboard minesweepers in October 1939, entering the U-boat service in June two years later. Between November 1941 and July 1942 he had sailed as watch officer aboard the veteran Type IX *U103* of Lorient's 2nd U-Flotilla before being posted to command training boat *U560*. In August 1944 he became commander of the U-boat base at Kristiansand Süd where the Type XXIIIs were based, assuming command of *U2324* in March 1945.

Hass's patrol illustrated the major flaw in the Type XXIII as an offensive weapon. Though fast and manoeuvrable, the small U-boat possessed only a pair of torpedoes, fewer even than the Type II U-boat with which Germany had begun the war. The comparisons between the Type IID and Type XXIII are interesting. The Type IID carried five torpedoes, was capable of a range of 5,650 nautical miles surfaced, but only 56 submerged, with a top surfaced speed of 12.7 knots and 7.4 submerged. The Type XXIII carried two torpedoes and was capable of a range of 2,600 nautical miles surfaced, 194 submerged and top speeds of 9.7 knots surfaced and 12.5 submerged.

Undoubtedly the newer design was more mobile and effective as a submerged weapon of war, but despite its greater likelihood of survival compared to the Type II, the Type XXIII carried no more weaponry than the *Seehund* midget submarine (though the latter only possessed a maximum range of 300 miles at seven knots surfaced and sixty-three miles at three knots submerged).

By the time that Hass had returned from Scotland a second Type XXIII had also sailed for active service. *Oberleutnant zur See* Fridtjof Heckel took *U2322* from Kristiansand on 6 February, again destined for the Firth of Forth. On 15 February near St Mary's Head, Heckel attempted an attack against a British freighter estimated at 5,000 tons, though he missed and opted to retreat rather than waste his last torpedo. It was not until ten days later that he sighted convoy FS1739 south of Berwick and launched his last attack. *U2322* had received radioed instructions from BdU that both itself and *U309* – reckoned incorrectly to be nearby – were granted freedom to manoeuvre. Shortly thereafter FS1739 hove into view. The convoy was small and escorted by what appeared to be only a pair of small escorts. Heckel fired his last torpedo and hit the Danish ship SS *Egholm*, which had been requisitioned by the British Ministry of War Transport in 1940. Fatally holed, the 1,317-ton freighter sank in twenty-five metres of water with five men aboard killed. The Type XXIII had finally achieved victory in combat and Heckel headed for Stavanger, arriving on 3 March.

It was not only the two Type XXIIIs that had seen action during February in British waters. The beginning of the month saw twenty-six other boats at sea alongside *U2324*. Of these only nine were actually on station on 1 February 1945: *U278* and *U313* on the English east coast patrolling against potential British carrier groups; *U245* off North Foreland; *U1014* in the North Channel; *U963* in the Irish Sea; *U275*, *U1017*, *U1018*, *U480* and *U244* in the English Channel. *U275* was forced to break away from action during the early part of February with *schnorchel* damage. However, instead of heading for Norway *Oberleutnant zur See* Helmuth Wehrkamp took his damaged U-boat south to the encircled port of St Nazaire, where the besieged 30,000-strong garrison continued to hold out against the Allies. Enough material was still stored within the bomb-proof shelters to enable

A Type VIIC undergoes maintenance of its port fuel bunker. Shipyard capacity within Norwegian yards could never meet the requirements of the combat U-boats.

U275 to successfully perform emergency repairs of the troublesome *schnorchel* installation.

On 20 February *U1004* reached its operational area at the western entrance to the English Channel. *Oberleutnant zur See* Rudolf Hinz had taken his boat from Bergen at the end of January on his second patrol of British waters. On 22 February southeast of Falmouth *U1004* found the small fourteen-ship coastal convoy BTC76 sailing from Bristol to the Thames. That afternoon Hinz fired a single T5 *Zaunkönig* and two LUT torpedoes and managed to sink two ships. The first was the 1,313-ton British freighter SS *Alexander Kennedy* loaded with coal. A single crewman was lost with the master, John William Johnson; fifteen crewmen and two gunners were later rescued. For his bravery during the sinking Johnson was later awarded the Lloyds War Medal (established in 1940 and bestowed on 541 merchant seamen for gallantry during the war).

Nine minutes after SS *Alexander Kennedy* was hit, *U1004* hit the single Canadian escort, corvette HMCS *Trentonian* starboard aft; she sank quickly with the loss of one officer and five ratings. The commander, Lieutenant Colin Glassco later recalled:

We had barely cleared the convoy when we were hit. The torpedo struck the ship at the starboard after depth charge thrower, blowing a large hole in the hull, and flooding the engine room. She settled very quickly and when the Engineer Officer and First Lieutenant said it was beyond repair, I gave the order to abandon ship. The men behaved with great courage and cheerfulness. Fortunately the men in charge of the depth charges had set them to safe, otherwise they would have gone off when the ship got down to the prescribed depth and the explosion would have killed most of us. The need for wearing life jackets was borne out by the fact that we lost no one by drowning despite the fact that more than fourteen of the crew could not swim. We were in the water for forty-five minutes waiting for the Fairmiles (motor launches) to pick us up, the men sang to pass the time and to keep spirits up. The crew's biggest complaint was the wasted effort they had just put into giving the ship a new coat of paint. The water was thirty-three degrees, and the effect on one's strength was very noticeable when climbing up the scramble net.

In all situations of this kind there is always a Court of Inquiry, and this was held at the Naval Base in Plymouth. The officers and crew were mustered outside the door where the Inquiry was to be held, and along came a warrant officer bearing a sword and placed it on the table. My heart sank as in my rather nervous state it looked as if the Court of Inquiry was to be dispensed with and they were going straight into a Court Martial. Happily it was all a mistake and the little warrant officer came back saying cheerfully, 'Sorry sir, wrong room'.

To my relief, the President of the Court confirmed the correctness of our tactics, and that we had intercepted a torpedo aimed at one of the 10,000-ton Liberty ships. The first paragraph of Atlantic Convoy Instruction reads; 'The safe and timely arrival of the convoy is the first duty of the escort'; so in this case we really carried out our duty, and in the process lost our ship."[5]

U1004 narrowly missed hitting a third ship; the explosion of the second LUT torpedo as it sank at the end of its run was clearly heard inside the German hull and causing Hinz to claim a third victim sunk.

In Berlin, BdU fought blind as they traced the presumed positions of their U-boats, optimism often overruling caution in the précis of action presented by Dönitz to Hitler:

The Führer is particularly pleased about the reports of the latest submarine successes. In this connection, C-in-C Navy reports that seven submarines have recently returned from operations in the areas around the British Isles. These ships had to operate in narrow sea lanes and in shallow waters near the coast. They all report that the enemy defences are not very effective. This proves therefore that the superiority of the enemy submarine defences has been overcome by the introduction of the *schnorchel*. The number of submarines in operation will be increased further in the near future. Since the beginning of February thirty-five submarines have left for operational areas, and twenty-three more will follow before the end of the month. The Führer asked . . . about the

The bridges of late war U-boats had become crowded with radar and radar detection gear. Forced to operate submerged made the operation of such equipment more problematic, but also initially diminished its necessity somewhat.

use of the new submarine types and was informed that two of Type XXIII are already operating along the east coast of the British Isles and that the first ship of Type XXI will be ready for operations along the American east coast by the end of February or the beginning of March.[6]

One further boat, *U907*, was on weather-reporting duty near Iceland, a seemingly thankless task for any U-boat crew, but something that BdU not only valued, but also could interpret in a way that emphasised the supposedly favourable position that the new U-boat offensive had created:

One to two boats have been detailed continually in the North Atlantic during the past year, to make weather reports every day. These weather reports were and are included in the formation of the general weather conditions in Europe, and also in a review of the conditions at the front, of the defences of the Reich and all such operations in which a report on the enemy air forces is of such great importance. The weather boats were increased to three at the beginning of December, to ensure that enough reports were received daily as were necessary for us to start the West Offensive.

Although the boats, whose positions were well known to the enemy owing to their extensive use of wireless telegraphy, were attacked now and then at the beginning of the year, this has no longer been the case during the last three months: It shows that the enemy's Atlantic air patrols have decreased over the open sea to enable them to cover the coastal waters to a width of about 400 miles, that is to say, their own outward and supply routes to Norway.[7]

German U-boat casualties mounted almost immediately from the beginning of February 1945, as the boats operated in bad winter weather near the British Isles. The new Type VIIC/41 *U1279* captained by *Oberleutnant zur See* Hans Falke had been at sea only four days when, on 3 February, it was detected by the British frigates HMSs *Bayntun*, *Braithwaite* and *Loch Eck*, which were sailing to their new billet at Scapa Flow, north-northwest of the Shetlands. The boat was sunk by depth charges with all hands.

The following day the Type VIIC/41 *U1014* was located in the North Channel

U309 pictured after rescuing the crew of *U981*, sunk by mine during the evacuation of La Pallice in August 1944. Forced to return to the French port, *U309* eventually joined the inshore battle later that month as part of the first wave.

and sunk by HMSs *Loch Scavaig, Loch Shin, Nyasaland* and *Papua. Oberleutnant zur See* Wolfgang Glaser had only arrived in his operational area a few days previously at the end of January. HMS *Loch Scavaig* detected the boat lying on the bottom north of Portrush, and began depth charging as four other frigates of the 23rd Escort Group joined the attack, eventually destroying *U1014* and its crew. Another VIIC/41 *U989,* which had survived a patrol in the English Channel during the August of 1944, was also sunk on 14 February east of the Shetlands, having been located by four frigates of the 10th Escort Group while bound from Horten to British waters. The captain, *Kapitänleutnant* Hardo Rodler von Roithberg and one crewman actually succeeded in escaping the submerged and sinking U-boat and were picked up by their British attackers, but both died shortly afterward, possibly due to internal injuries caused from escaping a U-boat from too great a depth. It was von Roithberg's 27th birthday. His U-boat career had begun in September 1940 as second watch officer aboard *U96* – the boat made famous by the book and film *Das Boot.*

On 16 February Type VIIC *U309* was also destroyed. *Oberleutnant zur See* Herbert Loeder had taken his boat into the Moray Firth, the first U-boat reported by the Allies in that region for five years. After stalking convoy WN74 north-northwest of Kinnairds Head, *U309* was found and attacked by the Canadian frigate HMCS *St John.* The Canadian's ASDIC detected *U309* in fewer than seventy metres of water and the frigate immediately attacked, bringing some oil to the surface. Two further attacks were mounted using the ship's Hedgehog, which produced more upwelling oil before a fourth attack with depth charges resulted in visible wreckage including charts, signal books and fragments of cork insulation material. Apparently a further attack the following day released a body from the destroyed U-boat after ripping the bow from the wreck.

New VIIC/41 boat *U1278* was the next to be destroyed, found and destroyed on 17 February by HMSs *Bayntun* and *Loch Eck* north of the Shetlands while outbound from Norway. Sister ship *U1276* was also destroyed, although not before it had attacked and sunk an enemy warship minutes earlier. *Oberleutnant zur See* Karl-Heinz Wendt operated in the Irish Sea from early February before moving into St George's Channel. There, on 20 February he attacked the 63-ship convoy HX337 south of Waterford, torpedoing and sinking the escorting corvette HMS *Vervain,* which went down with three officers and forty-six crewmen. *U1276's* victory was short lived, however, as its position was betrayed and within thirty minutes the sloop HMS *Amethyst* depth charged the boat out of existence, apparently blowing the bow off. The identity of the U-boat was established from clothing recovered by Lieutenant Commander David Harries aboard HMS *Peacock,* which had supported *Amethyst* during the attack.[8]

On 27 February new Type VIIC U-boat *U1208* was sunk by frigates HMSs *Duckworth* and *Rowley* southwest of Land's End. It appears that *Korvettenkapitän* Georg Hagene had made the boat's first kill when he torpedoed and sunk the coal-carrying SS *Oriskany* from convoy BTC78. The ship's master, convoy commodore (Commander I N Macmillan RNR), twenty-one crew members, seven naval-staff members and four gunners were all lost in the sinking, leaving no survivors. The pair of frigates from the convoy's escort then located and destroyed Hagene and all of his crew with depth charges. Originally it was thought that this U-boat had been the *Alberich*-coated *U480* commanded by *Oberleutnant zur See* Hans-Joachim Förster, but it now appears that this boat, which had already survived one patrol in the English Channel during August, was destroyed by minefield 'Brazier D2' laid at the beginning of 1945.

The same day that *U1208* was destroyed, a Warwick of 179 Squadron detected the *schnorchel* of new Type VIIC/41 *U927* on a fine clear evening south of the Lizard. Radar contact with the small object was made at a range of two miles. Flight Lieutenant A G Brownhill took his aircraft down from the 600-feet altitude at which he was patrolling, until the *schnorchel*, extended some five feet above the water surface with its exhaust, was plainly visible. Flying up along the *schnorchel's* wake Brownhill released six depth charges on the target, which had sea periodically breaking over its *schnorchel*, and three depth charges perfectly straddled each side of the submerged U-boat. Front and rear machine gunners also opened fire as the Warwick overflew *U927* until the target disappeared in the spume of explosions. Switching on his Leigh Light, Brownhill flew back and saw oil and debris already rising from the shattered boat. Ships of the 3rd Escort Group were homed on to the scene but there were no survivors. This was the sole combat victory achieved by a Warwick aircraft, which were gradually replacing the elderly Wellingtons.

Two more U-boats fell on 27 February. The first, *U327*, was depth charged in the west part of the English Channel by frigates HMSs *Labuan*, *Loch Fada* and the sloop HMS *Wild Goose* with no survivors, after an unsuccessful maiden voyage from Norway. The second was the fractionally more successful *U1018*. *Kapitänleutnant* Walter Burmeister attacked convoy BTC81 southwest of the Lizard, hitting the Norwegian freighter SS *Corvus*. This 1,317-ton steamer was laden with coal when the torpedo hit during the mid morning. The ship's starboard side was torn apart and the ship immediately developed a heavy list before capsizing and sinking within a couple of minutes. Because of the speed of the capsizing the crew were unable to launch lifeboats, though a single raft was thrown overboard. Out of twenty-two crewmen and three gunners, six crew and two gunners died with the ship. The escorts immediately began hunting *U1018*, HMS *Loch Fada* taking the search's inshore sector. Heading into Mount's Bay the frigate obtained ASDIC contact and carried out a Squid attack that destroyed *U1018*. Fifty-one of its crew including the commander were killed and two were rescued: the boat's IIWO *Leutnant zur See* Werner Banck and Engineering *Maat* Franz Merling.

Additional to those U-boats that had been hunted to destruction, *U683* was also lost during February. The final passage report from *Kapitänleutnant* Günter Keller

Type XXI, VII and XXIII U-boats photographed by RAF reconnaissance aircraft
in Kristiansand after the war's end.

was received in Berlin on 20 February after which the boat disappeared, lost in the
maelstrom of mines and depth charges.

To add to the terrible toll taken on the combat U-boats around the British Isles
during February, one of the new Type XXIII boats involved in training, *U2344*,
was rammed and sunk by *U2336* on 18 February north of Heiligenhaven. The Type
XXIII's conning tower was damaged and the pressure hull ruptured near the
electric motors, causing the boats to sink so quickly that only the commander and
two watchmen escaped.

Although BdU in Berlin were unaware of the scale of the disaster beginning to
overtake the outdated Type VIIs in British waters, February 1945 marked the
beginning of the end for the offensive. Reliant as Berlin had become on U-boats
returning from patrol before they were able to gather reliable information, the
slaughter remained largely unknown, the first inklings coming during March as
boats remained overdue. Thus outbound U-boats – except those aiming for the
British east coast – were sent first to a staging area west of Ireland, before receiving
the most up-to-date instructions and patrol-area allocations possible.

Germany had experienced difficulties in keeping so many Type VIIC boats
operational against Britain. Fuel was in desperately short supply. The Kriegsmarine
only received a fraction of its already slim allocation due to the disruption of
supply networks. The problem was only overcome once oil was siphoned from
laid-up Kriegsmarine surface ships, including the cruisers *Admiral Scheer* and
Lützow, which were languishing in Kiel's military harbour.

The initial optimistic exchange rate of Allied shipping sunk against U-boats lost
had plummeted, as the Royal Navy and its allies began to reap the dividend of
adapted tactics. The concentration of U-boats brought a corresponding
concentration of escort ships and U-boat hunters attached to their convoys.

Aircraft were startlingly ineffective in British waters against the U-boats, but in the transit areas of the Kattegat and Skagerrak they took a heavy toll of U-boats. Here *U2359* is under attack by a Mosquito of the Banff Strike Wing, sunk by rocket and cannon fire.

Though the difficulties of underwater terrain remained an issue throughout the inshore campaign for Allied ASDIC operators, once U-boats had betrayed their presence by mounting an attack, surface ships probing the depths smothered the surrounding sea. Aircraft had been somewhat relegated to the poor relation in terms of the successful destruction of U-boats in comparison to surface escorts, though they could still have successes, as proven by the destruction of *U927*. Their presence also guaranteed the U-boats' unwillingness to remain surfaced and operate with true freedom to manoeuvre and the ability to have all round visibility. The battle of attrition was spiralling out of German control once more. The sinking of U-boats was actually of secondary importance to the Allies. Even though it felt less 'aggressive', as long as the convoys were escorted safely to their destinations, and the U-boats were prevented from attacking, then the Allies were achieving their objective, while depriving the U-boats of theirs.

CHAPTER FIVE

Mines and Tactics

THE BRITISH ADMIRALTY had been receiving a steady stream of intelligence from early 1944 onwards regarding German development of a new generation of U-boats capable of a reported submerged speed of up to sixteen knots. This would nullify one of the greatest advantages possessed by the Allied ASW units over conventional German U-boats: once conventional U-boats were forced under their ability to manoeuvre at any kind of speed was curtailed. If a U-boat could operate at sixteen knots submerged – compared to a maximum of nine knots for the Type VIIC – it would mean that they could attempt to outrun pursuit. Although the submerged U-boats could still not match the overall endurance of the surface convoy escorts, their speed enabled them to nullify Allied ASDIC, since the escorts would have to match that speed. ASDIC aboard the Allied escort ships would be deafened by the rush of water if attempting to keep pace with the target U-boat. Thus the U-boats could still hope to outmanoeuvre and ultimately outdistance their pursuers. In one fell swoop Allied radar would be nullified by the U-boat's ability to remain submerged, and ASDIC by the speed at which the submerged boat could operate. Fresh ideas, technology and tactics were required – and potentially required very quickly.

To begin the development of new methods to combat a fast submerged U-boat, HMS *Seraph* – the submarine made famous by delivering 'The Man Who Never Was' in the Mediterranean – was urgently modified at Devonport's shipyard. The submarine was streamlined, the size of the bridge reduced, the gun removed along with one of the periscopes and the radar mast, and torpedo tubes blanked over. The motors were upgraded and higher-capacity batteries were fitted, and the propellers were replaced with the coarser-pitched models – ie, one with a high blade angle and thus capable of a larger 'bite' of seawater with each rotation – used on the larger *T*-class submarine. This allowed *Seraph* to achieve a high underwater speed so that trials and exercises could be carried out against it by Allied surface forces in order to replicate action against a submarine with similar capabilities to the Type XXI. The result with *Seraph* was an increase in her underwater speed from nine to twelve knots. HMSs *Sceptre, Satyr, Statesman, Selene, Solent* and *Sleuth* were similarly converted.[1]

The trials conducted proved extremely useful to the Royal Navy, and also pointed the way forward to future ASW necessities against not only German U-boats, but also, as it turns out, future enemies (the Soviets) equipped with the technological advances pioneered by the Kriegsmarine.

Elsewhere, other Allied weaponry and tactics were being used and improved to hunt the existing threat posed by the *schnorchel*-equipped conventional U-boats. Difference of opinion regarding the effectiveness of depth charges against bottomed U-boats in shallow water became an issue widely debated amongst Allied naval planners, not least of all in the Royal Canadian Navy's upper echelons. Their warships were engaged in both the British inshore battle and in home waters, which were being similarly attacked by large Type IX U-boats sailing close to the coastline in conditions similar to those found around the United Kingdom:

> Information from escorts and groups at sea was crucial, however, given such innovations in German tactics and technology as bottoming U-boats, where they mimicked wrecks to avoid detection, and *schnorchel* ... Policy makers and researchers had to know whether the equipment in hand was up to the task or had to be replaced, so reports like that of Escort Group 11, in July 1944, were subject to much discussion. Based on experiences in British coastal waters from 5 June to

During the inshore campaign in British waters, depth charges appeared to be beginning to lose their effectiveness in comparison to improved weaponry such as the Hedgehog and Squid.

12 July, and hence encompassing Operation Neptune [the D-day landings], the group's commander related how his ships mistakenly attacked over three dozen wrecks, its only success the destruction of *U678* with the aid of HMS *Statice.*[2]

Indeed the traditional ten depth-charge pattern was found to be of little use against U-boats that were lying on the seabed. Illustrated by elementary physics, the maximum force exerted by an exploding depth charge would expend itself along the path of least resistance. Thus, the majority of the explosive force was directed upwards towards the surface rather than against the seabed or the solid object of a U-boat hull. The 'ten-charge pattern' had been developed for blue-water fighting, the theory being that five charges would detonate below the target and five above. Therefore at least five of these depth charges would essentially be wasted on a bottomed U-boat:

> The only submarine to be definitely destroyed on the June-July patrol had been attacked with at least twenty-five tons of minol – a poor explosive developed as a potential substitute for TNT, which was in short supply. It is suggested that this is due to the fact that depth charges explode on or near the bottom . . . and cause comparatively little lateral disturbance. It is believed that some of our own submarines have stood up to an amazing amount of hammering when bottomed without being seriously damaged.
>
> For this there was no cure, except to get the weapon as near the victim as possible, a principle that led Vice-Admiral L W Murray, the Commander-in-Chief Canadian Northwest Atlantic, to comment [on 1 September 1944] that 'I consider that Senior Officer EG 11's theory of effect of sea bottom in diminishing effectiveness of depth charges is erroneous. Depth-charge attacks on bottomed submarine should be more effective than in deep waters, since the error in estimation of depth is absent' allowing a more accurate setting for fuses.
>
> According to EG 11, it also allowed a change in technique. 'The most effective method of bringing up wreckage, and therefore presumably of causing lethal damage, has been found to be by means of towed charges fired electrically' and so 'it is recommended that all ships should be fitted to carry out this form of attack.'[3]

However, Commodore Western Approaches, G W Simpson, suggested that the Canadian Escort Group commander had confused the:

> . . . destruction of a U-boat with the obtaining of the necessary evidence of destruction. The use of the towed charge electrically fired is a good idea. But the disintegration of the hull cannot reasonably be expected, however many charges are dropped on it.

The hard evidence required by the Admiralty to confirm the destruction of a U-boat had led Allied ASW ships to pulverise the location of what they presumed was an enemy target in order to bring enough debris to the surface for retrieval. The debate about the best weaponry to use against a shallow inshore enemy would continue until the end of the war. Squid mortars were considered the most effective, with their large forward-thrown timer charges, followed by the smaller but more numerous Hedgehog, contact-fused projectiles, with depth charges regarded as the most inferior weapon.

However, despite the apparent difficulty in obtaining firm kills with it, depth charges were still considered a powerful psychological weapon for use against hunted U-boats. ASDIC sweeps through the water followed by sporadic depth charges were widely reported by rescued German survivors to have caused extreme anxiety within the U-boat's cramped and damp interior. In fact many Allied surface ships also reverted to older pattern depth charges that had been deemed unsuitable in the open ocean. The improved Mark X depth charge had been issued to counter previous deficiencies when it was discovered, after the capture of *U570* by the British, that U-boats could exceed depths previously ascribed to them. The Mark X was designed to sink quickly in order to attack targets deeper than previous depth charges had been able to reach. However, in shallow British waters they often failed to fire due to hitting the bottom too quickly. Thus older depth charges were frequently taken aboard the ASW ships in order to combat Dönitz's new tactics.

The Allies had also been furnishing their ASW forces with charts plotting the reported thermocline features of the Atlantic, a factor that now became ever more crucial with U-boats exploiting the physical properties of differing temperature layers in shallow waters around both the British and Canadian coastlines. It was a German scientist, Dr H Lichte who first theorised that sound waves travelling through water would refract both upward and downward on encountering slight differences in temperature, salinity, and pressure. In the United States scientists at the Woods Hole Oceanographic Institution in Woods Hole, Massachusetts, had been assisting US Naval vessels in dealing with the phenomenon using a new device called a bathythermograph, invented in 1937 by Athelstan Spilhaus of the Institute. A small torpedo-shaped device, the bathythermograph used sensors to detect changes in water pressure and temperature as it dropped through the water column. Because the measurement of pressure in decibars was approximately equal to depth in metres, technicians could correlate depth with temperature. It was confirmed that, in the warm upper layer of the ocean, sound is refracted toward the surface. As sound waves travel deeper into colder water, they slow down and are refracted downward, creating a so-called 'shadow zone' just beneath the dividing line between the warmer and cooler layers of water in which U-boats could hide. While United States submarines and surface vessels were regularly equipped with a bathythermograph during the Second World War, the technology was slower in reaching British and Canadian forces. But charts compiled by their Allies were more readily available, and highlighted areas of particularly strong thermoclines where ASDIC detection could prove problematic.

Other technology used in combating the resurgent enemy was not new to the battle against the U-boats. Sonobuoys had first been successfully launched during an attack by a USAAF B18 bomber in July 1942. The first sinking directly attributed to detection by a sonobuoy took place on 30 October 1942 when *U568* was sunk by depth charges from a RCAF Hudson from 145 Squadron. Sonobuoys too became a frequent asset in the Allied armoury within British waters; they were considered particularly crucial in the expected impending battle against the near silent German electro-boats.

The sonobuoy was frequently used in conjunction with the MAD – Magnetic Anomaly Detector – that had been developed in the interwar years. The MAD had been designed for the scientific measurement of changes within the earth's magnetic field, though the usage of airborne MAD gear for the detection of submerged submarines was fairly obvious. And, by 1943, most ASW aircraft were equipped with MAD. However, in shallow waters the limitations of the equipment became rapidly apparent, primarily its inability to distinguish between sources of magnetic variance. Frequently wrecks or local magnetic disturbances were

The cramped cockpit of a Mosquito fighter-bomber, showing, at right, the eyepiece for the airborne radar that plagued German naval craft.

classified as submarines, though the more experienced the operator the greater the chances of correctly identifying a U-boat. By 1944 MAD gear was being used in combination with sonobuoys, which proved of more use. The MAD allowed an aircraft to localise a contact made with sonobuoys and the sonobuoys provided confirmation that the contact was, indeed, a submarine. In this combination MAD became the secondary system to the sonobuoy and would later become a mainstay feature of postwar NATO ASW techniques in the Atlantic.

The sudden loss to the Allies of both radio-direction finding and Enigma code-breaking due to the lack of radio transmissions from the U-boats had contributed to the initial slump in success in locating and sinking Dönitz's U-boats engaged in inshore attacks. Radar had been largely nullified by the U-boats' ability to remain submerged, while the German perfection of mounting radar detection equipment to the *schnorchel* head allowed the submerged boat to detect incoming Allied search aircraft before the radar could find the small signature generated by the *schnorchel*. Coupled with the prescribed manning by U-boat crews running submerged of the sky search periscope, U-boats finally possessed some measure of detecting enemy aircraft and thus improved chances of escaping Allied aircraft attack.

However, a U-boat's freedom to manoeuvre in enemy waters was immediately removed once it had launched an attack. Allied methods of hunting a U-boat to exhaustion were as effective as ever once the enemy had betrayed its presence. Despite their initial optimistic performance, the role of the attacking U-boats was still enormously complicated. The difficulties of operating a conventional U-boat that remained almost continually submerged were numerous, and included the lack of precise navigation. Though periscopes could sometimes be used for terrestrial navigation this required the U-boat to be extremely close to identifiable features on land. The ability to take star sights – should stars be visible during the heavy weather of the winter of 1944/45 – was beyond the Kriegsmarine, a device to enable this still being under construction during 1944. Once in the combat zone, particularly if attempting to run silent under the keels of enemy ASW forces, noise-generating equipment such as a gyro-compass and echo sounder were frequently turned off, thus complicating navigation. In general officers aboard the U-boats that were engaged in the war in British waters – including navigation NCOs – were young, often with little experience of navigation in the difficult tidal areas such as those found in the combat zone. Older, more experienced seamen had, by 1944, been promoted ashore to training establishments, or were preparing new crews for rejoining the war aboard the large Type XXIs.

The presumed effectiveness that BdU attributed to its Type VIICs in British waters ensured fresh departures of more of this Type, for the frontline from Norway throughout February and March 1945. In fact twenty-nine U-boats had sailed into action during February, the highest commitment during a single month to date.

Despite this high concentration of U-boats at sea, successes were slim. *U1058* claimed a 9,000-ton freighter sunk at some point after 13 February, but it remained unconfirmed. Likewise for *U1104* which claimed both a 7,000-ton tanker and 3,000-ton freighter sunk at the northern end of the Minch. On 21 February *Korvettenkapitän* Karl-Hermann Schneidewind recorded within his KTB aboard *U1064*, three ships hit and sunk in the North Channel, giving an aggregate total of 17,000 tons. In fact he had hit a 1,564-ton Icelandic steamer SS *Dettifoss* carrying 1,300 tons of general cargo. *U1064* hit the ship during an attack on convoy UR155 east of Belfast, the steamer sinking within seven minutes, taking twelve crewmen and three passengers to the bottom. *U1203* sank a single ship during ten and a half weeks at sea, the British ASW trawler HMT *Ellesmere*, rather optimistically claimed by *Oberleutnant zur See* Sigurd Seeger as a 5,000-ton freighter. Seeger's run of unconfirmed ships continued during the last week of February, when he reported a Liberty ship and unknown patrol vessel also hit and torpedoed, but no such attacks exist in Allied records.

The penultimate confirmed sinking for February was made by Taschenmacher's *U775* on the last day of the month. At 1015hrs a single torpedo hit the unescorted – unescorted vessels were always far easier targets than those ships sailed in convoy – American steamer SS *Soreldoc* travelling in ballast from Liverpool to Swansea. The ship broke in two after being hit to port, the forepart, with wheelhouse, sinking within thirty seconds, killing the master. The stern remained afloat for four minutes allowing only enough time for fifteen of the twenty-nine crewmembers to jump overboard, accompanied by six armed guards and a US Army security-officer passenger. That day *U1302* sank the small 646-ton motor ship MV *Norfolk Coast* southwest of Strumble Head. Travelling from Cardiff to Liverpool, seven of the fifteen men aboard were killed. Both these U-boats had not yet finished their run of sinkings.

The beginning of March found *U775* cruising west of Ireland where Taschenmacher reported two ships torpedoed for 6,000 and 8,000 tons respectively. The claims remained unconfirmed, though on 6 March it appears that *U775* did probably torpedo and damage British steamer SS *Empire Geraint* from convoy MH44. It was the end of *U775*'s achievements, as the boat headed for Norway where it docked on 30 March.

Kapitänleutnant Wolfgang Herwartz's *U1302* attacked convoy SC167 during the evening of 2 March with great success. Launching torpedoes in the St George's Channel off Milford Haven, Herwartz sank the British motor ship MV *King Edgar* and the Norwegian SS *Novasli*. The *Novasli* had its rudder and propeller blown off by the explosion, the hull splitting just aft of amidships with water flooding the engine room. The drifting ship was abandoned by most of the crew in three lifeboats while the master, first mate, radio operator, steward and mess boy remained on board to facilitate the towing of the drifting ship. However, with water rising in the engine room the stern gradually sank deeper into the water until the engine and boiler rooms were totally flooded and the ship was abandoned completely. The ASW trawler HMT *Helier* picked up the five men, after which it shelled and depth-charged the wreck with its 1,124 strands of lumber aboard. The second ship to be hit, MV *King Edgar*, was also taken in tow, but soon sank with four men killed and 1,667 standards of lumber, 2,038 tons of plywood and 500 tons of lead and zinc lost.

But for Herwartz and his forty-seven crewmen the victory came at the ultimate price. They had now tipped their position to the enemy and a five-day search for the U-boat began. On 7 March warships of the 25th Escort Group located *U1302* northwest of Dinas Head in St George's Channel. Three Canadian frigates – HMCSs *Hulloise, Strathadam* and *Thetford Mines* – began a systematic depth-charge attack, which destroyed the trapped U-boat with its entire complement.

Faulty navigation destroyed the next boat lost during March. *Oberleutnant zur See* Werner Gebauer's *U681*, which claimed an unconfirmed ship hit on 6 March, struck a rock while running submerged near the Bishop Rock north east of the Isles of Scilly, a perilous stretch of reef-strewn water. The boat was badly damaged in both the pressure hull and propellers and began flooding, ruptured diesel lines spraying fuel into the engine room. Gebauer was forced to abruptly surface where *U681* provided one of the few hard radar contacts for patrolling aircraft. An American Liberator of VPB103 – the first squadron of the US Navy to have

U260 returning from patrol, showing a typical late-war flak weaponry layout.

Members of *U260*'s crew above decks at the end of a patrol. The boat would be lost to British mines off southern Ireland.

completed their training with the RAF Coastal Command after a phasing out of the USAAF anti-submarine squadrons – sighted *U681* running at speed on the surface and immediately began a bombing run, straddling the U-boat with depth charges, which further damaged the German. *U681* was ordered abandoned and scuttled. Once the surviving crew were overboard the U-boat was left to submerge with hatches open, the demolition charges exploding once it had submerged. The Royal Navy later rescued Gebauer and thirty-nine crewmen.

Further west *U275* was also destroyed on 6 March. *Oberleutnant zur See* Helmut Wehrkamp's boat had sailed into the besieged port of St Nazaire during February to undergo repair to its damaged *schnorchel*; the boat slipped from the harbour once more on 25 February. The western coast of France was now heavily patrolled by Allied warships, while land forces kept a watchful eye seaward for U-boats engaged on running supplies to the trapped garrisons of Lorient, La Pallice, St Nazaire and the Gironde. Nevertheless Wehrkamp still successfully rejoined the battle, and headed back into his operational area of the English Channel. On 8 March *U275* attacked convoy ONA289 northwest of Fecamp, torpedoing and sinking British steamer SS *Lornaston*, which was carrying 6,002 tons of coal ultimately bound for Casablanca. The German radio monitoring service, B-Dienst, confirmed the sinking, which Wehrkamp was unable to report. Managing successfully to evade detection by the convoy's escort ships Wehrkamp slipped

Die Dienststelle hat den oberen Teil vor Aushändigung hier abzutrennen und bei Nichtbenutzung der Eisenbahn unbrauchbar zu machen!

Urlaubsschein = Dienstreiseschein D) № Ma   945806 ✳

Gültig nur in Verbindung mit Soldbuch, Truppenausweis, Personalausweis Wehrpaß od. dgl.¹) Nr.

Kennwort: ¹)   ==//==   , Frontleitstelle: ==//==

Grund und Verfügung: D) Meldung beim Ob.d.M., gen. Befehl Ob.d.M. vom 20.1.45

Oberleutnant zur See Klaus B e c k e r

(Dienstgrad und Name des Reisenden)

von Feldpostnummer M49764   Urlaub vom ==== bis ====

Dienstliche Reise vom 23.1.45 bis 25.1.45   Rückreise am D) 25. Januar 45

Zwischenaufenthalt in D)   ====================   genehmigt

Alle Reiseziele bzw. Urlaubsorte: ¹) Berlin- Bernau

Vermerke und Bescheinigungen der Einheit

1. Abgefunden mit:

Wehrsold (Gr. ...) bis einschl. 31.1.45. Tabakwaren: 4. **Besondere Vermerke:**
Frontzulage   als Portion   bis einschl.
Bekl.-Entschädigung   als Market.-Ware
Verpflegungsgeld   Raucherwaren
Feinseife   Raucher-Kontr.-Karte
Raserseife   Raucherkarte
    Sonst. Market.-Ware

2. Verpflegungsnachweis: (Heeresverpflegungstage für Fronturlauber.)
Verpflegungszulage für Bombenschäden, Verwundete oder Kranke.¹).

Monat: Januar 45 | Monat: | 1

2	3	4	5	6	7	8	9	10	11		2	3	4	5	6	7	8	9	10	11
12	13	14	15	16	17	18	19	20	21		12	13	14	15	16	17	18	19	20	21
22	23	24	25	26	27	28	29	30	31		22	23	24	25	26	27	28	29	30	31

Bei Abgabe von Truppen- oder Marschverpflegung oder Lebensmittelkarten sind entsprechende Tagesabschnitte durch die abgebenden Stellen — auch Kartenstellen — mit Tinte oder Tintenstift unbrauchbar zu machen.
Bescheinigung der Lebensmittelkartenzuteile: Rückseite.

3. Mitgeführte Geldbeträge:

Reisekosten
Gebührnisse
Sonstige Geldmittel
Geldumtauschvermerke: Rückseite

genehmigt vom Ob.d.M.
Großadmiral Dönitz

1) Nichtzutreffendes deutlich durchstreichen.
2) Bei mehreren: Name des Transportführers und   (Anzahl) Mann
U) Nur für Urlaubsschein ausfüllen.
D) Nur für Dienstreiseschein ausfüllen.

Ausgefertigt am 22. Januar 194 5
Feldpostnummer M49743
(Truppenteil bzw. Feldpost-Nr.)
(Unterschrift)
Korv. Kapitän
(Dienstgrad u. Dienststellung)
Dienstlich gedruckt.
Nachdruck wird nach den Kriegsgesetzen bestraft.

Even in early 1945 some U-boat commanders were travelling from Norway to Berlin for briefings from Dönitz, this travel pass issued for *Oberleutnant zur See* Klaus Becker of *U260*.

away, but two days later unwittingly blundered into a minefield south of Newhaven. The U-boat triggered one of the deadly devices and immediately flooded; all forty-eight men aboard were killed.

Mines were found during postwar examination to have been more successful during March 1945 than previously had been accepted by examination of U-boat records. As well as *U275*, both *U260* and *U1021* were lost to defensive mine barrages within a day of each other.

Oberleutnant zur See William Holpert's *U1021* had left Bergen on 20 February 1945 for its first war patrol in British inshore waters following an abortive attempt in mid-February due to *schnorchel* failure. Like many other U-boats engaged on this perilous campaign, there is no record of any signals having been received from

U1021 after the boat's departure from port. On 1 March BdU advised the boat to proceed towards the sea area off southwest Ireland as a holding area pending further redirection. A week later *U1021* was allocated the operational area along the coastal convoy route on both sides of Land's End. The main operational area was between Cape Cornwall and the Cape Cornwall Bank. Although *U1021* failed to answer a request on 10 March for a routine passage report when passing to the west of Ireland on its way south, BdU nevertheless believed the boat to have arrived in its operational area. On 14 April, assuming *U1021* to have, by then, already commenced its return to base, it was routinely allocated to Trondheim as the port of destination. When the boat failed to return to port, it was posted as missing on 5 May 1945 with effect from the same day.

After the war the Allied A/S Assessment Committee attributed the loss of *U1021* to a series of depth-charge attacks by the frigates HMSs *Rupert* and *Conn* on 30 March 1945. However, this attack was later assigned to the destruction of *U965* after the wreck was found and identified. It was only later that the wreck of *U1021* was discovered in the position of the British minefields off Padstow, the boat's bow completely blown away from the rest of the hull. On the night of 14 March 1945 the merchantman SS *Rolsborg* was passing Trevose Head when it reported hearing a loud explosion; large oil slicks were subsequently spotted.

There was no mistaking the cause of the destruction of *U260* south of Ireland. *Oberleutnant zur See* Klaus Becker had sailed his boat from Horten on 18 February bound for Liverpool as *Dieselmaschinist* Werner Banisch remembered:

My main memory is from 13 March 1945. That date is very significant to me and I have always celebrated my second birthday on that date. Our crew only just escaped disaster.

Our order was to attack British battleships in Liverpool. Of course we were informed of this at sea and not before leaving port. I think we were chosen because our boat got into the port of Reykjavik some operations before. There, we had informed our leaders about American warships without attacking them with torpedoes. We were on our way toward Liverpool when the mine hit us near Fastnet Rock.

It happened at a depth of 80 metres – which was the regular depth for dangerous operations – so I was off duty at the time as we were running on electric motors. The mine destroyed the boat's bow and it dropped sharply toward the seafloor with the water that we were taking in. The outside hull had been destroyed and although the pressure hull wasn't totally holed, we were still leaking badly. We reached a depth of 192 metres. Fortunately we didn't hit any rocks down there!

Twice we tried to turn up tightly toward the surface, but we couldn't reach it. We ran the electric motors in full reverse and blew high-pressure air into the intact diving tanks. But every time the boat was near the surface the air pressure inside the tanks was higher than the water pressure outside and the air kept escaping the

Oberleutnant zur See Klaus Becker (left) atop his conning tower on *U260*.

U-boat, water filled the tanks and we would sink again. Finally the *schnorchel* saved us. We had had it installed the mission before and used it between France and Norway – but we used it terribly! It was difficult to say the least.

With the help of the *schnorchel* we started the diesel engines at a depth of about fourteen metres. Once they were running, we channelled the exhaust gases into the diving tanks, which forced out the water and allowed the boat to become light enough to reach the surface. Our captain, Klaus Becker, headed for the Irish coast and we were able to hold her there for long enough for all the crew to abandon ship into the life rafts. I was standing by the diesel engine throughout this time so I was one of the last ones to leave the U-boat. An eight-man lifeboat awaited me, but there were eleven of us! We rowed all night and reached the lighthouse at Galley Head as the first boat. So that is my second birthday.

Becker had managed to communicate his predicament by radio to BdU, who had finally received proof of deep-laid minefields. Fresh reminders of previously issued instructions for traversing areas known to be mined were issued; U-boats were instructed not go deeper than thirty metres in confirmed danger zones; BdU considered it unlikely that surface mines would be present lest they cause damage to Allied military and merchant vessels.

The confirmed loss of *U260* and radio silence from virtually all of the other U-boats in British waters during March prompted Dönitz to consider a full withdrawal of U-boats from coastal waters, allowing those who had found enemy ASW defences too strong to penetrate to return to Norway. Defeat loomed once more, though the true scale of the losses would not become completely apparent until the conflict was over. But the retreat would not be immediate, and the month of March continued to exact a bloody tool on both protagonists.

CHAPTER SIX

A New Dawn

DURING FEBRUARY *U1019* had experienced a close brush with disaster courtesy of enemy aircraft west of the North Channel. On 16 February the boat was attacked by a Liberator, which deployed both a sonobuoy and 'Fido' homing torpedo. Fortunately for the German crew, *Oberleutnant zur See* Hans Rinck managed to evade the attacker and *U1019* slipped away into the Irish Sea. On 12 March Rinck reported an 8,000-ton steamer sunk by torpedoes, but Allied records leave it as unconfirmed. It was the sole recorded 'victory' for Rinck; *U1019* put into Trondheim on 9 April 1945.

There were four U-boats operational within the North Channel during February: *U296*, *U483*, *U1003* and *U1064*. With no results obtained, and an increasing ASW presence within the area, BdU released the four U-boats to allow them to roam either into the Firth of Clyde or the Irish Sea in search of targets. To no avail, for *U483* returned empty handed to Norway on 26 March, while *U1003* and *U296* were both lost and *U1064* returned to Norway after sinking a single Icelandic freighter after a brief stint as weather boat. It had been a costly expenditure for BdU, though the extent of this cost was not yet suspected within the Berlin office.

Kapitänleutnant Hans-Joachim Schwebcke's *U714* had been operational since October 1943 within the Atlantic battleground, and was one of the first wave of U-boats that sailed for British waters from France in August 1944. In all of that time, however, from four war patrols, the boat had sunk nothing, but had been hunted and harried by air and surface forces. Schwebcke had taken his boat from Horten for his second British patrol on 3 March, heading for Scotland's eastern seaboard where he stalked the Firth of Forth. Seven days after putting to sea he made the first successful attack of the boat's career when he torpedoed and sank the Norwegian auxiliary minesweeper *Nordhalv II* off Dundee. The Norwegian had been part of the dispersed convoy FS1753d, and was serving with the Dundee-based 71st Minesweeper Group when *U714* hit her. Four Norwegian crewmen, one British gunner and the commander, Lieutenant A Olsen, were killed. Ironically it was Olsen's first voyage as captain, having transferred from the often perilous duty aboard MTBs. The seventeen shocked survivors were rescued by another Norwegian minesweeper *Syrian*. It may not have been the most glorious of combat victories for Schwebcke, but it was a triumph nonetheless. And he wasn't finished yet.

On 14 March *U714* torpedoed and sank the 1,226-ton Swedish vessel SS *Magne* from convoy FS1756. Ten of the twenty-one men aboard were killed in the attack and the nearby destroyer HMS *Wivern* closed to rescue survivors. Also nearby was the South African frigate HMSAS *Natal* which was engaged on shake-down trials after sailing for the first time from the Tyne bound for Scapa Flow. Ironically, the South African was then due to head to Tobermory on the Isle of Mull for anti-submarine training. Shortly after leaving port a southbound vessel, SS *Sheaf Crown*, signalled that a merchantman had just been torpedoed and sunk in her vicinity, five miles to the north of HMSAS *Natal*, near St Abbs' harbour. *Natal* immediately turned to investigate, the crew still familiarising themselves with their new ship as action stations was sounded.

When *Natal* arrived at the scene, HMS *Wivern* was already rescuing the

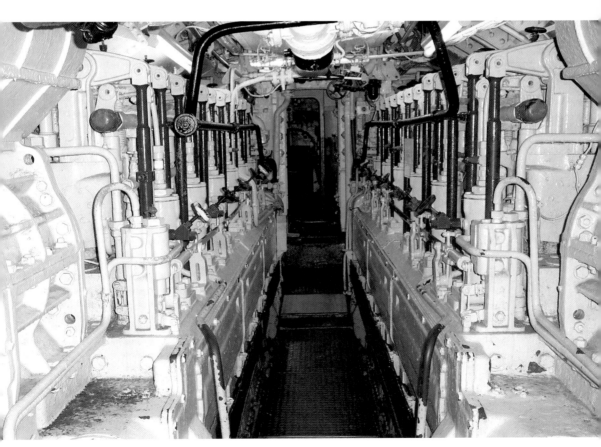

The engine blocks aboard a Type VIIC/41. The conventional U-boats' Achilles Heel was its reliance on diesel propulsion.

survivors. Shortly after offering assistance the South African's ASDIC operator established a firm contact off the port beam, using her new-type 'Sword' scanning equipment (Set 147B). This was an improvement on the so-called 'Q-attachment' that had been introduced to standard ASDIC equipment during 1942. This had enabled the sonar to detect deep-diving U-boats – a capability revealed to the Allies by the capture of *U570* – that could operate below ordinary ASDIC range. In 1943, the Type 147 was introduced, which operated at fifty kilohertz and could provide a lateral as well as vertical fix on the target. *Natal* immediately attacked the located U-boat using its new Squid mortar and, after firing two salvoes, a quantity of light diesel oil and pieces of wreckage – including a metal tank – broke the surface, and ASDIC contact was immediately lost. Schwebcke and his fifty crewmen were entombed on the seabed. Their grave was hammered by depth charges two days later when a hunter-killer group from the Tyne, led by HMS *Ascension*, depth charged the position of the attack, bringing fresh debris to the surface, which included a hand-carved shield depicting a diving U-boat that was later forwarded to *Natal* as a trophy of its maiden kill.

To the west *Oberleutnant zur See* Werner Strübing's *U1003* was engaged in patrolling the North Channel. On 20 March the U-boat was running on *schnorchel* as it had for the majority of its time in action, when ensuing events clearly showed the danger of insufficient ability to make clear observations (whether due to poor sea and weather conditions or inadequate vigilance by the crew) and nullified hydrophone use by running submerged on diesel engines. Canadian frigates HMCSs *Beacon Hill*, *Sussexvale*, *New Glasgow* and *Ribble* had all sailed that night from Londonderry bound for training at Loch Alsh. Shortly after the group passed the Foyle buoy they formed into line astern with a mile gap between each ship, zigzagging independently at fourteen knots with CAT gear streamed – (Countermeasure Anti-Torpedo) was a towed array of clanking metal bars that masked propeller noise and thus acted as a decoy for acoustic torpedoes. Suddenly lookouts aboard *New Glasgow* sighted the periscope and *schnorchel* of *U1003* and immediately turned to intercept, ordering a shallow-set depth-charge pattern to be made ready. However, the target was only twenty metres from the ship's bow, and the call to action stations had barely been made when the frigate rammed *U1003*; the impact was so strong that hammock lashings snapped in the Canadian crew quarters. The U-boat had impacted just below the frigate's bridge, twisting the propeller shaft and holing the hull; water immediately began to flood into the disabled warship. *New Glasgow* managed to limp back to Londonderry, reaching port two days later after an anxious transit for officers and crew, since the frigate would have been extremely vulnerable to U-boat attack. Its rammed opponent had disappeared. A massive U-boat hunt immediately took place with fourteen Allied ships from Escort Groups C4, 25 and 26 scouring the sea area for hours for what must have been a badly damaged U-boat. Depth charges at the scene failed to produce any evidence of a sinking.

As the conning tower of this stricken U-boat sinks lower into the sea,
its British attacker closes to rescue survivors.

Unbeknown to the Allied hunters Strübing and his crew were still near the location of the collision, but in dire shape. The unexpected impact had thrown the German crew off their feet, and severely damaged both the *schnorchel* and periscope which were leaking badly. *U1003* was immediately bottomed where it remained for forty-eight hours amid the periodic depth-charge attacks, while the crew struggled to control the boat's flooding.

Early on 22 March Strübing managed to lift his boat from the seabed and attempted to surface to assess the damage to the boat's superstructure. It was immediately apparent to the shocked U-boat crew that they had been badly damaged by the impact, but sounds of an approaching ship quickly forced *U1003* back underwater where it continued leaking badly while creeping northward. Due to its inoperative *schnorchel*, *U1003* was forced to surface periodically to recharge its batteries, but was constantly forced to cut this time short as the ASW ships continued their hunt in the area. Finally the batteries failed as charge was expended, and the crew faced the ominous threat of chlorine-gas poisoning from cracked and flooding cells. Electrically operated bilge pumps no longer functioned and in the early hours of 23 March, the U-boat surfaced where the crew abandoned ship letting it sink to the depths once more. The commander and fourteen crewmembers were lost, while thirty-three men were picked up by HMCS

Thetford Mines. Two of them – *Kapitänleutnant* Karl Meier and *Maschinenober-gefreiter* Paul Zander – later died and were buried at sea from the Canadian's deck.

Oberleutnant zur See Heinz Buhse's U-boat *U399* had torpedoed and damaged the American Liberty ship SS *James Eagan Layne* from convoy TBC103 northeast of Eddystone Rock on 21 March, while the freighter was steaming as the lead ship in the convoy's starboard column. A single torpedo struck the freighter's starboard side throwing a pillar of water over the main deck and blowing hatch covers into the air. The hull was cracked and the propeller shaft and steering gear damaged. Fifteen minutes after the torpedo had hit the ship was abandoned, though the master, fourteen crewmen and four armed guards reboarded the ship one hour later and prepared the freighter for towing to Whitesand Bay. There she was later beached and settled on the bottom with only her masts and stack showing at high water. The ship was declared a total loss.

Buhse escaped retribution from this attack but on 26 March attacked convoy BTC108 west of the Lizard and sank Dutch MV *Pacific*, a small 362-ton merchant ship. A hunt by 3rd Escort Group followed, and *U399*, within fifteen minutes of the Dutch vessel being hit was destroyed; *U399* was depth charged by HMS *Duckworth* in Mount's Bay near Land's End in the English Channel. A single survivor, *Oberbootsmaat* Gerhard Pflock, was rescued.

The surface ships of 3rd Escort Group would claim another U-boat kill within days and almost at the same spot, when they reacted to the torpedoing of HMCS *Teme*, which had been hit by a T5 *Zaunkönig* torpedo while escorting convoy BTC111 off Land's End. The Canadian frigate lost sixty feet of her stern and was later towed to Falmouth and declared a total loss. Ironically, the attacker *U315* wriggled free from the immediate and protracted U-boat hunt, which instead produced the destruction of *U1169* and its entire crew by depth charges from HMS *Duckworth*. *U315* on the other hand had had one of the more successful March U-boat patrols, sinking the 6,996-ton British merchant ship SS *Empire Kingsley* on 22 March after attacking convoy TBC103 northwest of Land's End with a spread of LUT torpedoes. Surviving both this and the attack on HMCS *Teme*, *U315* returned to Norway on 24 April. There, in Trondheim harbour, the boat that had been in action since February 1944 and was plagued by diesel-engine problems, was decommissioned on 1 May.

On 27 March two more U-boats fell to the enemy. *U722* was sunk by depth charges from HMSs *Byron*, *Fitzroy* and *Redmill* of 21st Escort Group east of Eriskay in the Hebrides. *U905* was destroyed in the Minch Channel by depth charges from the frigate HMS *Conn*. Both boats were lost with their entire complement. *U905* had had no success on its patrol, while *U722* had torpedoed and sunk a single British freighter, the 2,190-ton SS *Inger Toft*, on 16 March after attacking convoy RU156 in the southern part of the Little Minch.

Three more U-boats were to be lost before the end of a disastrous month for BdU. On 29 March Liberator 'O' of 224 Squadron sighted a wake at three miles range northeast of the Færoes. After closing to within a mile it was positively identified as a *schnorchel*. Depth charges were readied and dropped in a text-book attack. The stern of a U-boat rose to the surface amid the churning water before sliding to the seabed. Later a sonobuoy pattern was laid over the reported position of the U-boat, which detected the sound of banging and machinery noises, as well as an intermittent propeller beat. But none of the forty-six crew of *U1106* was ever seen again. On 30 March *U965* was also destroyed, this time lost to depth charges from HMSs *Rupert* and *Conn* north of Scotland. Again, there were no survivors. The final U-boat lost was *U296*, which had been missing since 12 March, possibly to minefields laid within the Minches where the boat was directed to patrol. None of these three boats had achieved anything while at sea.

The entire British inshore campaign seemed to be achieving little. Both *U1005* and *U978* patrolled the Minches to little effect in February and into March. Both reported a ship sunk apiece, the former an escort destroyer sunk off Cape Wrath, the latter a 6,000-ton freighter on 4 April; neither claim is substantiated by Allied records. *Kapitänleutnant* Günther Pults's *U978* also attempted to attack an *Illustrious*-class aircraft carrier on 6 April. It fired three LUT torpedoes, though only end-of-run detonations were heard within the submerged U-boat. However, despite their poor combat showing, at least both these boats survived what would transpire to be their final combat patrols. They returned to Norway where the long wait for space in hard-pressed and over-subscribed shipyards for the necessary overhaul of their U-boats would prevent either taking to sea again before the war's end.

The remaining four U-boats that had sailed and were at sea during February – *U246*, *U953*, *U1002* and *U1195* – were all concentrated on the English Channel, an area to which eleven of the 27 U-boats despatched in February had sailed. Of these two would fail to return and only one would achieve a sinking. *Oberleutnant zur See* Herbert Werner's *U953* entered the western portion of the English Channel during March after the arduous *schnorchel* voyage from Norway. Werner later wrote a book about his experiences in the U-boats, *Iron Coffins*, which remains highly regarded despite some controversy in certain quarters regarding its historical veracity. Nonetheless his description of that patrol to the English Channel accurately portrays the daunting situation in which the U-boat men found themselves, including the difficulties of running on *schnorchel* with an unskilled chief engineer handling the delicate task of accurate depth keeping:

> For a while, *U953* floated peacefully at the designated depth, course northwest, direction Atlantic. But soon the Chief demonstrated his inexperience and, worse, his lack of aptitude. Incapable of holding the boat level on *schnorchel* depth, he repeatedly exposed her to the watchful Tommies and allowed her to tumble down toward the floor. Each time the Chief disturbed the buoyancy, it sent the whole company through new tortures. The vacuum it created sent the men twisting and vomiting in agony while they were tossed about wildly by the

boat's pirouettes. Each time the punishment became unbearable, I again assumed control and again tried to teach my Chief the fundamentals of *schnorchelling*.

We continued our tumultuous progress, though the mission seemed futile. By the time of our sailing, the Allies had called in vast dispersed naval forces and concentrated them in the water around the British Isles. Destroyers in overwhelming numbers were posted near the Shetland and Færoes Islands to catch our few lone wolves, whose comings and goings had been reported beforehand to the British Admiralty by Allied sympathisers or agents. None of our preparations for a spring offensive had remained a secret. During the first days of February, six U-boats had been sunk, all on their first patrol. One by one they sailed into the enemy's bristling defence; they were too slow to evade his skilled air-and-sea teamwork and most of their officers were too inexperienced to know the tricks of survival. The seas around England had become a sort of private pool in which the British eagerly played their game of killing off a helpless U-boat now and then; and if the hundreds of aircraft and surface vessels failed to sink our boats, then the hundreds of square miles of minefields did.[1]

Werner, and *Oberleutnant zur See* Hans-Heinz Boos in *U1002* both at least survived the torment of sailing the enemy-controlled waters with the almost constant sound of distant depth charges. Their boats returned successfully to Norway at the end of their final patrols, though of course both were empty handed. The days of fluttering victory pennants streaming from raised periscopes seemed almost a bygone age, along with those memories of French ports and battles in the high seas of the mid-Atlantic.

Kapitänleutnant Ernst Raabe's *U246* was not so fortunate, reporting for the final time on 7 March while moving from the fruitless English Channel into the Irish Sea. The boat then vanished, presumed lost during April 1945 south of the Isle of Man. On 30 April the British destroyers HMSs *Hesperus* and *Havelock* depth-charged a reported U-boat contact made by a 201 Squadron Sunderland aircraft, and they were credited with the sinking of *U242* in Admiralty assessments. However, they had in fact bombarded the already dead remains of *U246*, bringing some personal belongings of a crewmember to the surface for recovery.

U1195 experienced slightly more success. *Kapitänleutnant* Ernst Cordes had left Bergen on 25 February, traversing the seas north of the British Isles bound ultimately for the English Channel, which he finally entered after twenty-seven days. Cordes had operated in the English Channel before as commander of *U763* during the weeks following the D-Day landings. Then, his boat had actually drifted off course into the British naval anchorage of Spithead, within easy sight of Portsmouth; he succeeded in extricating himself from possibly one of the most dangerous areas for a U-boat to have found itself in. His experience of the difficult navigational conditions found within the Channel at least appeared to offer his largely inexperienced crew slightly greater odds of survival. On 21 March convoy TBC102 was passing in heavy fog about nine miles from the Lizard when Cordes fired, hitting the first ship in the convoy's port column, the 7,194-ton Liberty ship SS *John R Park*, which was carrying the convoy commodore. A single torpedo struck the ship's port side, throwing water and sand ballast over the bridge and onto the main deck as well as cracking the hull and destroying the aft life rafts. The American vessel's steering gear was also wrecked and the propeller shaft buckled in the explosion. Swinging out of line the ship began settling by the stern as all seventy-five men aboard abandoned ship. Despite subsequent attempts to save her, the ship sank stern first about six hours after *U1195* had launched its attack. Meanwhile Cordes had slipped from the scene.

U1195 did not announce its presence again until the early morning of 6 April near Portsmouth. The U-boat was stationary, bottomed and lying in wait in one of the Channel's busiest transit points. The propeller noise of convoy VWP16 brought Cordes to periscope depth to investigate, whereupon a small coastal convoy of six destroyers escorting a single ship confronted him. While warships were valid targets, it was the centrepiece of the group that proved the most tempting, the 11,420-ton troopship SS *Cuba* bound from Le Havre to Southampton where she was due to load men for transport to France. The *Cuba* had begun life in French service as part of the Compagnie Générale Trans-atlantique before being taken over by Vichy in June 1940. On 31 October of that year the liner was captured by a British warship and transferred to the Ministry of War Transport where she was converted to a troop transport. Cordes fired two *Zaunkönig* torpedoes, one hitting SS *Cuba*, which had accelerated for harbour, the propeller cavitations drawing the torpedo towards her. Almost miraculously only one man from the 265 aboard was killed in the attack; the ship was abandoned and went under in forty-five metres of water.

This time, however, Cordes was not able to slip the net of retribution from the convoy escorts. He immediately took *U1195* to the bottom, but the surrounding terrain was more shifting sands than rock, and in such shallow waters the U-boat's hull bounced back a clean ASDIC echo to the hunters above. The destroyer HMS *Watchman* carried out a perfect Hedgehog attack and the hull of the U-boat was fatally ruptured. Water immediately began to flood into *U1195* and the bow compartment was knee deep within two minutes. Cordes ordered the compartment sealed as he vainly tried to lift his boat from the bottom in order to abandon and scuttle her. Finally, with water steadily rising, electrical systems failing and deadly chlorine gas seeping through the hull from flooded batteries he ordered the crew to prepare to make a submerged escape. The terrified men clustered in both the control room and stern torpedo compartment, waiting in the darkness for the water to rise sufficiently to allow pressure equalisation between the interior and exterior of the boat, whereupon the outer hatches could be opened. Finally equalisation was reached, the hatch was opened, and more cold water flooded into the U-boat as the first men swam for the surface. Eighteen men survived the ascent, while Cordes and thirty others remained within their shattered U-boat tomb. His success against the troopship was later confirmed by B-Dienst interception of Allied radio transmissions.

Ten U-boats had been sunk in British waters during February, a further fourteen during March. For these twenty-four U-boats – representing 1,020 men killed, and 120 captured – the Kriegsmarine's inshore British campaign had managed to sink a confirmed nineteen merchant ships totalling 65,389 tons; two corvettes; one minesweeper and one converted trawler during the same period. It was a ruinous exchange rate that could not be supported. And it showed no sign of improving as the first eight days of April demonstrated with the loss of *U1195*, *U321*, *U242*, *U1001* and *U774*.

U321 was sunk on its first patrol on 2 April southwest of Ireland by a Wellington of 304 (Polish) Squadron. The aircraft's navigator spotted the U-boat's *schnorchel* and periscope in the midst of a rain shower as the Wellington investigated an intermittent radar contact. The aircraft was approaching from a mile away when the U-boat submerged, perhaps having spotted the threat. Six depth charges were dropped along its projected path as the nose gunner opened fire on the shallow-diving U-boat. *Oberleutnant zur See* Fritz Berends and his forty crewmen were killed.

Oberleutnant zur See Heinrich Riedel had taken *U242* from Kristiansand on 4 March on the boat's first war patrol under his command. Riedel was by no means inexperienced, having entered the U-boat service in June 1941 and served as second watch officer aboard training boat *U612* until that boat's sinking after a collision with *U444* in the Baltic. Two men were lost in the accident, the remainder, including Riedel, transferred to combat boat *U230*, which saw action within the Atlantic and the difficult battleground of the Mediterranean Sea. Though *U242* was Riedel's first command the boat had already been on a war footing since May 1944 captained by *Oberleutnant zur See* Karl-Wilhelm Pancke. During the D-Day landings *U242* had been part of the eleven-strong *Mitte* group that had formed a patrol line stretching from Trondheim to Lindesnes in anticipation of an Allied assault on Norway. Following this, the boat was transferred to Finland as part of 8th U-Flotilla where it operated from Reval and Helsinki on torpedo and minelaying patrols, as well as landing saboteurs behind Russian lines. When at the beginning of March Riedel assumed command of *U242*, curiously the boat was assigned not to the 11th U-flotilla but 5th U-Flotilla, ostensibly a training unit. His tenure as commander was not a long one. On 5 April at 0715hrs, *U242* detonated a mine in the mine barrage QZX within the St George's Channel; the fate of the boat remained unknown for years after the end of the war.

By curious coincidence the next U-boat destroyed – on 8 April – was also of the 5th U-Flotilla and had had a combat career similar to *U242*'s. It too had taken part in the *Mitte* group and served in the Baltic Sea operating from Reval, Danzig

U-boat officers in Bergen during the final days of the war. From left to right: Günter Pulst (*U978*), Rolf Thomsen (*U1202*), Horst von Schroeter (*U2506*), Herbert Pankin (LI *U861*), Jürgen Oesten (*U861*) Adalbert Schnee (*U2511*), Konrad Lüdes (IWO *U2511*), Reinhardt König (LI *U2506*), Günter Lüth (*U1057*), Heinrich Lehmann-Willenbrock (Chief 11th U-Flotilla), Gerd Suhren (LI *U2511*).

and Libau. In March 1945 *Kapitänleutnant* Ernst-Ulrich Blaudow had taken *U1001* to Kristiansand in preparation for its first patrol of British waters. Once at sea and bound for the English Channel, *U1001* was one of seven U-boats diverted to a holding area in the Western Approaches where the boat was found on 8 April and sunk by frigates HMSs *Byron* and *Fitzroy* of 21st Escort Group with all forty-six crew lost. *Kapitänleutnant* Werner Sauskimat's *U774*, on its first war patrol, was another of the seven redirected boats; it was found and destroyed by depth charges from frigates HMSs *Bentinck* and *Calder* of the 4th Escort Group that same day.

Ironically the two lost boats had been diverted away from the area perceived to be the most perilous by Dönitz. The scale of the fresh disaster that had befallen his inshore waters campaign had slowly begun to dawn on Dönitz and his BdU Staff. And it was not solely in this theatre of operations that the U-boat continued to suffer. Though he did not know it yet, fifty-seven U-boats would be lost in the month of April in all areas. Thirty-three were to be sunk at sea while twenty-four were destroyed by air raids or other causes. In return, the U-boats would sink only thirteen Allied merchant ships. During the late afternoon of 7 April Dönitz met with Hitler in the depths of the Führerbunker beneath the Reich Chancellery in Berlin to assess the continuation strategy of the U-boat campaign, while still awaiting the long awaited miracle of the electro-boats:[2]

Using a submarine chart *Kapitän zur See* [Heinz] Assmann [SKL Operational liaison to OKW] reports on the present submarine situation. There are now twenty-five submarines in the operational area, thirty-seven vessels are on the way there, twenty-three are returning, and sixteen additional submarines are lying in Norwegian harbours. This makes a total of 101 submarines in operation. The C-in-C Navy reports in this connection that the fact that we have concentrated our submarines in the coastal waters around the British Isles, as has been the case for several months now, has caused the enemy to also concentrate his defences in these areas. Although enemy defence forces can no longer find our submarines by locating devices, as soon as the submarine discloses its position by attacking, such a concentrated defence action sets in that the vessel is often lost . . . Because of their low underwater speed the old types of submarine cannot escape once they are discovered, but the new types can leave the danger area at high speed and thus escape the concentrated enemy defence.

To counter the above situation, the C-in-C Navy intends to take the submarines out of the coastal areas for the present and to send Type VIIs to the open ocean just west of the British Isles . . . His purpose in doing this is twofold: on the one hand he hopes that the submarines will be able to make successful surprise attacks in new regions with only slight defence opposition; on the other hand he wants to force the enemy to disperse their defence forces and thus to improve the submarine warfare conditions in the waters near the British coast.[3]

During February and March only thirty of the 114 U-boats that sailed into the Atlantic, either for more far-flung destinations or for the hook southeast into British waters, reported their arrival in the Atlantic. Fewer still made reports during their return passages. Fears for many boats that had not been contacted since January and were thus at the end of their operational endurance were mounting, while confirmation from *U260* that new minefields were a greater danger than supposed resulted in the slowly dawning comprehension of the reality of the situation at sea within British waters. Thus, with several confirmed losses and ominous silence from the remaining U-boats at sea Dönitz ordered a withdrawal from coastal waters. On 30 March and 10 April seven U-boats planned for the English Channel – *U326*, *U774*, *U776*, *U826*, *U1001*, *U1063* and *U1107* – were diverted to the new hunting areas 200 and 300 miles west of the Channel entrance. On 15 April six more boats that were headed for the North Channel – *U293*, *U636*, *U956*, *U1017*, *U1105* and *U1305* – were also redirected, this time to the seas thirty to 100 miles north of Donegal Bay. Three U-boats bound for the Irish Sea – *U325*, *U825* and *U1023* – were granted operational freedom of movement.

As the disengagement began the destruction of U-boats at sea continued. *Kapitänleutnant* Hans-Joachim Gutteck's *U1024* had been in the Irish Sea since late March, claiming its first kill on 5 April with the sinking of one unidentified, and unconfirmed, corvette. Two days later Gutteck torpedoed the American Liberty ship SS *James W Nesmith* from convoy HX346 north-northwest of Holyhead. The freighter was a valuable target carrying 3,375 tons of tobacco, fertilizer, lumber, crated aircraft parts and eight P47 aircraft as deck cargo. The torpedo hit the ship to port, damaging the steering gear and causing immediate flooding. But the Liberty ship stubbornly refused to sink and with all crew and passengers still on board was towed to Holyhead by HMCS *Belleville*. She was beached and later refloated and towed to Liverpool for repair. Gutteck, perhaps unwisely, remained in the same general area, and on 12 April attacked convoy BB80 sailing from the Clyde to Bristol. Gutteck fired a full salvo of torpedoes and reported three ships hit; two sunk of 8,000 and 12,000 tons each and a third damaged. In actuality he had hit the American SS *Will Rogers* that was hauling 4,995 tons of general cargo. While one torpedo was seen to pass astern of the ship a single torpedo hit on the starboard side and caused extensive flooding. Again, however, it was not a mortal blow and *Will Rogers* was also towed to Holyhead and beached alongside Gutteck's earlier victim. The latest Liberty ship to be left high and dry was also refloated and towed to Liverpool where she was repaired and returned to service. The two ships were the last of the Second World War to be torpedoed within the Irish Sea.

But Gutteck had once more confirmed his position to the Allies, and frigates arrived to begin the hunt several hours afterward. Proven strategy for the U-boats was to depart the scene at all possible haste before strong ASW groups could achieve saturation coverage of the area. Gutteck apparently had not been able to place enough distance between *U1024* and his pursuers – ships of 2nd and 8th Escort Groups – as, that evening, the U-boat was detected by HMS *Loch Glendhu* of 8th Escort Group. Although the frigate's advanced Type 147B ASDIC was not working, a Squid attack was still immediately launched at 2042hrs and three minutes later the stricken shape of *U1024* burst through the surface and came under immediate fire from all of the Escort Group ships. HMS *Loch Achray* closed to deliver a pattern of depth charges as the German crew emerged on deck. Gutteck was the first to reach the conning tower, leading his men into a maelstrom of gunfire and being hit in the hand. As his crew began throwing themselves over the side the Allied ships checked their fire, though for Gutteck the situation proved all too much and he shot himself in the head.

Beneath the fleeing German crew *U1024* was not sinking and an opportunity immediately presented itself to 8th Escort Group who despatched a boarding party from HMS *Loch More*. The badly damaged U-boat was secured and the British sailors lowered themselves into the battered interior, retrieving what were considered 'valuable documents' and, apparently, holding the surviving crewmen below decks on *U1024*. *Loch More* took *U1024* in tow toward Douglas on the Isle of Man, but as the weather deteriorated the ships became shrouded in thick fog, during which the towline parted and *U1024* foundered twenty-three miles north-west of Holyhead. Eight of the German crew had been killed, an unknown number during the actual armed boarding, while the boat's second watch officer, five senior ratings and thirty-one junior ratings were rescued.

Despite the late stage that the war at sea had reached by April 1945, it was still an unusual event for a U-boat to be successfully boarded and taken in tow. The loss of Gutteck atop his conning tower no doubt contributed to the temporary capture of *U1024*. The loss of both the chief engineer and first watch officer also conspired to prevent the successful scuttling of the boat. As recently as 9 January 1945 BdU had issued fresh instructions to U-boat crews, recorded as an appendix within the BdU KTB:

> The enemy's interest in new devices, the 'M' cypher and cypher material is such that he tries in every way to get alongside submarines unable to submerge or unmaneouverable and even submarines which are sinking.
>
> Returned prisoners of war report that as soon as the submarine has surfaced, the enemy lowers a boat and tries to come alongside, usually under cover of light arms fire. In several cases the enemy was known to have come alongside a slowly sinking submarine which had already been abandoned by the crew.
>
> Therefore: If a submarine which is not battle-worthy and is unmaneouverable is forced to surface in the vicinity of enemy sea forces, in order to disembark the crew, measures are to be taken to ensure that she is then sunk at once under all circumstances. The Captain and the Engineering Officer and the most experienced members of the crew are to remain on board until the very last moment before sinking.

Also active within the Irish Sea during March was *Kapitänleutnant* Rolf Thomsen's *U1202* on its second British patrol. *Maschinenmaat* Anton Wrobel, his duty station at number-two electric motor, later recalled this arduous voyage:

> It was mid-March and the Kommandant had us running at periscope depth, when a ship engaged on the 'outer coastal watch', an American destroyer came towards us. The Kommandant was convinced that he hadn't seen us as he continued on his normal zig-zag course . . . We stayed at thirty metres and the destroyer kept getting closer. Finally the Kommandant fired a T5 (*Zaunkönig*) . . . from the stern tube as the destroyer was now behind us. A hit! We heard the detonation and clear sinking noises. That same day we hit an escort carrier and heard sinking noises. We decided to stay in that area where we had had so much success. Five days later there was another convoy and we sank three steamers totalling 21,000 tons. Three days later the next convoy. We stayed at periscope depth in our attack position, the torpedo tube caps were open and the shooting solution had been put into the *Vorhaltrechner* (Torpedo computer) and fed to the torpedoes in their tubes. Suddenly an English destroyer comes towards us. That old game. We dived down to thirty metres and there was barely water over the periscope head. The destroyer came straight for us. We heard the 'ping-ping' of

Kapitänleutnant Rolf Thomsen of *U1202* receives the Oak Leaves to his Knight's Cross from FdU West Rösing on 29 April 1945. The reality of his combat achievements was less than impressive despite his aggressively handled patrol, though even survival at sea demonstrated great skill by 1945.

Thomsen and Rösing, 11th U-Flotilla commander *Fregattenkapitän* Heinrich Lehmann-Willenbrock second from left.

his sonar throughout the hull. It was chilling. From the listening room came a last message 'Destroyer, 5-4-3-2-1-0'. At the moment the ship veered away. We were overjoyed. Back we went to periscope depth and the Kommandant went into the conning tower to use the attack periscope. He reacquired the convoy and corrected the firing solution in the torpedoes as the target had moved on its way a little. Then the command came: 'Tubes 1 to 4 ready for underwater firing, Fire!' Each tube was fired within eight seconds. During this time as the torpedoes left the boat the 'torpedo cells' were flooded, the additional weight taken in to replace that of the torpedoes and to keep the boat on an even keel. The boat lay stopped and in that eight seconds the Kommandant looked around with the attack periscope to search for threats in the sea and air . . . All he saw was a grey wall. The destroyer behind us had stopped and switched off most of his machinery. The Englander had then spotted our periscope with his glasses. Of course with nearly all of our machinery also turned off, the only direction our boat could go in was down, there were no other possibilities . . . [The Kommandant] yelled 'Alarm! Take her deep!' As we dived the first detonation hit us, it was only our good luck that the boat was offering a slim silhouette as a target so they had not fixed us. Then another explosion . . .

U1202 was battered by depth charges as it dropped rapidly in the water column. Disaster nearly overtook them when it was discovered that the torpedo in tube four had not left the boat and was a 'hot runner' with propeller turning. The crew needed to get the stuck 'eel' out of their boat but could only do so in shallow depths where the compressed air pressure would be capable of forcing the torpedo out and the outer caps could be closed. The dive was arrested and the torpedo crew struggled to release the weapon. Miraculously, *U1202* survived and managed to free the torpedo and leave the scene without further damage. The salvo Thomsen had fired before being forced to evade retribution resulted in two claimed steamers sunk totalling 14,000 tons. The next day *U1202* encountered a hunter-killer group and in the ensuing battle claimed to have sunk two corvettes and achieved a hit on another destroyer.

It had been a remarkable patrol for Rolf Thomsen and his men. The claims from *U1202*'s second war patrol amounted to one destroyer, two corvettes and two steamers sunk, two hits on an escort carrier, followed by audible sinking noises which prompted a claim of a possible kill, and another destroyer damaged by a single hit. *U1202* headed back towards Norway, approaching Bergen on 27 April.

We had received a message warning us of an English submarine that had fired at U-boats entering or leaving port. We finally left periscope depth and began to surface the watch getting ready to head up top. Suddenly from the listening room: 'Torpedo! Full ahead, take her down! All men forward.' The men ran like rabbits to the bow room. In the electric motor room the stern was not even

U2321 undergoing rust treatment in Hamburg, late 1944.

under water when I heard two torpedoes fly past. The Kommandant then resumed his course for home, surfacing only in safer waters on the way to our base. It had been the longest time that I had been without daylight when I went above decks. How beautiful the world was, how green the water, brown mountains, white snow; a gloriously colourful world after such a long time with nothing but electric lights.[4]

Thomsen and his crew were fêted upon their return, one of the few U-boats to enter port flying sinking pennants from its raised periscope, and decorations soon followed such an incredibly aggressive and successful voyage. On 27 April Thomsen and several of his men including *Maschinenmaat* Anton Wrobel, were awarded their bronze U-boat combat clasps, while other, less experienced members of the crew received the coveted U-boat combat badge. Three days later FdU West Hans Rudolf Rösing presented Thomsen with Oak Leaves to his Knight's Cross won during the previous patrol. Six Iron Cross First Class and eight Second Class were awarded to various members of the crew. Thomsen's was the 852nd such award to be made and the penultimate for a U-boat commander.[5] The final irony was that, despite the accounts of crewmembers aboard *U1202* and Thomsen's own claims, not a single sinking was confirmed by Allied records. *Kapitänleutnant* Rolf Thomsen, recipient of the Knight's Cross with Oak Leaves, had only a single confirmed sinking to his name: the 7,176-ton Liberty ship SS *Dan Beard*. It was the end of combat missions for Thomsen, who transferred from command of *U1202* to a role within the administrative section of 11th U-Flotilla in Bergen.

Oberleutnant zur See Helmut Christiansand's Type VIIC/41 *U1305* was in the

U2321 in transit along the Elbe river, 1944.

North Channel during April on the boat's first war patrol. On 24 April eighty miles from Sligo Christiansand torpedoed the 878-ton British steamer SS *Monmouth Coast*, which was sailing unescorted from Sligo to Liverpool carrying 841 tons of sulphates. The small ship was virtually destroyed by the blast; of the seventeen crew only messroom boy Derek Cragg survived and was rescued by Irish fishermen. It was the sole victory for *U1305*, which was still on station at the war's end.

Several of the U-boats that sailed in March for the British Isles achieved nothing during their patrols, but at least survived in an area that had become increasingly deadly as the Allies mastered the seas around the British Isles once more. *U778*, *U826*, *U1109* and *U776* were all on their first war patrols and made no reported attacks. On 21 March *Kapitänleutnant* Uwe Kock's *U249* departed Bergen for its first war patrol, planned for the English Channel. Two days from port the U-boat came under attack by a flight of RAF Mosquitoes of 235 Squadron, Banff Strike Wing. During the fierce exchange of gunfire that followed, *U249* was damaged, though not before an attacking aircraft, Flight Lieutenant Williams' Mosquito 'Q' was brought down, crashing into the sea. Kock rescued Williams and later transferred him and his own crewmen wounded during the attack to the escort/flak ship *V1703* 'Unitas 5' ashore in Bergen after the boat had returned to port for repairs.

The second Type XXIII to enter combat sailed from Horten on 9 March. *Oberleutnant zur See* Hans-Heinrich Barschkis' *U2321* had arrived in Norway from Kiel four days previously to begin preparation for the boat's inaugural war patrol. Barschkis was bound for the Scottish east coast near St Abbs. On 30 March he made a failed attack on a 5,000-ton freighter, leaving a single torpedo with which to continue his patrol. Six days later he attacked once more, targeting a fast-moving independently sailing freighter that was sailing in ballast from Grangemouth to Blyth, two miles from St Abbs. The single TIIIa (FAT2) torpedo impacted 1,407-ton SS *Gasray* and sent the ship rapidly to the bottom. The merchant ship's master, R E Baker, eleven crewmen and four gunners were rescued, six crewmembers and two gunners lost with their ship. Barschkis was no doubt elated to have not wasted his second torpedo and *U2321* headed back to Norway, docking in Marviken on 13 April. Neither he nor his crew would sail again before the war's end.

The sinking of SS *Gasray* was the second achieved by the small Type XXIII U-boats. Other than this fact there is little to mark the passing of the small steamer or the eight men lost aboard her. The two gunners would be marked on some memorial somewhere, but the dead of the merchant navy have received very little recognition for their ultimate sacrifice. Recently, however, there has been a movement in Sunderland, led by local historian Alan Burns, to have such men of the merchant navy remembered in a memorial. A recent article also illustrated the tragic human side of the all too numerous casualty statistics suffered by both sides of this U-boat campaign:

Hannah Hall has more reason than most to support Alan Burns' call for a merchant navy tribute. Her father, Richard Henry Hopper, was shipwrecked four times during the war – tragically drowning in the final incident.

'My dad's name is on the tribute in London, and in Alan's book, but it would be lovely to have a tribute up here, too', she said. 'The men of the merchant navy risked their lives just as the men in the forces, but they seem to have been rather forgotten.' Richard was born in Jarrow but moved to Sunderland before the war, as he worked on the Wear-based ship SS *Tynehome*.

'He was a donkeyman', said Mrs Hall. 'He was responsible for making sure there was enough steam for the engine. The ship used to take coal to Holland and then return with tinned foods. It was a hard life, but one that he really enjoyed. Richard continued on the *Tynehome* after war broke out, moving vital food supplies and other goods around the country by sea. On January 8, 1940, however, the ship was cut in half by another British ship just outside of Hull during the blackout.

'My dad couldn't swim, but managed to get his arm around a rope-ladder attached to the other ship', said Mrs Hall. 'It was pitch dark, but he was spotted by torchlight and hauled aboard by an Irishman, who saved his life. When he got back home he looked like a black jelly. He was covered in bruises from where he'd hit the ship so many times'.

Richard's doctor forbade him from returning to sea because of his injuries, so he found himself a job at a factory on the Tyne. 'He went for just half a day, then came back and told my mam: "I can't stand that, I'm off back to sea",' recalls Mrs Hall. Richard, then aged about 60, survived two more shipwrecks over the next few years before signing on to the SS *Gasray*.

'He must have had some kind of sixth sense because, after seeing the ship, he

U218 photographed in France. This boat was responsible for the last sinking of a ship attributed to U-boat action – trawler HMT *Kurd* sunk by one of its mines on 10 July 1945.

told us he had to get off it as quickly as possible, as that was the one that would "get him",' said Mrs Hall. 'He was right, too. He was only three hours away from the end of his final voyage when the ship blew up near Blyth in April 1945. Mam was absolutely devastated. I was at Edward Dukes in Nile Street, which made tent pegs and infantry boxes, when I was told I was needed at home,' she said. 'I remember running all along Tatham Street, praying nothing had happened to my dad. Mam was just sitting there when I got home; one of my older sisters had to tell me what had happened.'[6]

The destruction of SS *Gasray*, which was locally attributed to either aircraft, mine or U-boat, seemed all the more poignant to a population that could almost feel the end of the war as a tangible reality. Minelaying was in fact returning to Dönitz's priorities during planning sessions held in Berlin that March.

It had become a trend in U-boat operations that, upon the disengagement of torpedo operations from an area, minelaying was undertaken in its place. To this end five minelaying missions were planned for execution in British waters during April 1945. The Type VIID minelayer *U218* – which had sailed from Brest in August 1944 in the vanguard of the new commitment to inshore British waters –

was to deliver its payload to the Firth of Clyde, *U1065* to Dundee, *U1055* to Cherbourg, *U975* to Hartlepool and *U963* to Portland Bill. The first of these, *Kapitänleutnant* Rupprecht Stock's *U218*, sailed from Bergen on 22 March with a payload of 13 SMA mines, which he successfully placed off Ailsa Craig on 18 April, before arriving back in Norway on 8 May.

The deadly magnetic mines claimed their first victim within two days. The small 200-ton trawler *Ethel Crawford* of the Ardrossan Trawling Co Ltd was destroyed while fishing, all ten men aboard killed. It would not be the last victim that the mines would claim, though months would pass before *U218*'s lethal tally increased.

Fortunately for the Allies, *U218* was the only one of Dönitz's minelaying boats to successfully carry out its mission. The second minelaying U-boat scheduled to depart for the waters off Dundee, the Type VIIC/41 *U1065*, was attacked while sailing from Germany to Norway in preparation for its mission. On 9 April an anti-shipping sweep through the Skaggerak and Kattegat by 143, 235 and 248 Squadrons RAF spotted three U-boats – *U1065*, the Type IXCs *U804* and *U843* – travelling north while surfaced. All three U-boats were immediately attacked by the rocket-firing aircraft and sunk. There were no survivors from any of the U-boats; one of the U-boats exploded with such force that one Mosquito carrying a film unit recording the attack was caught in the explosion and lost. Three others were so badly damaged that they were forced to make emergency landings in Sweden, code-named 'Brighton' in their distress calls. Aboard *U804* was *Kapitänleutnant* Ruprecht Fischer, captain of *U244*, travelling as a passenger back to his boat in Norway.

The remaining U-boats of Dönitz's minelaying force were never called upon to undertake their missions; the end of hostilities nullifying their orders from BdU before leaving port.

The transit points between Germany and Norway had become increasingly perilous with a lethal combination of RAF minelaying and the fast and fierce aircraft of the Banff Strike Wing. With ground mines widespread U-boats were forced by the shallow waters to periodically travel surfaced through the areas of the Kattegat and Skaggerak. There they were denied the protection of *schnorchel* travel and thus they emitted the strong radar signatures that had stricken their war within the Atlantic years before.

Nonetheless, many U-boats succeeded in the perilous transit voyage, guns manned and radar detectors feverishly scanning the skies that now held an ominous threat of sudden and violent air attack. Indeed the first of Dönitz's 'wonder weapons' the Type XXI had succeeded in reaching Norway; *U2511* departing Germany for Horten on 16 March 1945 and reaching harbour two days later. The new design seemed to be on the eve of its baptism of fire under the command of the highly experienced *Korvettenkapitän* Adalbert 'Adi' Schnee and a crack crew. However, as if to mirror the constant reverses suffered by the ambitious

U-boats stationed in Norway faced air attack while in transit as did those vessels used to run supplies between Germany and the Norwegian bases. *U1060*, a Type VIIF torpedo transport, was badly damaged by aircraft near Trondheim, beached and later scuttled.

building and training programme of the Type XXI, its maiden patrol had to be postponed after damage during deep-diving trials off Horten. Chief Naval Construction Advisor Diestelmeier had accompanied *U2511* to Norway, where the boat was scheduled to take advantage of the steep sided Oslo fjord in order to test its performance at depth. This test was performed satisfactorily but had been limited to 160 metres by Diestelmeier as two interior frame rings supporting the pressure hull had been cut away slightly to accommodate a shaft brake. Following the successful completion of the first trials, work was done in Horten at strengthening the frames, causing further delay in the boat being cleared for operations. *U2511* then proceeded onwards to Kristiansand where a second deep-diving test, with no set depth limit, was undertaken to test the improved pressure hull strength at the beginning of April. This time, however, the test was abandoned at 170 metres after loud cracking noises were heard from 160 metres depth, seeming to signify to Diestelmeier that the pressure hull was buckling. *U2511* languished in port while Diestelmeier returned to Kiel to compare the area of concern in *U2511* to other Type XXIs in Kiel. After lengthy discussions, it was found that the cracking noises could be attributed to externally fitted plastic components moving against the elastic pressure hull, and were not actually related to pressure-hull integrity at all. But time – time bought by the Type VIIs in action within coastal waters – was running out for the new U-boats to have any effect in combat at all.

Two more U-boats that had sailed during March were later listed as missing in April. *U396*, which had been assigned weather-reporting duties after patrolling near the Hebrides disappeared without trace, as did *U325*. Initial post-war assessment of the loss of *U325* concluded that the boat had simply vanished, another of the many U-boats to be 'missing in action, whereabouts unknown'. However, recent research by diver Innes McCartney in conjunction with German historian Dr Axel Niestlé seems to have unearthed the whereabouts of the missing U-boat.

Oberleutnant zur See Erwin Dohrn's *U325* had departed Trondheim on 20 March 1945 for its second war patrol in British inshore waters. On 29 March 1945 U-boat Command ordered the boat to occupy an area southwest of Ireland in the Western Approaches with an operational radius of thirty nautical miles. This order was however cancelled the next day and on 31 March 1945 the boat was advised to continue its southward passage west of Ireland. On 7 April 1945 U325 sent the routine passage report indicating that the boat had hauled far to the west on its outbound route. Three days later U-boat Command ordered *U325* to operate on the coastal convoy route on both sides of Land's End from Bull Point to Lizard Head. At the time of the cessation of hostilities U-boat Command still considered *U325* as operational. However, exhaustive research of wrecks discovered have led the two experts to believe that *U325* was another victim of the minefields laid off the Cornish coast, the boat sunk during the second half of April 1945 in the British minefield HW A1.

CHAPTER SEVEN

Der Todeskampf

FIVE U-BOATS sailed into action on April Fool's Day 1945, destined for the death throes of Dönitz's inshore campaign. The war in Europe was staggering towards its culmination in the shattered streets of German towns and cities. During the previous night, 361 Lancasters, 100 Halifaxes and eight Mosquitoes of RAF 1, 6 and 8 Groups attempted to attack the Blohm & Voss shipyards, where the Type XXI U-boats were being assembled, but the target area was completely cloud-covered. Nonetheless, local German reports described 'considerable damage' to houses, factories, energy supplies and communications over a wide area of southern Hamburg and Harburg. The RAF lost eleven aircraft, primarily to an unexpected and increasingly rare Luftwaffe attack at night by day fighters. This was to be Bomber Command's last double-figure aircraft loss of the war from a raid on one city.

On the ground the US First and Ninth Armies linked up at Lippstadt on 1 April; this cut off *Feldmarschall* Model's third-of-a-million troops defending the Ruhr industrial heartland, while the US First Army entered Hamm forty miles northeast of Essen. Within twenty-four hours the British 7th Armoured Division reached the Rhine on the Dortmund-Ems canal sixty miles from Essen. To the east, Russian and Bulgarian troops – the latter erstwhile Allies to Nazi Germany before a change of heart and loyalties in August 1944 – captured the main Hungarian oil-producing regions that fuelled the Wehrmacht. Hungary was cleared of German troops.

At sea *U636* and *U739* sailed on 1 April for the Minches and North Channel, *U1274* for the Firth of Forth, *U293* for the Western Approaches and *U825* for the Irish Sea. *Oberleutnant zur See* Hans-Hermann Fitting's *U1274* followed a tragically familiar pattern for the new U-boats. Twenty-five year old Fitting, a former Marine Artillery officer before beginning a long service within U-boat training establishments, was on his first patrol as a combat commander. It was the maiden voyage for boat, commander and crew and on 16 April Fitting opened fire on convoy FS1784 off England's northeast coast. The 8,966-ton tanker MV *Athelduke* carrying 12,600 tons of molasses, was hit and sank with one man from the forty-seven crew killed. But with his presence betrayed by the attack, Fitting was then hunted by British escort ships; he was found by HMS *Viceroy* and depth-charged into oblivion with all hands. Wireless Operator Kenneth Foster was aboard the British destroyer:

While on the *Viceroy* we sank a U-boat which created a lot of wreckage. There was a huge container that should have contained life rafts, but instead it was full of bottles of schnapps. We sent a presentation of the schnapps to Churchill. He wrote back congratulating us for the attack and thanked us for the brandy. I've still got the Prime Minister's letter, signed by him.

Indeed Churchill had received his gift and replied with a letter on 12 May 1945 which read:

Thank you so much for sending the presentation case of brandy from the U-boat which I shall keep as an interesting souvenir. Will you convey my thanks to captain 'D' Rosyth Escort Force and the Commanding Officer and Ship's Company of HMS *Viceroy* for all the trouble they took in producing the very handsome casket and offer them my congratulations on the successful attack.

U636, a more experienced boat but under the command of new captain *Oberleutnant zur See* Eberhard Schendel, lasted three weeks at sea, patrolling without success west of the North Channel. On 21 April the U-boat was found west-northwest of Bloody Foreland by ships of the 4th Escort Group and sunk with all hands in the ensuing depth-charge attacks.

The final death ride had begun for Dönitz's men during April. *U1206* was lost on 14 April off northeast Scotland. The boat had a peculiar fate, forced to surface and scuttle following a malfunctioning toilet. *U1206* was a Type VIIC/41 and thus capable of deep diving. Correspondingly, such U-boats had been equipped with 'high-pressure heads' that could be safely used at greater depths than before. However, they required a complicated array of levers to be operated in the correct order to prevent any malfunction that could lead to seawater – plus the toilet contents – being flushed back into the U-boat's interior. It appears that either *Kapitänleutnant* Karl-Adolf Schlitt or one of his officers had attempted to use the device and called on a trained man to assist him in flushing the contents away. However, disaster overtook them as the toilet malfunctioned and began to flood uncontrollably into the pressure hull, the bilge pump also failing to operate. Seawater entered several battery cells and the boat was ordered to surface rapidly in order both to relieve the pressure that was building inside the hull and also to thoroughly ventilate the boat. Once surfaced, *U1206* soon came under air attack and Schlitt ordered the boat abandoned and scuttled. Three men were killed during the debacle, the remainder captured by the British naval forces that were soon on the scene.

The following day, 15 April, was darker still for the U-boats; *U285* and *U1063* were both lost to depth charges with all hands, the former southwest of Ireland, the latter west of Land's End after detection while attempting to attack convoy TBD128. Neither boat had had any success. The Type VIIC/41 *U1055* disappeared during April and its patrol of the waters west of the English Channel, her last passage report received on 23 April before the boat was lost, probably to enemy mines. *U398* was also believed to have been lost on or about that date in the North Sea, probably again to mines, this time off the east coast of Scotland.

Kapitänleutnant Peter Mattes' *U326* was one of the few U-boats of the campaign lost to aircraft. The boat was proceeding at *schnorchel* depth south of Ireland when a Liberator of USN VP103 sighted the exhaust. Lieutenant D D Nott's aircraft was equipped with Mark 24 'Fido' homing torpedoes and he dropped a salvo of them directly on to the U-boat. The ensuing explosion blew the *schnorchel* into the air and brought a large oil slick to the surface. The American crew could also plainly see a body floating in the disturbed water – all forty-three crewmen were killed.

Another aircraft accounted for *Oberleutnant zur See* Werner Riecken's *U1017* as the boat cruised toward its operational zone west of the North Channel on its second patrol to British waters. This time it was a Liberator of RAF 120 Squadron that sighted the wake from the boat's *schnorchel* and launched an immediate attack. The Liberator was patrolling off Malin Head when the second pilot Flight Sergeant A A McPhee sighted the U-boat. As they approached to investigate, diesel exhaust from the raised *schnorchel* could be clearly seen and a salvo of four depth charges was readied for an attack, alongside a sonobuoy. Making a perfect run in, all four depth charges released and straddled *U1017*. A second *schnorchel* was also sighted at a distance of one and a half miles but swiftly submerged so that no attack could be made. After the depth-charge explosions subsided, continued loud and drawn out detonations could be heard underwater via the sonobuoy, more of them launched to surround the area and monitor what were the death throes of *U1017* and its thirty-two crewmen.

On 30 April *U1107* was also destroyed. *Kapitänleutnant* Fritz Parduhn had departed Norway on his and his U-boat's maiden patrol a month previously and headed via the circuitous route around the northern waters of the British Isles to his operational area at the western entrance to the English Channel. The boat was coated with *Alberich* and on 18 April launched an attack against convoy HX348 west-southwest of Brest. Parduhn fired a spread of three torpedoes at the inbound convoy and hit two ships; the 7,181-ton Liberty ship SS *Cyrus H McCormick* and the British tanker MV *Empire Gold*. The Briton's Master, Henry Cecil Cansdale, thirty-seven crew members and five gunners were lost. Four survivors were picked up by the British rescue ship *Gothland* as the tanker went to the bottom burning fiercely, laden as she was with 10,278 tons of motor spirit. A single torpedo on the starboard side hit SS *Cyrus H McCormick*, flooding number one and two holds. With water being taken on at an alarming rate the ship settled quickly by the head and went under in less than four minutes taking its cargo of 6,384 tons of cranes, engineering equipment, locomotives and trucks to the bottom. One officer, three men and two armed guards died with the ship, the forty-seven survivors also rescued by *Gothland*. Perhaps ironically enough, the *Cyrus H McCormick*'s Master,

Heinrich Herman Kronke, was a German-born immigrant to the United States who had been at sea since 1919 at the age of sixteen. Kronke's ship had taken part in the resupply of troops on Omaha and Utah beaches during the Normandy invasion. He was the last captain of a Liberty ship compelled to order his ship abandoned – the two ships sunk by Parduhn were the last from any Halifax convoy sunk during the war.

Perhaps aided by his boat's *Alberich* coating, Parduhn managed to avoid escort ships bent on retribution and slipped away from the scene. *U1107* continued to hunt in the Western Approaches until the last day of April when an American 'MAD-Cat' Catalina of VP63 detected it. The 'MAD Cats' were equipped with Magnetic Anomaly Detectors, a device that had been largely nullified in coastal waters but which was in its element in the open seaways of the Bay of Biscay. The Catalina was equipped with retro-bombs, which when fired backwards at a velocity equal to the speed of the aircraft, dropped directly down upon a target beneath the aircraft. Lieutenant F G Lake aimed well and *U1107* was destroyed in the attack, all thirty-seven men aboard perishing with the boat.

The day that Parduhn and his men were lost was also a tumultuous one in the fortunes of the Third Reich. German armed forces in Italy had signed the surrender document the previous day as the bodies of the murdered dictator

A single Type VII and three Type XXIs in Bergen. *U2511* is second from left.

Benito Mussolini and his mistress Clara Petacci were hung by their heels in a Milanese square. In Berlin Adolf Hitler had married his mistress Eva Braun during the previous night and on 30 April, as Russian troops began their final assault on the Tiergarten, he shot himself in the head, his wife taking poison. While men of the Wehrmacht and Waffen SS were being urged to fight to the last round their Commander-in-Chief committed suicide. The Chief of the German General Staff, Hans Krebs, immediately asked Russian forces for a truce as the bodies of his erstwhile commander and Eva Braun were cremated in the shell-churned courtyard of the Reich Chancellery in order to escape a final humiliation similar to that shared by Mussolini and his mistress.

Grossadmiral Dönitz had relocated to Plön in Schleswig-Holstein on 22 April immediately before the Russians had entered Berlin. From there he learned that evening that he had been named as successor to Adolf Hitler as head of the German state in his Last Will and Testament. The following day a signal arrived from the Berlin Chancellery stating: 'Will now in force'. Hitler was dead and Germany in ruins. The bombing of U-boat construction yards and bases had intensified in 1945. On 12 January 32 Lancasters and a single Mosquito of 617 and 9 RAF Squadrons had attacked U-boat pens and shipping in Bergen harbour, four of the attacking Lancasters being lost in the raid, three 'Tallboy' bombs hitting and

The vulnerability of Germany's U-boat building yards to bombing is immediately apparent in this photograph.

penetrating the 3.5-metre-thick roof of the pens and causing severe damage to workshops, offices and stores inside. Horten also came under attack on 23 February from seventy-three Lancasters and ten Mosquitoes. During March and April the onslaught against U-boat yards continued, raids on Hamburg, Bremen and Kiel battering the cities and their shipyards.

For their part in the bombing offensive the USAAF had also stepped up its attacks on U-boat related targets. Seventy-three B17s bombed the Hamburg Blohm & Voss yards on 17 January. Two hundred bombers also hit the Deschimag U-boat yards at Bremen in February, while on 11 March 1,256 bombers and 814 fighters were despatched to make H2X radar attacks on U-boat yards at Germaniawerft, Kiel, and Deschimag, Bremen, and the Blohm & Voss and Deutschewerke shipyard and refinery area at Hamburg. The bombing continued until 4 April when twenty-four B17s flew a 'Disney' mission, attacking the Finkenwarder U-boat yard at Hamburg without loss. (The 'Disney' raids were so-named after the 4,500lb rocket assisted 'Disney' bomb, designed to penetrate thick concrete. The bomb's initial free-fall would be augmented at a height of 5,000 feet with the ignition of a rocket motor that would accelerate the bomb to an impact speed of 2,400 feet per second.)

The destruction and disruption was catastrophic. Since the beginning of 1945 eleven Type XXIs, one Type XXIII and eighteen other types had been destroyed by bombing either within shipyards or German harbours. Many more were damaged to varying degrees and required extended stays within the hard-pressed and increasingly shambolic yards for repair.

During April 1945 the first of these battered U-boat yards in which the Type XXIs and XXIIIs were under construction was captured by the enemy; Bremen surrendered to British and Canadian forces on 26 April. Still the fighting continued. Dönitz remained driven by a desire to prolong the struggle in order to evacuate as many people as possible from the path of the advancing Red Army. To that end the U-boats continued to sail into action. Elsewhere his weary men found themselves transferred to an unfamiliar battleground:

> In the port of Hamburg were a number of U-boat crews who could no longer be sent to sea. They were put into field grey uniforms and placed at General Wolz's [Officer commanding Hamburg district] disposal. The latter formed them into an anti-tank battalion under *Korvettenkapitän* Cremer and *Kapitänleutnants* Peschel and Thäter. Aware though I was of the fighting qualities of the submariners, I felt very doubtful whether they would be able to master the technique of this unfamiliar fighting on land. General Wolz used the battalion, in conjunction with Police and Luftwaffe units, for a series of skilfully planned commando exploits. They penetrated into the area already occupied by the British to the southwest of Hamburg and between April 18 and 20 destroyed some forty British tanks and armoured fighting vehicles . . . As a result of these

high and unexpected losses the British halted their offensive for the time being in that sector, and the advance on Hamburg was delayed.[1]

The reality of the situation was more than likely some way removed from Dönitz's own view of the situation. Indeed on 1 May he dictated a brief summary of the war situation as he saw it, including the conviction that: 'The U-boat arm was on the eve of a revival of the submarine warfare campaign, as, from May onwards, the new types of boat would be coming into service in increasing numbers.'[2]

While wonder weapons that would unleash a new phase of undersea warfare had kept a buoyant faith alive within the Kriegsmarine during the previous months, by April there could have been little doubt as to the outcome of their war at sea. Nevertheless the U-boats continued their struggle. Despite having been withdrawn to seaward of many regions of British coastal waters, April still saw the commitment of dozens of boats to continue the inshore campaign as best they could.

Thirty-two U-boats put to sea from Norway during April to continue the campaign centred on British waters. Of these, six would return to Norway with no confirmed success, one to Wilhelmshaven in Germany and twelve would eventually surrender at sea. Seven were lost in action and three scuttled, two of them off the coast of Portugal. From the thirty-two boats that sailed in April,

U637, U901 and *U1171* docked at Stavanger, May 1945.

twenty-eight of them achieved no enemy ships confirmed as either sunk or damaged.

U637 came perilously close to becoming another combat casualty statistic on 26 April. Three days after leaving Stavanger armed with a combined torpedo and mine weapon load, fire broke out aboard the Type VIIC. Though there were no serious injuries, enough damage had been done to convince *Kapitänleutnant* Wolfgang Riekeberg to return to Norway. Riekeberg had begun his naval career as artillery officer aboard the auxiliary cruiser *Stier* in 1942. After transferring to the same post aboard *Hansa* he then volunteered for U-boat training. His first command was *U1054* until that training boat was decommissioned in September 1944, having been rammed by the ferry *Peter Wessel* off Hela.

While running *U637* eastwards on *schnorchel* it appears that Riekeberg sighted what he believed to be two escort vessels near Utsira Island, west-southwest of Haugesund. Surfacing to make the rendezvous, the commander and his bridge watch were completely taken by surprise as tracer fire arced from the small ships and hit the U-boat. *U637* had actually surfaced before two Norwegian MTBs – *711* and *723* – of the 54th MTB Flotilla. A fast-moving battle swiftly developed. Torpedoes launched by the MTBs narrowly missed *U637*, which had charged forward at full speed, running in zigzags as flak guns opened fire. A red flare was sent into the air to warn nearby German coastal defences and soon the batteries on the island of Karmøy opened fire. MTB *711* dropped four depth charges near the U-boat's hull, causing severe damage to the boat, which began to flood. Riekeberg was badly hit in the face and collapsed while fire intensified all round. The Norwegians too had suffered casualties, one man wounded and another killed. As a Kriegsmarine trawler neared the skirmish and continued artillery fire the two Norwegians broke off their attack. *U637* appeared to be sinking behind them as they headed back to their base at Lerwick in the Shetlands.

U637 was indeed in a bad state with Riekeberg severely wounded and seven men killed, including the *Oberbootsmaat*. The boat's commander then drew his service pistol and shot himself in the head, and the Chief Engineer *Oberleutnant (Ing)* Klaus Weber assumed command. Under escort from the trawler, *U637* limped into the small harbour at Akrahamn where temporary emergency repairs could be made. *U637* finally returned to Stavanger on 28 April.

The transit points between Germany and Norway were still proving perilous for U-boats heading north to their front-line harbours from where they could prepare for combat. The Type XXIII *U2359* was lost to attack by Mosquitoes of the Banff Strike Wing on 2 May in the Kattegat. The small U-boat was spotted by the RAF aircraft while sailing in line astern with another U-boat, under minesweeper escort. *U2359* was hit numerous times by rocket fire, and she and the minesweeper sank soon afterward. *Oberleutnant zur See* Gustav Bischoff and eleven men were lost. *U2338* was sunk on 4 May by Beaufighters of 236 and 254 Squadrons in shallow water near the Danish coast while heading for Norway. Alongside *U2338* were the

Though not the primary killer of U-boats during the British inshore campaign, aircraft remained deadly if able to locate the enemy, not to mention the value of keeping the U-boats submerged and thus robbed of some manoeuvrability by their very presence.

Type VIICs *U393* and *U236* and a pair of escort *Vorpostenboote*. Both these U-boats and one of the escorts were destroyed; *Oberleutnant zur See* Hans-Dietrich Kaiser and eleven of his crew aboard *U2338* were killed by the combined rocket and cannon fire, but two survivors swam ashore. These were the only Type XXIIIs destroyed by direct enemy attack. However, two other casualties can possibly be attributed to the air assault. *Oberleutnant zur See* Uwe Christiansens' *U2365* was attacked by a 224 Squadron Liberator bomber also in the Kattegat. The U-boat was possibly damaged in what was later described as a 'complete balls up' of an attack:

> The attack was ... assessed very critically by Captain Peyton-Ward and Co [wartime Naval assessor]. When we first sighted the U-boat it was travelling so fast we thought it was a speedboat and therefore turned too late to get lined up, toppling the gyros in the Mk14 bombsight in the process of a very steep turn. The depth charges missed by miles and only our gunfire could have done any damage. The boat crash dived but almost immediately reappeared and, since there was so much discolouration of the sea surface, we thought (afterwards) that it must have ricocheted off the bottom in shallow water. However, we had

another go, quite well lined up this time, but the bomb aimer had mis-selected his switches and nothing came off the racks. The sub then resubmerged and stayed down.[3]

It is quite possible that damage resulting from the abortive bombing run caused the later scuttling of *U2365* on 8 May.

On 5 May *Oberleutnant zur See* Heinrich Schröder's *U2367* was also under air attack in the Great Belt when the boat collided with another unidentified U-boat while attempting to zigzag out of harm's way. The U-boat was so badly damaged that it was subsequently scuttled.

The Type XXI U-boats fared no better, many either completely destroyed by bombs and rocket fire while en route to Norway, or so badly damaged that their crews were forced to scuttle their boats and head for shore in life rafts. It was left largely to conventional U-boats to continue their desperate struggle.

Once again *U245* was in action on the second of its 'Operation Brutus' missions against the Thames-Scheldt convoy traffic. Schumann-Hindenberg had left Heligoland on 9 April and headed southwest toward his target area. In fact *U245* had departed the island in good time, as nine days later 969 aircraft – 617 Lancasters, 332 Halifaxes and 20 Mosquitoes – of all Bomber Command groups attacked the naval base, airfield and town on this small island. The bombing was accurate and the target areas were transformed into crater-pitted moonscapes. That same day Schumann-Hindenberg attacked convoy TAM142, hitting and sinking two freighters, the 4,991-ton Norwegian MV *Karmt* and the 4,856-ton British steamer SS *Filleigh*. The Norwegian was carrying a cargo of 7,539 tons of West African produce: groundnuts, palm oil and general as well as valuable minerals, including gold and tin concentrate. The torpedo hit the motor vessel to starboard causing considerable damage and killing four mechanics whose cabins were above the explosion to aft. Survivors immediately headed for their three remaining lifeboats, two having been destroyed in the blast. The ship was abandoned, but did not sink at once. Several uninjured crew decided to row back to attempt to salvage the vessel but she slowly turned over to port and went under before they could reach her. The British steamer went to the bottom with 6,000 tons of military cargo and five men killed. *U245* also fired a *Zaunkönig* at an escorting corvette and heard an end-of-run detonation after sixteen minutes. The German B-Dienst service suggested that the attack on the corvette had been successful judging by intercepted radio transmissions, but it remains unconfirmed by Allied records. One final attack was mounted by *U245* on 26 April, claiming an unconfirmed steamer and tanker hit and sunk.

On 12 April *U1105* sailed from Marviken on its first combat mission. The boat was clad in the black synthetic *Alberich* sheeting, its appearance earning the nickname 'Black panther' – a symbol adopted by the boat and adorning her conning tower on its metal shield. The aptly named commander, *Oberleutnant zur*

The colour difference between *U1105* at left with its black rubber *Alberich* coating and a standard Type VIIC illustrates why the former was known as the 'Black Panther'.

See Hans-Joachim Schwarz, took his boat toward Fair Island between the Orkneys and Shetland Islands, whereupon *U1105* would loop southwards towards the west coast of Ireland towards the boat's patrol area near Black Rock off the Irish coast. There Schwarz hoped to encounter convoy traffic bound for the British harbours of the west coast. During the evening of 25 April *U1105* encountered and managed to evade an Allied escort group. Two days later, west of Mayo, the fast rhythmic thump of military propellers heralded the arrival of three more enemy warships, but this time as potential targets. From a range of 2,000 metres Schwarz fired two T5 *Zaunkönig* torpedoes and immediately dived to 100 metres to begin their escape. After fifty seconds the first torpedo struck, followed shortly thereafter by the second. Schwarz's target had been the three frigates of 2nd Division, 21st Escort Group. HMS *Redmill* was hit and severely damaged by the explosions, which killed thirty-two crewmen. The stricken frigate remained afloat and was subsequently towed to harbour where she was written off as a constructive loss.

Aboard *U1105* the immediate crash dive after firing had slipped out of control, and the boat careered down to 174 metres before the descent was arrested by arrival at the seabed. There, Schwarz bottomed his boat, ordered all off-duty men to turn in, excess machinery switched off and the boat remained motionless as the hunt ensued above. For thirty-one hours Allied ships hunted for the U-boat dropping more than 300 depth charges, but to no avail. The U-boat was neither located nor inadvertently damaged. At 1600hrs on 28 April the hunt was abandoned and *U1105* returned to the surface.

Schwarz slipped away and patrolled west of the North Channel, reportedly stopping at the remote Tory Island, nine miles off the Donegal coast, to enable minor repairs to be made to the boat. The boat was still on station on 4 May when transmissions from BdU were received.

The next reported sinking achieved by an 11th U-Flotilla boat in British waters occurred on 29 April when *U2322* reported a steamer sunk by torpedo. *Oberleutnant zur See* Fridtjof Heckel was operating against convoy traffic in the Thames area as part of 'Operation Zeus' – similar in scope to *U245*'s 'Operation Brutus'. The boat carried two TIIIa FAT 2 torpedoes and took part alongside *U245* in the attack on convoy TAM142 on 18 April. The successful torpedo shots from the Type VIIC were audible inside *U2322*, though Heckel achieved no success himself. However in the ensuing hunt for *U245*, the Type XXIII was damaged by nearby depth charges that affected one diesel, the *schnorchel* and radio transmitter. Apparently Heckel claimed sinking an Allied freighter off the Norfolk coast on 29 April, though Allied records hold no confirmation of this attack. The boat docked in Stavanger at 2045hrs on the last day of April.

Three other Type XXIII boats were in action during March. *U2324* sailed on its second patrol from Kristiansand under new command. Hans-Heinrich Hass had come down with diphtheria and was replaced by *Kapitänleutnant* Konstantin von Rappard, commander of the Kristiansand U-boat base. Von Rappard was initially ordered to the Thames estuary region, but BdU redirected the boat to the Firth of Forth. Near the Bell Rock lighthouse east of Perth, the distant thunder of depth charges was heard reverberating through the North Sea water, attributed by Von Rappard to attacks on *U1206*. *U2324* continued to hunt in vain, finally exhausting its small supply of provisions and drinking water and was forced to return empty handed to Stavanger where the boat tied up on 8 May.

U2329 had sailed on 11 April and was also directed to the Scottish coast, sailing the waters off Aberdeen. Four days after departing Norway *Oberleutnant zur See* Heinrich Schlott attacked a small convoy of four merchant ships and three escorts near Aberdeen, firing a single shot at the freighter SS *Aalsum*. The torpedo malfunctioned, however, becoming a 'ground runner' that prematurely detonated against the shallow seabed, exploding a mere twenty metres from the U-boat's bow. Schlott retreated immediately, escaping the attentions of the alerted escort. On 20 April a second failed attack before Tynemouth rendered the U-boat out of ammunition, and it returned to Stavanger six days later.

U2329 in Norway.

Oberleutnant zur See Karl Jobst's *U2326* on its first combat mission experienced no success either:

Ran out of Stavanger at 2300hrs on the 19th and were escorted as far as Sveinane. Dived at 0100hrs on the 20th and proceeded across the North Sea. While at fifty metres we ran into an English minefield and were obliged to dive deeply. On the afternoon of the 23rd at about 1400hrs I sighted a convoy from Aberdeen escorted by several frigates and smaller escorts. As the convoy was too far away no attack was carried out. On the way south we had an alarm at about 1730hrs. At 1830hrs four to five depth-charge explosions were heard every ten minutes. Proceeded southwards in the direction from which the explosions were coming, at twenty metres, as I suspected that this was the position of the convoy. At 2100hrs we heard noises on the hydrophones. There was still nothing to be seen through the periscope. The noises were those of screws turning at high speed. At 2130hrs I saw two corvettes and a Liberty ship of about 9000 tons. The inclination was quite large (about ninety) and its outline clear. Estimated speed of the enemy was ten knots. Submerged attack had to be broken off at 2245 as it had become too dark. At 2250 we surfaced and followed the merchant vessel. The distance between the boat and the target was gradually closing. Found that the merchant vessel was not being escorted by two corvettes but being towed by two tugs. In spite of bright moonlight I decided to remain surfaced. The target's outline was very clear and it seemed as though it had grown to love me. At about 2355 I fired both torpedoes but at the moment of firing the merchant vessel altered course eighty degrees to starboard. Both torpedoes missed on account of this. On the 24th at about 0010hrs I crash-dived ahead of an escort which had been gaining on me from the northward, and got away at best speed towards the minefield west of us. Our depth was then fifty metres as it had been beforehand. Only a few depth-charge explosions were heard quite a long way away from us. I immediately made my way back to Stavanger, which we reached at 0800 on the 27th April.[4]

There, alongside *U2345* newly arrived from Germany, Jobst discovered that there were no torpedo reloads available for his boat. Both torpedoes were transferred from *Oberleutnant zur See* Karl Steffan's new boat to enable Jobst to return to action. Meanwhile FdU West issued priority instructions for more ammunition to be despatched and five torpedoes were transferred from Kristiansand to Stavanger. Jobst would sail once more on 4 May 1945, bound again for the Scottish east coast.

On 1 May *U2336* sailed from Norway for Scottish waters. *Kapitänleutnant* Emil

Kapitänleutnant Heinrich Schroeteler, final recipient within the U-boat service of the Knight's Cross.

Klusmeier was new to the U-boat. The previous captain *Oberleutnant zur See* Jürgen Vockel who had taken the boat from its Hamburg shipyard in September 1944, had been killed by splinters from RAF bombing of the Deutschewerft on 30 March. During the same raid *U2340* had been destroyed as the boat lay in the yards. The expedient of taking Klusmeier as well as his IWO, senior non-commissioned officers and a single rating from his crew and placing them aboard *U2336* – which had escaped damage – was taken, and the boat sailed for Norway on 18 April in preparation for its maiden war patrol at the beginning of May.

At 2000hrs on 1 May *U2336* sailed within a small convoy of escort vessels for the North Sea, diving and proceeding on *schnorchel* once free of the coastal waters and its escorts. In sporadic bursts of rain and drizzle the boat headed for the Firth of Forth, oblivious to larger developments in the war as radio reception suffered with the poor atmospherics. On 7 May at around midday the first hydrophone traces of convoy traffic were detected aboard *U2336* and Klusmeier turned his boat to investigate. By nightfall Klusmeier had three freighters with a three-destroyer escort in view and he prepared to attack. The convoy actually comprised five freighters and an escort of armed trawlers, HMTs *Angle*, *Wolves* and *Leicester City*, which formed convoy EN91 sailing outbound from Methil bound ultimately for

U1023, one of the last boats in action, in British hands. The boat's wolf's head emblem, drawn by crewman Otto Krempl, is clearly visible.

Belfast. Men aboard the convoy were relaxed for the first time in years, since news of Germany's order to cease fire at sea was common knowledge within Britain.

That same evening, far to the southwest, the Type VIIC/41 *U1023* also was preparing for its last torpedo attack, under the command of *Kapitänleutnant* Heinrich Schroeteler. Schroeteler had impressed Dönitz with his zeal in attack even before his final strike. He had previously served as captain of *U667* within the Atlantic for four patrols before being posted ashore to the BdU staff to replace 'Adi' Schnee who had returned to front-line duty as captain of *U2511*. But the fiery Schroeteler had pleaded for a combat post with fellow Staff Officer and veteran captain, Günter Hessler – Dönitz's son-in-law – and was rewarded with a return to active duty. Thus he had been assigned to *U1023* for the boat's maiden patrol. His reported successes of three large freighters totalling 26,000 tons sunk by 2 April prompted the award of the Knight's Cross from Dönitz, granted by radio that day. It was the last Knight's Cross to be awarded within the U-boat service.

Schroeteler had been at sea since early March aboard *U1023*, his first claimed kill of the patrol having taken place during April. On 9 April *U1023* had fired a spread of three LUT torpedoes at what it took to be an 8,000-ton freighter that was part of convoy SC171 in the North Channel. Two clearly heard detonations led to the claim of a damaged ship, though he had in fact missed his target. The explosions had buffeted nearby escorting frigate HMCS *Capilano*. Schroeteler escaped unscathed.

The U-boat then passed into the Irish Sea where it made its next attempt on convoy traffic on 19 April, firing another three LUTs and recording a detonation observed through the periscope and another audible from the convoy body. Schroeteler claimed an 8,000-ton freighter as sunk and moved on to continue his aggressive patrol. Four days later *U1023* attacked convoy TBC135 with a pair of LUT torpedoes, hitting and damaging the 7,345-ton British steamer SS *Riverton*, which was travelling in ballast. Claiming the steamer as 10,000-tons and definitely sunk, Schroeteler moved on and would make one final attack on 7 May at 2145hrs.

On the evening of 7 May the target was military and a single *Zaunkönig* hit the 335-ton Norwegian minesweeper HNMS *NYMS 382* off Lyme Bay, Schroeteler claiming the victim as a corvette. The small ship sank within two minutes; her captain and twenty-one crew members were lost while other Norwegians of 3rd Minesweeping Unit, stationed in Cherbourg, picked up ten injured survivors.

Later that same evening, to the northeast Klusmeier in *U2336* fired its two torpedoes at the small convoy. Both were direct hits; the 2,878-ton Canadian freighter SS *Avondale Park*, followed by the 1,791-ton Norwegian steamer SS *Sneland I* hit squarely amidships. *Avondale Park* slewed to a stop as the ship began to sink rapidly, and the Chief Engineer George Anderson and donkeyman (a rating that attends to the small so-called 'donkey boiler' that powered machinery used while the ship was in harbour) William Harvey were lost in the attack.

The Norwegian steamer was in the convoy's starboard column when SS

Avondale Park was hit. *Sneland I* was forced to alter course to port in order to avoid the torpedoed Canadian, but suddenly was also struck on the starboard side. Within two minutes the ship had sunk. The first and third mates attempted to launch the ship's port lifeboat, but the rapidity of the ship's sinking prevented them. SS *Sneland I* capsized and the survivors were pitched into the sea. There they clung to debris before being picked up by HMTs *Valse* and *Leicester City*. Seven men, including the captain, were killed. HMT *Leicester City* blindly dropped several depth charges before proceeding to pick up survivors from the torpedoed ships. The nearby Norwegian destroyer HNMS *Stord* arrived and also began hunting for *U2336*. Klusmeier evaded the ensuing depth charges and escaped unscathed to begin his return to base. Two days later *U2336* received news of Germany's capitulation.

Tragically all three sinkings contravened an order transmitted on 4 May 1945 from Dönitz to his U-boats at sea, whether deliberately or not remaining a matter for idle speculation to this day:

ALL U-BOATS. ATTENTION ALL U-BOATS. CEASE-FIRE AT ONCE. STOP ALL HOSTILE ACTION AGAINST ALLIED SHIPPING. DÖNITZ.

During 3 May *Generaladmiral* Hans Georg von Friedeburg – Dönitz's successor as head of the Kriegsmarine upon his ascension to head of state – had proceeded to Field Marshal Montgomery's headquarters to negotiate surrender on behalf of Dönitz who controlled the military zone of northern Germany. Montgomery agreed to the proposal for the surrender of north Germany, along with Holland and Denmark with the proviso that the German Fleet be included and no ships or U-boats scuttled before the surrender, which was to take place at 0800 on 5 May. Correspondingly Dönitz had issued the order to cease fire after agreeing the British terms.

On 10 May, after finally receiving and acknowledging the order to surrender his U-boat, Schroeteler aboard *U1023* transmitted one of the last encoded German messages from a combat U-boat:

During our recent sixteen-day long *schnorchel* operation we sunk one steamer (8,000GRT) and one destroyer in a convoy. In addition we torpedoed one large freighter (10,000GRT). With faithful confidence we shall now carry out the most difficult order. *U1023* (Schroeteler)

After transmission the U-boat surfaced, hoisted a black flag on its extended periscope and transmitted its coordinates to Allied forces, awaiting escort into Weymouth harbour where the U-boat surrendered.

The instructions issued by the Allied naval command were very specific and included the requirement that U-boats be surfaced and flying a black flag of

Geheim!

Funkspruch-Ausgang

Eingang Fernschreibraum	Schaltung	Leit-Nr.	Ausgangszeit	Funkspruch Nr.
	Alle Wellen			
Ausgeschrieben — B. U. Offz.	Hubertus			Offen!
	Nordmeer			
Bem.:		alle 2 Stdn. wiederholen		

An alle Boote!
U-Bootsmänner!Nach einem heroischen Kampf ohne Gleichen habt Ihr
die Waffen niedergelegt.Ihr habt Unerhörtes geleistet.Das härteste
Opfer müsst Ihr für Euer Vaterland noch bringen,indem Ihr bedingu-
gungslos die folgenden Anweisungen ausführt.Dadurch fällt kein
Makel auf Eure Ehre,jedoch werden schwerste Folgen für Eure Heimat
vermieden.Der mit FT 88 q/13 F/34 L/66 D und mit Sonderschlüssel
294,314,316,319 auf Küste erteilte Befehl ist aufgehoben.
Euer Grossadmiral

Uhrzeitgruppe	20 26 0 8 82
F. T. O. b. Wache	
Lfnr.	2125.
	8.5.45

Abschr. erledigt:

175 Druckerei M OKM 10 000 6 43

Nr.: 52

The end. Dönitz begins transmitting messages to all his combat U-boats
to cease fire and return to port.

surrender. In the early hours of 7 May a Catalina IV of 201 Squadron sighted a *schnorchel* and periscope northwest of Bergen, the white smoke of diesel exhaust clearly visible. Within one minute the submerged U-boat, *Oberleutnant zur See* Heinz Emmrich's *U320*, was attacked, as it still appeared to be operating on a war footing. Four depth charges exploded astride the diving boat and a large patch of oil soon appeared on the surface. Hours later a sonobuoy contact was made with *U320*, an audible sound of hammering being picked up, indicating that repairs were underway on the bottomed boat. The hammering sounds continued for two hours as oil continued to rise to the surface. After eleven hours, the Catalina was forced to leave the scene and *U320* appeared to complete some kind of emergency repair as the following day the boat surfaced and was scuttled. She was the last U-boat sunk as a result of enemy action.

The 'miracle' weapon of the Type XXI had never reached the fruition so longed for by *Grossadmiral* Karl Dönitz and his men. A single example, 'Adi' Schnee's

The wonder U-boat that never saw action; commanders of several Type XXI U-boats still in training in German waters as the war drew to a close.

U2511 had put to sea for operations in the western Atlantic and Caribbean, sailing on 3 May into action. However, unlike *U1023* and *U2336*, Schnee received and obeyed the cease-fire order. His mock attack against a British warship group centred on HMS *Norfolk* within hours of receiving the order on 4 May remains almost legendary. Schnee approached to within 500 metres of the British ships, plotted a firing solution and departed without any ASDIC contact from the enemy. Instead *U2511* returned to Bergen on 5 May where it was later handed over to the occupying British forces. Schnee later spoke with officers of HMS *Norfolk* and was able to prove to them that he had indeed made a dummy attack. The British were astonished that they had been so close to U-boat attack with no realisation at all that they were in peril.

CHAPTER EIGHT

Black Flag

ON 7 MAY 1945, formal instructions for their method of surrender were transmitted to all areas where combat U-boats still sailed.

To all U-boats at sea:
Carry out the following instructions forthwith which have been given by the Allied Representatives.
Surface immediately and remain surfaced.
Report immediately in Plain Language your position in latitude and longitude and number of your U-boat to nearest British, US, Canadian or Soviet coast W/T station . . .
Fly a large black or blue flag by day.
Burn navigation lights by night.
Jettison all ammunition, remove breechblocks from guns and render torpedoes safe by removing pistols.
All mines are to be rendered safe.
Make all signals in Plain Language.
Follow strictly the instructions for proceeding to Allied ports from your present area given in immediately following message.
Observe strictly the orders of Allied Representatives to refrain from scuttling or in any way damaging your U-boat.
These instructions will be repeated at two-hour intervals until further notice.

There then followed periodic transmissions of the correct port destinations and traffic lanes to use in order to reach them. With the official surrender not yet ratified and the knowledge that many U-boats could either deliberately ignore the instructions, or not have received them at all, the Allied naval forces took no chances when dealing with any U-boat suspected of violating the above instructions.

A narrow miss for a small coastal convoy was averted on 9 May. *Oberleutnant zur See* Karl Jobst's *U2326* had raced to head back into action from Stavanger, leaving harbour on the day of the ceasefire order:

Left Stavanger on 4 May at 0100 and was again escorted as far as Sveinane. Then dived to fifty metres and went across the North Sea and the English minefield just north of Aberdeen. In order to charge the batteries we *schnorchelled* every day between 2300 and approximately 0330. We also ventilated the boat for ten to fifteen minutes between 1200 and 1400. Just about half way from Aberdeen to Peterhead we altered course to the southward on the British convoy course. That was at about midday on the 7th.

It had been impossible until then to fix our position as the weather had been drizzly and soundings did not give an accurate fix. On the 8th we were abreast May Island. The clouds broke for a short while and the Island was quite clearly visible. At midday I was run over by two destroyers which were coming from the east on route up the Firth of Forth. The boat was not detected. During the night of the 8/9 May we bottomed in sixty metres near May Island. In the forenoon of the 9th we heard noises of ships' screws on the hydrophones. We came off the bottom and proceeded in the direction of the noise. Through the periscope I saw that a corvette and a frigate had already passed over me. Inclination was very great (160–180). About five minutes later a small escort ship passed along my port side about 200 metres away. This was too short a range at which to fire so I did not attack. Astern of the convoy – a tanker of 1,500 tons and a small coaster of 500–800 tons – were two more frigates. One of them turned towards me. I dived to forty metres and made off southwards towards Abbs Head. In the evening at 2200 I surfaced, both to charge the batteries and to try to get W/T reception.

Flying the black flag of surrender.

U2326, after surrender, in British hands in Dundee.

As I had heard no depth-charge explosions nor W/T messages, I decided to go north to Aberdeen and then eastwards into the North Sea. I hoped to hear W/T messages as I approached Norway. On the morning of the 10 May at 0010 I heard the news by Norwegian Radio that Germany had capitulated. At 0230 I passed a big convoy coming from the north but as I was not sure whether the Norwegian station had spoken the truth or not I did not attack the convoy. Our position was then between the convoy course and the English minefield. I altered course to the northward. At this time the batteries were fully charged. I proceeded further north at slow speed. At about 0430 we sighted a 10,000-ton tanker which was being escorted northward by a frigate. I had still had no orders by W/T. The frigate attacked me and I crash dived when she was 300 metres away. No depth charges were dropped. At about 1430 I was on the surface between Aberdeen and Peterhead. I then went eastwards through the minefield.

On 11 May I surfaced in order to wait for orders from operations. The English station gave us news of our surrender and said that German submarines in our area were to make for German Ports. In Kiel they said the British Admiral's Flag was flying. As I was already far into the North Sea and only knew the position of the minefields in the northern part of the North Sea near the Skagerrak and Kattegat I decided to make for Kiel. On the evening of the 11th and the morning of the 12th we had our first complete W/T instructions. On the 10th we had heard that all W/T transmissions were to cease. I had a black flag placed next to our ensign and told the crew of the instructions in the signal. The transmission of my PCS (positioning signal) was not heard by the British Station. At 0700 on the 12th a Liberator flew over us and demanded my number. This I gave and again proceded. Further flashing was very difficult for we could only read part of what was sent. The Liberator flew very low over us, circled and then dropped a bomb. After about two minutes I was ordered to steer 270. I turned to this and proceeded at best speed. This aircraft was later relieved by another. By this time the British Station GZZ 110 had heard our PCS signal and told us to make for Loch Eriboll. The last we heard from the aircraft was 'See you in Dundee'. From this I took it that I should go to Dundee. During the night of 12 and 13 of May we had no aircraft escort. I went westwards on the surface. On the morning of the 12th the destroyer L.33 came to meet me. I told him my number and my intentions of steering for Dundee. I was told to go to Edinburgh. On the afternoon of the 13th I sighted the defence vessel at one end of the minefield, and as I did not know my position I went straight up to him and said 'I have orders to go to Edinburgh and wish to know my position'. I was told to steer a westerly course. At the same time, along came an RAF rescue launch, and told us to follow him to Dundee. I took up station astern of the launch. On 14 May I waited in the proximity of Bell Rock for further instructions. The launch returned at 0500 and took me into Dundee where I secured alongside King George Wharf. The boat was searched and all firearms were removed. All secret codebooks etc, were given up and scuttling charges handed over. On the morning of the 16th we left Dundee to fire our Type T IIIA torpedoes near the minefield. This was done under the supervision of the Commanding Officer of P34. At 1900 we left for Loch Eriboll with two officers, 1 PO and a signalman from P34 on board. We were escorted by a frigate and made fast alongside another in Loch Eriboll on the morning of the 18th. In the afternoon the boat was visited by the senior British officer present. Escorted by a frigate we left for Loch Alsh and on the 19th K483 escorted us to Londonderry.

As the surrender order began to filter through to the U-boats at sea, the totality of their defeat was gradually accepted and more and more U-boats prepared to surrender. Some opted – against BdU orders – to follow the contingency plan of 'Operation Regenbogen' (Rainbow) and scuttle themselves rather than suffer the

U249 photographed by the RAF after surrender.

indignity of handing over their intact U-boats to the enemy. 'Operation Regenbogen' had been created on 30 April 1945 when Dönitz ordered that the entire German fleet be scuttled to uphold the honour of the Kriegsmarine, rather than submit to the same kind of humiliating surrender that had occurred in 1918. However, on 4 May the *Grossadmiral* was forced to rescind his order as it violated the Allied terms of the cease-fire that he had agreed. Although Dönitz himself officially forbade transmission of the code word '*Regenbogen*' to begin the scuttling, the order was nonetheless sent by others within BdU and by the end of it 218 U-boats, including eighty-two Type XXIs and twenty-nine Type XXIIIs, had been scuttled in the Western Baltic.

Fifty miles south-southwest of the Lizard, *Oberleutnant zur See* Uwe Kock received the order and in accordance with instructions began signalling his position *en clair* on 8 May, making him the first active U-boat to surrender following Dönitz's proclamation. Lieutenant Haskell-Thomas aboard HMS *Magpie* remembered being the first British ship to approach the long dark

Kapitänleutnant Uwe Koch of *U249* turns away from the camera after
signing the surrender document.

silhouette of what had so recently been their mortal enemy. 'We went to full action
stations as a sensible precaution.'

Magpie and its accompanying sloops of 2nd Escort Group kept their guns
trained on *U249* while a boat was launched carrying a boarding party towards the
waiting Germans. Once aboard, the British sailors attached a chain around the
periscope pedestal and dropped the other end into the conning tower to prevent
the hatch being closed and the U-boat diving once more:

> The sloops were advised that the U-boat had ten torpedoes on board, of which
> six were in the tubes – the boarding party went a mite pale. *U249* had left
> Peenemünde [sic] 40 days earlier and had been on continuous patrol since –
> drawing in air for her diesels from her snorkel. The air on board was rich! The
> boarding party had been supplied with the normal Navy rations – two loaves of
> bread, two tins of corned beef and a bottle of rum. The crew invited the party
> to share their food. Instead of RN rations, the boarders enjoyed sausages from

Poland, French cheese, Italian olives and German bread. The acorn coffee was a disaster – or was it the all-pervading smell of diesel fumes?

The Escort Group was ordered to bring *U249* into Portland harbour, though a rather bizarre and presumably symbolic gesture was made by the Admiralty before reaching the harbour. 'Possibly for some PR exercise reasons – spin doctoring is not new – *Magpie's* sailors were taken off *U249* and replaced by a group of Polish sailors, who then took the craft in'.[1]

Gradually, those U-boats that were at sea in their patrol areas obeyed the surrender orders and began to filter into British harbours under the watchful eyes of the Royal Navy. Large crowds of civilians were frequently on hand to witness the arrival of the hated U-boats, many families of the port cities having lost men in both the Royal and merchant navies to the torpedoes and mines of Dönitz's grey wolves. *U776* was the last of these boats that had been in the Western Approaches to enter a British harbour, sailing into Weymouth on 16 May and formally surrendering.

Perhaps strangely there appeared little hostility between the Allied and German fighting men as they finally came face to face. Royal Navy man Eric Williams was one of the victors that circulated among the surrendered U-boats, engaging their crews wherever possible:

> I built up a fascinating impression of these brave, clever and determined men. Discipline was the backbone of their character – implicit and unquestioning obedience. They preferred to be known as soldiers, not sailors, and they obeyed automatically. When I asked one officer whether he would obey an order he knew to be wrong, he smiled and said: 'But that would not happen. We do not get wrong orders.'[2]

Another Royal Navy veteran of minesweeper service, George Smith, recalled the moment when *U1009* emerged from the depths to surrender. The boat, which had sailed in British waters during January 1945, had been assigned weather-reporting duties in March and was still at sea when Germany capitulated:

> Tuesday the 8th of May, 1945, turned out to be a memorable day for me, a twenty-one-year-old Royal Naval telegraphist aboard a minesweeper [HMT *Beaumaris Castle*] at the top of the Minches in the Atlantic, near the Butt of Lewis in the Outer Hebrides.
> Our flotilla was on its second day out from Stornoway, with the ships stretched out on a routine sweep in full lookout for mines, but the ship's crews and officers were trying to come to terms with the fact that the war in Europe had ended, when in the late afternoon 'action stations' were sounded aboard our ship. To our shock and surprise a German U-boat rose menacingly to the surface,

U1009 after surrender headed, under escort, for Scotland.

and slowly at the masthead she hoisted a black flag. The German High Command had ordered all U-boats to surrender unconditionally to the nearest Allied naval ships, and the hoisting of the black flag was the surrender signal.

After the panic had subsided messages were rapidly exchanged with our flotilla leader and the naval base at Loch Ewe, and finally we were instructed to order the German U-boat to follow in our wake into Loch Ewe . . . Formal surrender was undertaken by senior British naval officers who boarded the U-boat and interrogated her captain and officers. Apparently other U-boats were also expected there. Our crew was ultimately allowed to board this U-boat and inspect what had been the hated scourge of all Allied shipping. Ironically we had formally to salute the U-boat's officers before boarding their boat, but grudgingly we all knew this was the crème de la crème of the German navy.

As a postscript to the U-boat's surrender in Loch Ewe, it was established that several weeks before VE Day a U-boat operating in the Irish Sea had laid magnetic mines in the Firth of Clyde. Our flotilla was sent post haste from Loch Ewe to the Clyde where we swept from dawn to dusk from Ardrossan to Stranraer for nearly three months. Many mines were found and destroyed in the area around Ailsa Craig.[3]

Oberleutnant zur See Rolf-Werner Wentz's *U963* was also at sea when the surrender order arrived. The boat had sailed from Trondheim on 23 April, bound for the sea area off Hartlepool. The boat had made eight war patrols, though only one with Wentz in command, when the boat had scoured the Irish Sea to no avail. In fact throughout its career span from August 1943 it had made no sinkings, though the

U249 and *U1023* in captivity. Both boats had been active during the inshore campaign, the single aircraft 'kill' marking from March 1945 clearly visible on *U249*.

crew attributed this to bad luck rather than bad leadership. *U963* passed uneventfully through the Iceland passage and proceeded down Scotland's west coast. The sole cause for concern had been the malfunctioning of the dipole antennae of the radar detector atop the *schnorchel* three days from port. Water had entered the cable from the aerial to the wireless compartment, with the result that the cable had to be severed and sealed off. The danger in which this placed the boat was finally demonstrated on 6 May in the early hours of the morning when *U963* was rocked by a single aircraft-launched depth charge while west of the Hebrides. Though *U963* evaded further attack, considerable damage had been caused already: the pressure hull was cracked abreast the conning tower to starboard, the port diesel engine was damaged and inoperative, starboard vents could be opened but not shut and the boat's main aerial was destroyed rendering *U963* 'deaf'. Wentz headed southwest as a continuous inflow of water from the cracked hull threatened to swamp the U-boat. *U963* developed a pronounced list to starboard, and there were frequent short circuits caused by regular failures of the overworked bilge pumps. Finally, on the evening of 19 May, near the Portuguese west coast, the main pumps failed altogether and were adjudged irreparable. The boat began to settle, and Wentz gave the order to abandon ship at 0300hrs the next morning. The entire crew of forty-eight men were interned in neutral Portugal.

U963 was not the last boat to reach the Portuguese coast. *Kapitänleutnant* Ehrenreich Stever's *U1277* had been at sea since 21 April in the Western Approaches. Upon receipt of the surrender orders from Germany he and his crew chose internment rather than handing their boat over and cruised toward Portugal. On 3 June *U1277* surfaced at dawn off Cabo do Mundo, near Oporto, and was scuttled, the crew paddling for shore in rubber dinghies, landing at the beach of Angeiras north of Oporto. There they were captured and interned by Portuguese authorities in the *Castelo de Sao Jose da Foz* in Oporto. A few days later they were handed over to a British warship in Lisbon, beginning their journey to spend three years in a POW camp before they could return to Germany. Ehrenreich also faced punishment by British court martial for contravening the German surrender terms.

Elsewhere only one other boat of the Type VIIs directed against England made a genuine bid for freedom. On 17 August 1945 the dishevelled appearance of *U977* in Mar del Plata, Argentina, marked the final act of Dönitz's last campaign. *Oberleutnant zur See* Heinz Schäffer had received the surrender order, but instead chose to put the matter to his men, barely able to believe – after the fierce defiant broadcast in the last hysterical days of the Third Reich – that a total collapse had taken place. Aware of the Allied demand for unconditional surrender and also the cruel intentions of the Morgenthau Plan which had been publicised in the German press, Schäffer put three options to his crew.[4] The first option was to surrender as apparently ordered, the second to scuttle the boat, the third was to escape and put into harbour in a country that had remained friendly to Germany throughout the war years. Eventually a majority – thirty of the forty-eight men aboard – opted for the last. Two desired to be landed in Spain and sixteen others with families still in Germany wanted to return to their homes. The men who wished to return were subsequently delivered under cover of darkness to a remote area of the Norwegian coast near Bergen, paddling ashore in rubber dinghies after *U977* inadvertently ran aground. Schäffer and his remaining crew extricated the boat from their perilous position as dawn approached and headed to sea:

> First slowly, and then with gradually increasing speed, we moved away – as with every moment the coastline emerged more clearly from the darkness. We could dimly make out our shipmates signalling with lights. They had reached the shore and were flashing out a farewell message: 'Bon voyage. If they catch us we'll say the boat struck a mine and we were the only survivors.' Then, to our surprise, followed a short burst of gunfire as coastal batteries engaged. We sank thankfully to the bottom.
>
> Morale was high. There was complete unity amongst us and our decision was duly entered in the log book. Any suggestion of running our ship on democratic lines was ruled out . . . We certainly worked efficiently, even with so few hands aboard. The youngsters in the engine room knew their jobs and carried on without the Petty Officers, and, incidentally, moved into their mess so that now we had room to stretch our legs.[5]

So began a marathon trek around the British Isles and into the Atlantic, sailing continuously for sixty-six days underwater on *schnorchel* and electric motors. Constant radar detection from the antennae mounted atop the *schnorchel* head showed that the Allies had still not given up the hunt for remaining U-boats. Many of those boats that had been lost in the final months of the war were still believed by BdU to be operational and with no evidence to the contrary, Allied naval forces continued their search:

> After eighteen days without a break the crew began to get on edge, with black rings under their eyes, and faces pale and even greenish-looking from lack of daylight and fresh air. The bulkheads too were turning green with damp. Since we were permanently dived now we couldn't get rid of the refuse from the galley and this piled up into a revolting mess, apart from the smell breeding flies, maggots and other vermin . . . With our bodies and minds both imprisoned, there was nothing to occupy or stimulate us, and nothing at all to enjoy – cut off as we were from nature and civilisation. However much we longed to let off steam somehow, to scream, pick a quarrel or hit someone, we dared not break down for fear of what that might lead to – self control is the first essential for the caged.[6]

Conditions in the boat deteriorated further as the voyage dragged on. The crew had not seen daylight for more than two months and the condition of the men and the vessel became extremely difficult to manage. The diesel engines were also beginning to show the strain of their unnaturally prolonged voyage. As *U977* cruised in equatorial waters the internal temperature rose, compounding the men's misery. Finally, after sixty-six days Schäffer allowed the U-boat to surface in an area he at last considered safe, and the marathon submerged journey was ended beneath a clear, starry night sky.

U977 continued south, alternating between surface and submerged runs as the crew began to recover slightly from their ordeal. Conditions aboard were still fragile and it remains a testament to Schäffer's leadership that the crew remained relatively united and functional throughout the trek. On 10 July a radio broadcast announcing the arrival at Mar del Plata of the other escaping U-boat, Type IXC/40 *U530*, which had been in operations off the American coast at the time of the surrender, raised morale within the crew aboard *U977*. This was only temporary, however, as it was also learned that *U530*'s crew had been handed over to the United States for imprisonment. Nonetheless, Mar del Plata remained Schäffer's

The one that got away – *U977* photographed in Argentina after its epic voyage that began as one of the last missions of Dönitz's onslaught in British waters.

destination and a surfaced *U977* entered harbour on 17 August where the German crew were interned before also being handed over to the Americans.

The arrival of *U977* in Argentina fuelled endless speculation about U-boats smuggling high-ranking Nazis from Germany after the surrender. While it is true that Argentina did indeed harbour many such men, the idea that they had been smuggled there via U-boat remains completely unsubstantiated. Even more ridiculous were reports that Schäffer had taken Hitler and Eva Braun on his epic voyage, or, the height of absurdity, that Schäffer and *U530* had acted as escort for a small convoy transporting Hitler and his entourage to their new redoubt in the frozen wastes of Antarctica. The truth remains more prosaic. *U977* was the final fragment of Dönitz's doomed campaign in the inshore waters of Great Britain, a campaign brought about by the loss of the Atlantic convoy war in 1943 and subsequent defeat on land and in the skies over Europe.

While Schäffer and his men had been heading south to Argentina there was one final echo from the inshore battle. The fifteen-year-old trawler HMT *Kurd*, which had been built originally for Shire Trawlers Ltd had been requisitioned by the Royal Navy on 5 September 1939 for conversion to a minesweeper. On 10 July 1945, *Kurd* was engaged on sweeping mines off the coast of Cornwall when a massive explosion devastated the small ship: 'I was on what was then known as Huff and

U1171, shown after surrender in 1945 and named the 'White Puma' for obvious reasons, with *schnorchel* gear fully upright.

Duff, later called ASDIC sweeping for loose mines. I just remember a loud bang; the sailor behind me took the initial blast, which saved me. I ended up in Truro Hospital and was told only seven of us survived'.[7]

In fact eleven men survived the blast that sank their 352-ton trawler off Lizard Head. Two officers and fourteen ratings were lost; the survivors were picked up by HMS *Almandine* and landed in Truro where six were hospitalised. The cause of the explosion was a moored SMA mine, one of the thirteen laid by *U218* at the beginning of the inshore battle in August 1944.

With the end of the war in Europe German U-boat technology was immediately scrutinised by the victorious Allies. While the technological developments such as *Alberich* and the German *schnorchel* designs were all examined closely, it was the electro-boat that was of greatest interest. The Russian, American and British navies also took the hulls of Walter boats and their hydrogen-peroxide propulsion units in the test boats into service. The United States soon dismissed the idea as unworkable due to its inherent complexities, coupled with the fact that they had practical experience of the power of nuclear reaction; their scientists were concentrating on the development of a reactor small enough for use aboard a submarine. Russia, too, discontinued its hydrogen-peroxide experiments shortly afterward, while the British commissioned a raised *U1407* into the Royal Navy as HMS *Meteorite* in trials to assess the viability of this non-nuclear alternative to air-independent propulsion. The boat was in service from 1946 to 1950, and was only ever regarded as 75 per cent safe. But it served as the catalyst for the construction of two improved versions, HMSs *Explorer* and *Excalibur*, which entered Royal Navy service between 1956 and 1958. These two submarines – know as the 'blonde' submarines (due to a humorous association with women who dyed their hair 'peroxide blonde') – never fully proved their worth other than as fast submarine targets for Royal Navy surface forces. The instability of Walter's fuel produced several explosions and other dangerous incidents that ultimately proved the unsuitability of the Walter drive.

It was the Type XXI model that attracted the most scrutiny by the Allied forces. The Russians went as far as to load the hull of the incomplete aircraft carrier *Graf Zeppelin* with incomplete Type XXI hull sections within the carrier's capacious hangar, towing the hulk toward Leningrad, though it struck a mine and sank in the Gulf of Finland. Almost immediately, design features of the Type XXI began to be incorporated in postwar submarine designs: the elimination of the deck gun, streamline hull and conning tower, large battery capacity and integral incorporation of the *schnorchel*, known to the British as the 'snort' and the Americans as a 'snorkel'.

The Allies also seized other captured German technology with relish. These included the V1 'Doodlebug' rocket, which inspired submarine-launched, guided-rocket systems. On 12 February 1947 off Point Mugu, California, USS *Cusk*, a *Balao*-class fleet boat heralded the ultimate task of modern-day ballistic-

The raised 'ring-float' *schnorchel* on this Type VIIC – pictured here in British hands and undergoing tests – indicates how far below the surface the boat could sail while using the breathing device.

missile submarines and their crucial role in the use of deterrence to maintain the international balance of power. On that day *Cusk* successfully launched a guided missile, known as a 'Loon' from her newly installed launch platform. The Loon missile was essentially an improved model of the V1, later redesignated as the LTV-N-2 missile by the US Navy. A little more than a year later, on 3 May 1950, *Cusk* again made history when, after launching a Loon the submarine went immediately to periscope depth and tracked the missile for a distance of 105 miles using AN/BPQ-2 guidance equipment. In 1954 USS *Cusk* also underwent what was known as 'Guppy II' conversion in the Mare Island Naval Shipyard. Again directly related to the Type XXI, this involved lengthening the hull and installing enlarged batteries as the 'Greater Underwater Propulsion Power' update.

Concurrent with such underwater advances were the critical elements of ASW strategy and tactics that were developed as a direct result of German advances. It was not only the virtually unblooded 'electro-boat' concept that galvanised such radical rethinking of ASW techniques, but also the myriad other German technologies that had seen action, particularly in Dönitz's inshore campaign in British waters: the *schnorchel* and pattern-running and acoustic torpedoes. While all had been used elsewhere and before the U-boats came into the shallows, it was only then that they significantly undermined Allied technological and tactical defences. Radar and ASDIC were suddenly no longer able accurately to locate the enemy that they had so comprehensively beaten in the open waters of the Atlantic. Even the initial U-boat attack on D-Day shipping within the English Channel had been largely defeated by aircraft as the U-boats raced surfaced to attack. The later campaign within the same waters did not involve such a reckless surface dash for the target areas, and so eliminated the advantage of Leigh Light-equipped, radar-carrying bombers.

Nonetheless, the tried and proven Allied convoy system remained ultimately both an offensive and defensive triumph. While U-boats prowling in search of targets could often evade detection, once the attack had been launched their position was immediately compromised. The initial German tactic of hiding inshore among the confused jumble of British shallow seabed topography certainly yielded initially promising results, but never invalidated the benefits of convoying. Results for the U-boats were still slim in terms of the percentage of enemy ships sunk from the convoy traffic attacked, while German losses mounted steadily after their first heady moments of success.

Also, although the immediate tactical initiative in the U-boat war during the onset of the inshore battle definitely passed to the Germans, the Allies never lost the strategic initiative. The bombing of German industry and transport networks as well as the general advance on all fronts of the land war were never really threatened by Dönitz's last gamble. Indeed, the planned completion and activation to combat status of the Type XXI by November 1944 was directly sabotaged by such Allied strategic advantages.

Nonetheless, the final developments within the Kriegsmarine's U-boat service yielded new headaches for the British and Americans in particular. Indeed in his epic account of the Second World War Winston Churchill summarised the end of Dönitz's forces with a genuine insight of what was to follow:

The *schnorchel*-fitted boats now in service . . . were but an introduction to the new pattern of U-boat warfare which Dönitz had planned. He was counting on the advent of the new type of boat, of which very many were now being built. The first of these were already under trial. Real success for Germany depended on their early arrival in service in large numbers. Their high submerged speed threatened us with new problems, and indeed would, as Dönitz predicted, have revolutionised U-boat warfare. His plans failed mainly because the special material needed to construct these vessels became very scarce and their design had constantly to be changed. But ordinary U-boats were still being made piecemeal all over Germany and assembled in bomb-proof shelters at the ports, and in spite of the intense and continuing efforts of Allied bombers, the Germans built more submarines in November 1944 than in any other month of the war. By stupendous efforts and in spite of all losses about sixty or seventy U-boats remained in action almost until the end. Their achievements were not large, but they carried the undying hope of stalemate at sea. The new revolutionary submarines never played their part in the Second World War . . . This weapon in Soviet hands lies among the hazards of the future.[8]

These concerns would increase once the victors had begun to run trials using captured Type XXIs and found that, despite their constructional deficiencies, they could outpace and outmanoeuvre escort forces used in exercises within the Atlantic. The high submerged speed remained at the core of the problem faced by ASW forces in the open ocean, while the *schnorchel* posed further difficulties both in inshore waters and blue-water operations. The US Navy estimated that the snorkel alone had initially reduced the effectiveness of radar-equipped aircraft as the primary killer of submarines by 95 per cent, the British by 90 per cent. The role of U-boat hunter passed firmly to surface ships. For the British the change from aircraft-assisted open-ocean battle to shallow-water coastal warfare meant that the *schnorchel* U-boats had quite literally vanished from radar screens, requiring a complete rethinking of both surface-ship ASW tactics and those employed by Coastal Command. While convoying never diminished in effectiveness, it took fresh technological advances to reinvigorate the aerial threat to submerged submarine attacks. The era of the sonobuoy and homing torpedoes had begun; the age of the hunter-killer submarine was about to dawn.

Notes

CHAPTER ONE

1 Quote from First Sea Lord Cunningham, Barnett, Correlli, *Engage The Enemy More Closely*, p 854.
2 *The U-Boat War In The Atlantic*, Hessler, Günter, p 71 (Volume III).
3 In fact *Oberleutnant zur See* Karl-Heinz Lange had sunk corvette HMCS *Regina* and Liberty ship SS *Ezra Watson* from coastal convoy EBC66 and American military transports *LST921* and *LCI99* from EBC72. *U667* itself was sunk by mine returning to La Pallice on 25 August, all forty-five men aboard killed.
4 Combat boats *U480*, *U247*, *U999*, *U485*, *U486*, *U1105* and *U4709* were all *Alberich* coated.
5 BdU KTB, 30 September 1944.
6 BdU KTB, 13 September 1944.
7 BdU KTB, 15 October 1944.

CHAPTER TWO

1 This first patrol had actually originally been focused on the Minch area, Hein ordered to Reykjavik after a lack of suitable opportunities for attack.
2 Fritz Hein had learned his craft serving as Watch Officer aboard *U333* for a year before commanding the newly commissioned *U300*. He and eight of his crew were killed on 22 February 1945 south east of Cape St Vincent when the boat was sunk en route to Gibraltar.
3 http://www.airmuseum.ca/rcn/robert10.html – Collection of Canadian veterans' memories, courtesy of the *Vancouver Sun*, April 30, 1999.
4 'The Challenge of Modernization: The Royal Canadian Navy and Antisubmarine Weapons, 1944–45', William Rawling. *The Journal of Military History*, Vol. 63, No 2. (April 1999), p 375. The article includes extracts from the 'Precis of Attack by HMCS Annan', 16 October 1944, 11: 026, COAC 7-14-2, RG 24.
5 Rohde, Jens, *Die Spur des Löwen, U1202*.
6 Skinner, Richard, *U249*, pp 11–13.
7 See http://www.oldwillingham.com/History/Spy/Tate_Spy.htm.
8 BdU KTB, 17 November 1944.
9 BdU KTB, 18 November 1944.
10 BdU KTB, 24 November 1944.
11 BdU KTB, 4 December 1944.
12 Lifeboats and Carley floats with the ship's name emblazoned on them soon washed up on the German-occupied Channel Islands confirming *U486*'s success.
13 BdU KTB, 19 December 1944.
14 Skinner, Richard, *U297*, p 18.
15 *The Battle Of The Atlantic*.

CHAPTER THREE

1 Mallmann-Showell, Jak P (ed) *Führer Conferences on Naval Affairs*, p 425.
2 *U278* reported torpedoing a single ship during this patrol, though this remains unconfirmed.
3 BdU KTB, 14 January 1945.
4 BdU KTB, 13 January 1945.

CHAPTER FOUR

1 Rössler, Eberhard, *The U-Boat*, p 168.
2 *Führer Conferences on Naval Affairs*, p 391.
3 Topp, Erich, *Odyssey Of A U-Boat Commander*, p 103.
4 On 14 September 1966, the German Type XXIII *Hai* also suffered accidental flooding, killing all but one of the crew.
5 http://www.angelfire.com/on3/hmcstrentonian/survivors.html
6 *Führer Conferences*, 17 Feb 1945, p 447.
7 BdU KTB, 14 February 1945.
8 HMS *Amethyst* later became famous for its part in the so-called 'Yangtze Incident' during the Chinese Civil War. On 20 April 1949 the sloop was fired on by Communist artillery while en route from Shanghai to Nanking on the Yangtze River where it was due to replace HMS *Consort* as guard ship for the British Embassy. By the time the shelling had ceased twenty-two men, including the commander and first officer, had been killed and thirty-one wounded. *Amethyst* had received over fifty hits, holes beneath the waterline plugged with hammocks and bedding. Delicate negotiations to free the trapped and damaged ship ended on 30 July when *Amethyst* succeeded in an audacious dash for freedom, making contact with HMS *Consort* at the river mouth, sending the signal 'Have rejoined the fleet off Woosung . . . God save the King'.

CHAPTER FIVE

1 HMS *Seraph* continued in her role as fast target submarine until 1963. The 'Man Who Never Was', officially known as 'Operation Mincemeat', was a classic disinformation operation and involved HMS *Seraph* carrying a metal canister in which a body was packed in dry ice, wearing a Royal Marines uniform and handcuffed to a briefcase filled with documents. The corpse was of an unidentified male and on 30 April 1943 the body, complete with documents, was fitted with a life jacket and put into the sea by the crew of *Seraph* near the port of Huelva, Spain. From there he washed ashore as planned, whereupon German intelligence retrieved the documents that clearly showed Allied intentions to land in the Balkans and Sardinia instead of Sicily as part of 'Operation Husky'.
2 'The Challenge of Modernization: The Royal Canadian Navy and Antisubmarine Weapons, 1944–45', William Rawling. *The Journal of Military History*, Vol 63, No 2. (April 1999).
3 Ibid.

CHAPTER SIX

1 Werner, Herbert, *Iron Coffins*, pp 288–9.
2 Interestingly, the daily situation conferences continued to be held by Hitler either in the

Bundesratsaal (Federal Council Chamber) within the old Reich Chancellery or his private study in the New Chancellery until mid-March 1945 when moved to the bunker due to the increased risk from bombing.

3   *Führer Conferences*, 7 April 1945, p 480.
4   Rhode, Jens, *Die Spur des Löwen æ U1202*, Quote from Anton Wrobel, (book pages unnumbered).
5   *Kapitänleutnant* Hans-Günther Lange, commander of 13th U-Flotilla's *U711*, which was active against Arctic convoys, was the last recipient of Oak Leaves within the *U-Bootwaffe*, awarded the same day as Thomsen.
6   *Sunderland Echo*, 19 July 2007.

CHAPTER SEVEN

1   *Memoirs*, Karl Dönitz, p 438.
2   Ibid p 448.
3   Franks, Norman, *Search, Find and Kill*, p 83. Quote from Pilot Sub Lieutenant John Downey.
4   Preliminary Interrogation of *U2326* Commanding Officer, *Oberleutnant zur See* Karl Jobst – covering patrols from 19–27 April 1945 and 4–14 May 1945.

CHAPTER EIGHT

1   Interview with Lieutenant Haskell-Thomas; http://www.navynews.co.uk/
2   http://www.navynews.co.uk/ww2/battle_of_atlantic2.asp
3   http://www.bbc.co.uk/ww2peopleswar/
4   The Morgenthau Plan, named after its creator Henry Morgenthau, Jr, Secretary of the Treasury of the United States, envisioned harsh measures inflicted on a defeated Germany in order to eliminate any capability for Germany to wage war again. Germany was to be partitioned into two independent states, with all heavy industry dismantled and centres of mining and industry either shared among conquering nations or annexed. This would leave Germany an agricultural nation. In September 1944 President Roosevelt and Morgenthau persuaded a reluctant Churchill to agree to the plan, though soon after the plan's details were leaked to the press, prompting strong denials from Roosevelt. To Propaganda Minister Josef Goebbels it was a perfect gift and he was able to use the plan's details to strengthen German resolve to continue the struggle.
5   Schäffer, Heinz, *U-Boat 977*, pp 168–9.
6   Ibid p 170.
7   Recollections of Royal Navy rating John Edwards, http://www.bbc.co.uk/ww2peopleswar/
8   Churchill, Winston, *The Second World War*, Volume 6 'Triumph and Tragedy', p 435.

Glossary and Abbreviations

Abwehr – German Military Intelligence Service.

ASDIC – Acronym for Allied Submarine Detection Investigation Committee. Royal Navy term for sonar used for submarine location.

B-Dienst – German radio listening service for gathering intelligence of enemy transmissions.

BdU – *Befehlshaber der Unterseeboote*, U-Boat Commander in Chief.

Coastal Command – Royal Air Force arm of service dedicated to defending Britain from naval threats. Formed in 1936.

Enigma – Name of coding machine used by German Armed Forces.

Falke – T4 acoustic torpedo designed to home on low-pitched merchant propellers.

FAT – *Felderapparattorpedo*; German T3 pattern-running torpedo.

FdU – *Führer der Unterseeboote*; regional U-boat command responsible primarily for the logistical coordination of that area's U-boat flotillas and bases.

FuMB – *Funkmessbeobachtungs Gerät*; radar detector.

G7a – Standard German air-driven torpedo.

G7e – Standard German electric torpedo.

Heer – German Army.

HMCS – His Majesty's Canadian Ship.

HMS – His Majesty's Ship.

HMSAS – His Majesty's South African Ship.

HMT – His Majesty's Trawler, Tug or Transport.

HNMS – His Norwegian Majesty's Ship.

Ib – Fleet operations (German)

(Ing.) – *Ingenieur*; German Engineer designation inserted after rank, e.g. *Leutnant (Ing.)*

Kleinkampfverbänd – included midget submarines, explosive motorboats and frogmen.

Kriegsmarine – German Navy.

KTB – *Kriegstagebuch*; German unit War Diary kept as daily record of military activities.

LI – *Leitender Ingenieur*; Chief Engineer.

Liberty ship – Mass-produced cargo ships manufactured in the United States, originally of British conception. Quick and easy to produce they became the backbone of Allied mercantile traffic.

Luftwaffe – German Air Force.

MV – Motor vessel.

OKM – *Oberkommando der Marine*, German Naval Command.

OKW – *Oberkommando der Wehrmacht*, German Military Forces High Command.

RAF – Royal Air Force.

SIS – Secret Intelligence Service.

SKL – *Seekriegsleitung*, German Naval War Staff.

SMA – *Schachtmine* or shaft mine.

SS – Steam Ship.

Stab – German staff.

Vorpostenboot – German patrol boats, typically a converted trawler.

VP – US Navy Patrol Squadron (aircraft).

VPB – US Navy Bomber Patrol Squadron.

Wehrmacht – German Armed Forces, excluding the Waffen SS.

Wintergarten – Nickname given to open railed extension of the conning tower to accommodate flak weaponry.

WO – German Watch Officer. Thus, IWO is First Watch Officer, IIWO is Second Watch Officer and IIIWO Third Watch Officer. There were three Watch Officers aboard a combat U-boat, the IIIWO a senior non-commissioned officer, the others commissioned.

Zaunkönig – T5 acoustic torpedo, designed to home on higher pitched warship engines.

Comparative Rank Table

German (Abbreviation)	British/American
Grossadmiral	Admiral of the Fleet/Fleet Admiral
Admiral	Admiral
Vizeadmiral (V. A.)	Vice Admiral
Konteradmiral (K. A.)	Rear Admiral
Kapitän zur See (Kpt. z. S.)	Captain
Fregattenkapitän (F. K.)	Commander
Korvettenkapitän (K. K.)	Commander
Kapitänleutnant (Kptlt.)	Lieutenant Commander
Oberleutnant zur See (Oblt. z. S.)	Lieutenant
Leutnant zur See (L. z. S.)	Sub Lieutenant/Lieutenant (j.g.)
Oberfähnrich	Senior Midshipman
Fähnrich	Midshipman
Stabsobersteuermann	Senior Quartermaster/Warrant Quartermaster
Obersteuermann	Quartermaster (also U-boat Navigation Officer)
Obermaschinist	Senior Machinist/Warrant Machinist
Bootsmann	Boatswain
Oberbootsmannmaat	Boatswain's Mate
Bootsmannmaat	Coxswain
-Maat (trade inserted as prefix)	Petty Officer
Maschinenobergefreiter	Leading Seaman Machinist
Matrosenobergefreiter	Leading Seaman
Mekanikergefreiter	Able Seaman Torpedo Mechanic
Maschinengefreiter	Able Seaman Mechanic
Matrosengefreiter	Able Seaman
Matrose	Ordinary Seaman

Appendix A – U-boats assigned to British waters during the 1944–45 inshore campaign (from September 1944 onwards)

Sailed August 1944

U-boat	Main operational area	Sailed	Returned/Lost
U218	English Channel	10 August	23 September
U680	Moray Firth	14 August	8 September
U484	*Scotland/Hebrides*	*14 August*	*Sunk 9 September*
U482	Shetland Islands	16 August	26 September
U296	Shetland Islands	16 August	29 September
U248	North Channel	17 August	14 October
U743	*Hebrides*	*21 August*	*Missing August*
U398	Hebrides/North Channel	23 August	15 October
U262	St George's Channel	23 August	5 November
U758	Bristol Channel	23 August	10 October
U285	North Minch	24 August	18 September
U247	*English Channel*	*26 August*	*Sunk 1 September*
U714	Bristol Channel	27 August	20 October
U1004	North Channel	29 August	23 October
U963	North Channel	29 August	7 October
U309	North Channel	29 August	13 October
U979	Iceland	29 August	10 October
U985	North Channel	30 August	23 October
U953	North Channel	31 August	11 October

Sailed September 1944

U281	Bristol Channel	4 September	29 October
U1199	Moray Firth	14 September	5 November

Sailed October 1944

U483	North Channel	3 October	21 November

U246	English Channel	4 October	12 November
U978	English Channel	9 October	16 December
U1006	*English Channel*	*9 October*	*Sunk 16 October*
U1003	North Channel	11 October	16 December
U991	English Channel	15 October	26 December
U1200	*Northwest Approaches*	*19 October*	*Sunk 11 November*
U1202	Irish Sea	30 October	1 January

Sailed November 1944

U296	North Minch	4 November	25 December
U979	St George's Channel	9 November	16 January
U322	*Irish Sea/English Channel*	*15 November*	*Sunk 29 December*
U680	English Channel	18 November	19 January
U482	*North Channel*	*18 November*	*Sunk 25 November*
U775	North Minch	18 November	21 December
U400	*St George's Channel*	*18 November*	*Sunk December*
U772	*English Channel*	*19 November*	*Sunk 17 December*
U1020	*Orkney Islands*	*22 November*	*Sunk November*
U297	*Orkney Islands*	*25 November*	*Sunk 6 December*
U1209	*English Channel*	*26 November*	*Sunk 18 December*
U486	English Channel	26 November	15 January
U485	English Channel	29 November	30 January

Sailed December 1944

U650	*English Channel*	*6 December*	*Sunk December*
U325	English Channel	9 December	14 February
U905	English Channel	11 December	31 January
U1009	North Channel	11 December	8 February
U1055	St George's Channel/Irish Sea	11 December	1 February
U312	Orkney Islands	14 December	4 January
U285	St George's Channel/Irish Sea	20 December	31 January
U1172	*Irish Sea*	*22 December*	*Sunk 27 January*
U313	Moray Firth	23 December	17 February
U278	Moray Firth	23 December	13 February
U315	Orkney Islands	25 December	6 January
U764	English Channel	26 December	4 February
U1051	*Irish Sea*	*28 December*	*Sunk 26 January*
U1017	English Channel	28 December	2 March
U825	Bristol/St George's Channels	29 December	18 February

Sailed January 1945

U1199	*English Channel*	*1 January*	*Sunk 21 January*
U480	*English Channel*	*6 January*	*Missing February*
U244	English Channel	9 January	13 March
U275	English Channel	13 January	10 February
U245	North Foreland	14 January	18 February
U1058	Irish Sea	15 January	26 March
U1203	English Channel	15 January	30 March
U1208	*English Channel*	*16 January*	*Sunk 27 February*
U963	Irish Sea	16 January	6 March
U1014	*North Channel*	*18 January*	*Sunk 4 February*
U1018	*English Channel*	*21 January*	*Sunk 27 February*
U1004	English Channel	27 January	20 March
U1276	*Irish Sea/St George's Channel*	*28 January*	*Sunk 20 February*
U1279	*Irish Sea*	*29 January*	*Sunk 3 February*
U2324	Firth of Forth	29 January	25 February
U327	*English Channel*	*30 January*	*Sunk 27 February*
U927	*English Channel*	*31 January*	*Sunk 24 February*

Sailed February 1945

U1104	The Minch	1 February	22 March
U683	*English Channel*	*3 February*	*Missing February*
U1302	*Irish Sea/St George's Channel*	*3 February*	*Sunk 7 March*
U1019	North Channel	3 February	9 April
U2322	Firth of Forth	6 February	3 March
U399	*English Channel*	*6 February*	*Sunk 26 March*
U483	North Channel	7 February	26 March
U775	St George's Channel	7 February	30 March
U989	*English Channel*	*7 February*	*Sunk 14 February*
U1064	North Channel	7 February	9 April
U309	*Moray Firth*	*8 February*	*Sunk 16 February*
U1278	*English Channel*	*11 February*	*Sunk 17 February*
U681	*English Channel*	*14 February*	*Sunk 10 March*
U315	English Channel	15 February	24 April
U260	*Irish Sea*	*18 February*	*Sunk 13 March*
U1005	North Minch	19 February	20 March
U1003	*North Channel*	*19 February*	*Sunk 23 March*
U1169	*Irish Sea*	*20 February*	*Sunk 29 March*
U1021	*St George's Channel*	*20 February*	*Sunk 14 March*
U1002	English Channel	20 February	9 April
U722	*Hebrides*	*21 February*	*Sunk 27 March*

U953	English Channel	21 February	3 April
U246	*English Channel/Irish Sea*	*21 February*	*Sunk during April*
U1195	*English Channel*	*25 February*	*Sunk 6 April*
U978	The Minches	25 February	20 April
U275	*English Channel*	*25 February*	*Sunk 10 March*
U296	*North Channel/Irish Sea*	*28 February*	*Missing during March*

Sailed March 1945

U1024	*Irish Sea*	*3 March*	*Sunk 13 April*
U242	*Irish Sea*	*4 March*	*Sunk 5 April*
U1202	Irish Sea	4 March	26 April
U714	*Firth of Forth*	*4 March*	*Sunk 14 March*
U778	Moray Firth	4 March	26 March
U965	*The Minch*	*5 March*	*Sunk 30 March*
U1023	Irish Sea	5 March	Surrendered 10 May
U826	English Channel	9 March	11 May
U2321	Firth of Forth	9 March	13 April
U1063	*English Channel*	*11 March*	*Sunk 15 April*
U1001	*English Channel/Western Approaches*	*11 March*	*Sunk 8 April*
U905	*The Minch*	*13 March*	*Sunk 27 March*
U396	*Hebrides*	*13 March*	*Sunk during April*
U774	*English Channel*	*14 March*	*Sunk 8 April*
U321	*English Channel*	*15 March*	*Sunk 2 April*
U325	*English Channel/Irish Sea*	*20 March*	*Sunk during April*
U249	English Channel	21 March	24 March
U1106	*The Shetlands*	*21 March*	*Sunk 29 March*
U218	Firth of Clyde	22 March	8 May
U1109	British waters	22 March	6 April
U776	English Channel/Western Approaches	22 March	Surrendered 16 May
U285	*English Channel*	*26 March*	*Sunk 15 April*
U326	*English Channel*	*28 March*	*Sunk 25 April*
U1107	*English Channel*	*29 March*	*Sunk 30 April*

Sailed April 1945

U636	*North Channel*	*1 April*	*Sunk 21 April*
U1274	*Firth of Forth*	*1 April*	*Sunk 16 April*
U293	Northwest Approaches	1 April	Surrendered 11 May
U739	North Minch	1 April	4 May
U825	Irish Sea	1 April	Surrendered 10 May
U956	North Channel	2 April	Surrendered 13 May
U2324	Firth of Forth	2 April	8 May

U249	English Channel	4 April	Surrendered 8 May
U1305	North Channel	4 April	Surrendered 10 May
U2322	Thames Estuary	4 April	30 April
U1055	*English Channel*	*5 April*	*Missing April*
U1206	*Firth of Forth*	*6 April*	*Sunk 14 April*
U245	North Foreland	9 April	Surrendered 9 May
U2329	Firth of Forth	11 April	26 April
U1105	Ireland West coast	12 April	Surrendered 10 May
U1017	*North Channel*	*14 April*	*Sunk 29 April*
U901	Western Approaches	14 April	Surrendered 15 May
U398	*Firth of Forth*	*14 April*	*Sunk during April*
U1010	Western Approaches	15 April	Surrendered 14 May
U244	English Channel	15 April	Surrendered 14 May
U1109	Western Approaches	17 April	Surrendered 12 May
U218	Firth of Clyde	18 April	8 May
U2326	Firth of Forth	19 April	27 April
U1165	Western Approaches	21 April	5 May
U1277	Western Approaches	21 April	Scuttled 3 June (Portugal)
U637	British waters	23 April	28 April
U963	Hartlepool	23 April	Scuttled 20 May (Portugal)
U1057	Western Approaches	26 April	9 May
U764	Western Approaches	26 April	Surrendered 14 May
U320	*Western Approaches*	*27 April*	*Scuttled 8 May after depth charge damage*
U1058	Western Approaches	28 April	Surrendered 10 May
U287	*Firth of Forth*	*29 April*	*Sunk 16 May*

Sailed May 1945

U2336	Firth of Forth	1 May	Surrendered 14 May
U977	Western Approaches	2 May	Interned 17 August
U2511	Færoe Islands (actually destined for the Caribbean)	3 May	6 May
U2326	Scottish coast	4 May	Surrendered 14 May

Appendix B – U-boat types engaged in the British inshore campaign

Type VIIC

Arguably the most famous U-boat type of the Second World War, the Type VIIC came about not through any perceived deficiency in the VIIB design, but by a desire for increased internal space. As production of the VIIB proceeded, a new active sonar, *S-Gerät*, was nearing projected completion and strongly desired to be fitted within new U-boats. While the VIIB served Dönitz perfectly as the backbone of his burgeoning U-boat service, it did not have enough internal space to carry the *S-Gerät*. Thus was born the Type VIIC. An extra frame was added to the central control room adding 30cm to either side of the periscope housing. This increased space for the new sonar equipment also allowed the conning tower to be enlarged 30cm in length and 6cm in width. Two pressure-tight negative buoyancy tanks (*Untertriebzelle*), one on either flank, were included within the saddle tanks to enable improved diving time in combat by remaining partially flooded. The engines were also upgraded, an oil-filtration system introduced to prolong the life of diesel lubricants and increase engine reliability. Also the starboard electrical compressor was replaced by a diesel-powered Junkers model, reducing the strain on the densely packed batteries. Finally, an improved AEG-designed knob-switch electrical control system was introduced to replace the archaic BBC knife-switch system used on the VIIB. Ironically the *S-Gerät* – the sole reason for the enhanced design – was deemed unready for installation and the Type VIICs sailed without it. Despite the fact that with the increased size there was no increase in performance – in fact, a minor decrease in submerged range – the Type VIIC became the standard design, frequently modified as war progressed, but remaining the backbone upon which Dönitz hung all hopes for his assault on the Allied convoys.

Specifications

    Displacement: 761 tons/865 tons (surfaced/submerged). Submerged fully loaded and manned 1070 tons.
    Length: 67.1m
    Beam: 6.2m
    Draught: 4.74m (keel to bridge: 9.6m)

Diving depth/theoretical crush depth: 150m/250m

Diving time: 30 seconds (normal)

Engines: 2 supercharged Germaniawerft, 6 cylinder, 4-stroke M6V 40/46 diesels totalling 2,800–3,200bhp. Max rpm: 470–490.

Motors: U69–U72, U89, U93–U98, U201–U212, U221–U232, U235–U300, U331–U348, U351–U374, U431–U450, U731–U750, U1051–U1058, U1063, U1068, U1191–U1210: 2 AEG GU 460/8-276 electric motors, totalling 750shp. Max rpm: 296.

U77–U82, U88, U90–U92, U132–U136, U401, U451, U452, U551–U650, U751, U821–U840, U929–U936, U951–U994, U1026–U1050: 2 BBC (Brown Boveri & Co) GG UB 720/8 electric motors, totalling 750shp. Max rpm: 296.

U301–U316, U329, U330, U375–U400, U701–U730, U752–U782, U1131, U1132: 2 GL (Garbe Lahmeyer) RP 137/c electric motors, totalling 750shp. Max rpm: 296.

U349, U350, U402–U430, U453–U458, U465–U486, U651–U698, U901–U912, U921–U928, U1101–U1106, U1161–U1162: 2 SSW (Siemens-Schuckert-Werke) GU 343/38-8 electric motors, totalling 750shp. Max rpm: 296.

Batteries: 2 x 62-cell AFA 33 MAL 800, producing 9160 amp hours.

Speed: 17–17.7kts/7.6kts (surfaced/submerged)

Range (nm/kts): 8,500/10 surfaced (combined diesel electric drive range 9,700nm at 10kts); 80/4 submerged.

Armament: 5 x 53.3cm TT (9 reloads, or 26 TMA or 39 TMB mines)

Several different flak weaponry combinations were used by the Type VIIC, becoming more prevalent as the war progressed. The following combinations illustrate some of these:

1. 1 x 2cm C30 AA gun

2. 1 x 2cm C30 and 2 x MG151 machine guns

3. 2 x 2cm C30 (on twin LC30/37 mounting) and 4 x MG151 machine guns (2 x 2)

4. 1 x 2cm C30 and 4 x Breda machine guns (2 x 2)

5. 2 x 2cm C30 AA weapons, one on each *wintergarten* level.

6. 4 x 2cm C38 (2 x 2 on upper *wintergarten*) and 4 x 2cm C38 Vierling (lower level).

7. 4 x 2cm C38 (2 x 2 on upper *wintergarten*) and 1 x 3.7cm automatic flak.

There were many variations, some official some not, as Allied aircraft became the principle threat to U-boat activity.

Crew: up to 60 (4/56).

Stored boats: One dinghy stowed under forward casing forward of torpedo loading hatch. Four five-man life-rafts held in watertight canisters on fore-casing (1944 onwards).

Type VIIC/41
For a brief account of the development of the Type VIIC/41, please see chapter 1 page 21.

Specifications
   Displacement: 759 tons/860 tons (surfaced/submerged). Submerged fully loaded and manned 1070 tons.
   Length: 67.2m
   Beam: 6.2m
   Draught: 4.74m (keel to bridge: 9.6m)
   Diving depth/theoretical crush depth: 180m/300m
   Diving time: 30 seconds (normal)
   Engines: 2 supercharged Germaniawerft, 6 cylinder, 4-stroke M6V 40/46 diesels totalling 2,800–3,200bhp. Max rpm: 470–490.
   Motors: U1191–U1199, U1271–U1279, U1301–U1308: 2 AEG GU 460/8-276 electric motors, totalling 750shp. Max rpm: 296.
   U995–U1025: 2 BBC (Brown Boveri & Co) GG UB 720/8 electric motors, totalling 750shp. Max rpm: 296.
   U317–U328: 2 GL (Garbe Lahmeyer) RP 137/c electric motors, totalling 750shp. Max rpm: 296.
   U1107–U1110, U1163–U1170: 2 SSW (Siemens-Schuckert-Werke) GU 343/38-8 electric motors, totalling 750shp. Max rpm: 296.
   Batteries: U320, U328, U1166, U1168, U1169, U1171, U1172, U1192, U1194, U1196–U1199, U1272, U1306: 2 x 62-cell AFA 33 MAL 800 W, producing 9160 amp hours. All others: 2 x 62-cell AFA 33 MAL 800 E, producing 9160 amp hours.
   A small number of boats operated with some batteries of each type, the difference between them being the casing of the individual battery cells only.
   Speed: 17–17.7kts/7.6kts (surfaced/submerged)
   Range (nm/kts): 8,500/10 surfaced (combined diesel-electric drive range 9,700nm at 10kts); 80/4 submerged.
   Armament: 5 x 53.3cm TT (9 reloads, or 26 TMA or 39 TMB mines), except all C/41s from *U1271* upwards had no mine carrying capability. Again, several different flak weaponry combinations were used by the Type VIIC, becoming more prevalent as the war progressed.

Type VIID
For a brief account of the development of the Type VIID please see chapter 1 pages 30–1.

Specifications

Displacement: 965 tons/1080 tons (surfaced/submerged). Submerged fully loaded and manned 1285 tons.

Length: 76.9m

Beam: 6.38m

Draught: 5.01m (keel to bridge: 9.7m)

Diving depth/theoretical crush depth: 100m/200m.

Diving time: 35 seconds

Engines: 2 supercharged Germaniawerft, 6 cylinder, 4-stroke F46 diesels totalling 2,800–3,200bhp. Max rpm: 470–490. Max fuel oil: 169.4 tons (115.3 tons within pressure hull).

Motors: 2 AEG GU 460/8-276 electric motors, totalling 750shp. Max rpm: 285.

Batteries: 2 x 62-cell AFA 33 MAL 800 E, producing 9,160 amp hours (*U217* W-type cells).

Speed: 16-16.7kts/7.3kts (surfaced/submerged)

Range (nm/kts): 11,200/10 surfaced (combined diesel electric drive range 13,000nm at 10kts); 69/4 submerged.

Armament: 5 x mine chutes, carrying a total of 15 SMA mines; 5 x 53.3cm TT (7 reloads, or 26 TMA or 39 TMB mines); 1 x 8.8cm C35/L45 deck gun with 220 rounds; 2 x 2cm (2x1) C30 AA guns with 4,380 rounds. After 1942 defensive armament changed to: 1 x 3.7cm Flak with 1,195 rounds 4 x 2cm C38 (2x2) with 4,380 rounds.

Crew: 44 (4/40)

Stored boats: One dinghy stowed under forward casing forward of torpedo-loading hatch.

Type XXIII

Designed for use within the Mediterranean or coastal waters, the Type XXIII was the smaller brother to the Type XXI design. With a streamlined hull formed by two flattened cylinders and prefabricated into four separate sections that were then welded together, the Type XXIII boasted no external weaponry or deck casing. In fact the interior was also so compact that the two bow torpedo tubes had to be loaded from the outside, the stern lowered into the water and torpedoes allowed to slide tail-first into the tubes. Thus the boat could not reload at sea.

Although relatively successful in action, the Type XXIII carried a weapons load inferior even to the Type II with which the Kriegsmarine entered the war. However, the last ships sunk by U-boat torpedo during the Second World War were the SS *Sneland I* and *Avondale Park* in the Firth of Forth by *Kapitänleutnant* Emil Klusmeier's *U2336* on 7 May 1945.

Specifications

  Dimensions: 34.2 x 2.98 x 3.74 metres (draught)

  Displacement: 232 tons (256 tons submerged)

  Armament: 2 x 53.3cm torpedo tubes at bow (2 x torpedoes carried).

  Propulsion: 1-shaft diesel/electric motors, bhp/shp 580/600. Silent creeping motors, shp 35 = 2 knots.

  Speed: 9.75 knots surfaced/12.5 knots submerged

  Endurance: 1,350 miles (surfaced) at 9.75 knots; 175 miles (submerged) at 4 knots.

  Rated depth: 160 metres

  Complement: 2 officers, 12 crew.

Appendix C – U-boat Command standing orders for schnorchel use, taken from the surrendered U249.

Current Order No. 2
  U249.
  Procedure when *schnorchelling.*
  Issued November 1944.

Many undertakings of 40–60 days duration were carried out without surfacing. The *schnorchel* proved very effective and through it operations were again possible in areas heavily patrolled from the air.

In General
Principle. Under all circumstances attempt to recharge battery completely every day. On account of enemy positions the *schnorchel* is not to be shifted. Continued reduction of the battery capacity can finally cause the boat to be in especially dangerous situation.

(1) Choose favourable conditions for *schnorchelling*, ie, in general at night, in a swell, poor visibility. By day only in clear weather with good visibility, the motion of the sea from force 2 and if the *schnorchel* does not smoke. Best at night, once 2–3 hours at the beginning and end of the night.

(2) The *schnorchel* is not undetectable by radar. If the *schnorchel* is correctly manipulated, that is to say, with the exhaust under water, it can be scarcely or only inaccurately intercepted. The motion of the sea reduces the possibility of being located. If the *schnorchel* is fully raised, it can be located and attacked, therefore it is wrong to let the *schnorchel* protrude too far when there is phosphorescence, so as to avoid a trail of foam. Then interception through location by radar is possible at a much greater distance and therefore more often than by a trail of foam. The range of location of the camouflaged *schnorchel* is about 10% of the boat when on the surface. In practice it is scarcely perceptible.

(3) Air attacks on dark nights are generally only possible with the use of artificial light. If a searchlight is detected shining directly on the boat or a flare above it,

sound the *schnorchel* alarm, and dive to at least 80 metres (260 feet). If searchlights and/or flares are detected searching a long way off, or their location is above the *schnorchel* dipole, only sound the 'quiet-*schnorchel*-alarm', that is to say, dive to 20–30 metres (65–100 feet).

(4) When the *schnorchel* is in use, periscope manned by the commander and officers of the watch in watches of roughly 1–2 hours. In boats of type VIIC, turn the main periscope continually by hand. In boat type IXC in general, only the periscope for air observation. The raising of both periscopes results in oscillations, and moreover increases the danger of being located by radar. Do not proceed at too high a speed (i.e., with both diesels on screw (*aufSchraube*)) this endangers the periscopes. They swing, bend and become leaky and cloudy; slight oscillations are frequently corrected by very small alterations of periscope height.

(5) Noise caused by *schnorchelling* is about the same as when the boat is running on both E-engines at a rate of 200 revolutions per minute. In areas where there is hydrophone activity do not refrain from using the *schnorchel* because of the fear of being heard. According to experiments, boats have proceeded unperturbed with the *schnorchel* in use, with hydrophone bearings of weak signal strength and with 'circular saw noises' of medium signal strength. 'Circular saws' on shadowing vessels cut out other noises.

(6) Circular acoustic sweeps for enemy positions every 15–45 mins. [Unreadable] – dive to a depth of 20 metres. It is possible that the shadowing craft makes towards a U-boat which it has intercepted by hydrophone and in order to remain undetected, will stop when the boat stops her diesels in order to make a hydrophone sweep. Therefore measures have to be taken to be ready for a circular acoustic sweep as soon as diesel engines are stopped.

Execution

(a) Order to engine room, central control and listening room: 'Ready for circular acoustic sweep'.

(b) Switch off charging, charging diesel engine, electric fan and condenser.

(c) Lighten the boat in order to avoid further pumping, once the diesel engine has been switched off. Vent the diving tank (exhaust gas through leaky 'blow distributor' in the tank.) Report readiness of rooms to central control.

(d) Engine room telegraph to 'Dive'. Cruising diesel is to be turned off and the E-engine run, utmost silence in the boat, and keep a listening watch.

(e) If charging was previously carried out, at the end of the acoustic sweep vent the starting battery. As soon as the diesel is running, vent the *schnorchel* battery.

(f) Complete the venting of the diving tank. After *schnorchelling*, or after reaching greater depth, cease venting and report to central control.

Methods of Proceeding

(a) *Schnorchel* in sea up to force 6–7 (according to type of boat) steer broadside on, 1–5 degrees, with the ballast forward, with as little flooding as possible, otherwise current and air unnecessarily consumed when pumping prior to the circular acoustic sweep. Choice of cruising speed depends on the motion of the sea, and the oscillations and angle of the periscope.

(b) Whenever possible ventilate the boat at least once during the day, for fifteen minutes with the *schnorchel*; this saves potash cartridges. If when *schnorchelling*, exhaust fumes enter the boat, let them circulate the *schnorchel* with the quick-action valves shut, suck out the air, then, after switching off the diesel, equalise the pressure. Ventilate thoroughly otherwise casualties through carbon-monoxide gases penetrate into the boat, the best ventilation only with either 'in' or 'out' ventilators, thus ensuring the maximum supply of fresh air possible. Switching on both ventilators does not cause such a great increase.

(c) Overhead fuel tank – keep always full, otherwise air in the pipes. Strictest attention to the maintenance of pressure in the oil pressure cylinder and to drainage between the stuffing box and the *schnorchel* mast. Any leakage of water into the oil pressure plant soon puts the periscope installation out of order.

Bibliography

Books

Barnett, Correlli, *Engage The Enemy More Closely*, Hodder & Stoughton, London, 1992.

Blair, Clay, *Hitler's U-Boat War*, Cassell & Co, London, 2000.

Brennecke, Jochen, *Die Wende im U-Boot Krieg*, Weltbild Verlag, Augsburg, 1995.

Churchill, Winston, *The Second World War Volumes 1 to 6*, Cassell and Co Ltd, 1954.

Franks, Norman, *Search, Find and Kill*, Grub Street, London, 1995.

Hessler, Günter, *The U-Boat War In The Atlantic*, HMSO, London, 1989.

Knudsen, Svein Aage, *Deutsche U-Boote vor Norwegen 1940–1945*, E S Mittler & Sohn Verlag, Hamburg, 2005.

Kramer, Reinhard and Müller, Wolfgang, *Gesunken und Verschollen*, Koehlers Verlag, Herford, 1994.

Lohmann, W and Hildebrand, H H, *Die Deutsche Kriegsmarine*, Podzun Verlag, Bad Nauheim 1956.

Mallmann Showell, Jak P (ed), *Führer Conferences on Naval Affairs*, Chatham Publishing, London, 2005.

Neitzel, Sönke, *Die deutschen Ubootbunker und Bunkerwerften*, Bernard & Graf Verlag, Koblenz, 1991.

Niestlé, Axel, *German U-boats Losses During World War II*, US Naval Institute Press, Annapolis, 1998.

Paterson, Lawrence, *U-Boats in the Mediterranean*, Chatham Publishing, London, 2007.

—— *Weapons of Desperation*, Chatham Publishing, London, 2006.

Rhode, Jens, *Die Spur des Löwen – U1202*, Self published, Izehoe, 2000.

Rössler, Eberhard, *Die deutschen Uboote und ihre Werften*, Bernard & Graf Verlag, Koblenz, 1990.

—— *The U-Boat*, Cassell & Co, London, 2001.

—— *U-Boottyp XXI*, Bernard & Graf Verlag, Bonn, 2001.

—— *U-Boottyp XXIII*, Bernard & Graf Verlag, Bonn, 2002.

Rohwer, Jürgen, *Axis Submarine Successes of World War Two*, Greenhill Publishing, London, 1999.

Schäffer, Heinz, *U-Boat 977*, William Kimber and Co., London, 1952.

Skinner, Richard, *U297*, Military Press, Pulborough, 2002.

Tarrant, V E, *The Last Year of the Kriegsmarine*, Arms & Armour Press, London, 1994.

—— *The U-Boat Offensive 1914–1945*, Arms & Armour Press, London, 1989.

Terraine, John, *Business In Great Waters*, Leo Cooper Ltd, London, 1989.

Topp, Eric, *The Odyssey Of A U-Boat Commander*, Praeger Publishing, Westport, 1992.

Werner, Herbert, *Iron Coffins*, Henry Holt and Co, New York, 1969.

West, Nigel, *MI5: British Security Service Operations 1909–45*. Stein & Day, New York, 1982.

Wynn, Kenneth, *U-Boat Operations Of The Second World War*, Chatham Publishing, London, 1998.

Articles and other documents

Palmer, Dr Michael A, 'The Influence Of Naval Strategy On National Security Planning, 1945–55', Contemporary History Branch, Naval Historical Center.

Rawling, William, 'The Challenge of Modernization: The Royal Canadian Navy and Antisubmarine Weapons, 1944–45'. *The Journal of Military History*, Vol 63, No 2 (April 1999).

Websites

The following websites have been extremely useful in compiling information for this book. Of particular note is the first, an exceptional source of details and facts.

www.uboat.net – Probably the most comprehensive and up-to-date website on the subject of the Second World War U-boats. Though it is free I urge anybody interested in the topic to subscribe to the members area in order to assist with the running of this huge site.

www.ubootwaffe.net – An excellent website with excellent resource material compiled by a team of dedicated enthusiasts.

http://www.warsailors.com – Superb collection of information about the Norwegian merchant fleet of the Second World War.

http://www.uboatarchive.net – Online collection of U-boat records and reports.

www.airmuseum.ca – A collection of Canadian veterans' memories, courtesy of the *Vancouver Sun*, April 30, 1999.

www.oldwillingham.com/History/Spy/Tate_Spy.htm – For the history of 'Tate'.

http://www.navynews.co.uk – Royal Navy News which often shares the recollections of veterans.

www.bbc.co.uk/ww2peopleswar – A steadily growing repository of memoirs from the Second World War on all fronts, including the often overlooked one of that at home.

Index